Networked Virtual Environments

This book is published as part of the SIGGRAPH Books Series with ACM Press Books, a collaborative effort among ACM SIGGRAPH, ACM Press, and Addison-Wesley Publishing Company. The SIGGRAPH Books Series publishes books on theory, practice, applications, and imaging in computer graphics and interactive techniques, some developed from courses, papers, or panels presented at the annual ACM SIGGRAPH conference.

Editor: Stephen Spencer, The Ohio State University

MEMBERSHIP INFORMATION

Founded in 1947, ACM is the oldest and largest educational scientific society in the information technology field. Through its high-quality publications and its services, ACM is a major force in advancing the skills and knowledge of IT professionals throughout the world. From a dedicated group of 78, ACM is now 85,000 strong, with 34 special interest groups, including SIGGRAPH, and more than 60 chapters and students chapters.

For more than 25 years, SIGGRAPH and its conferences have provided the world's forum for the interchange of information on computer graphics and interactive techniques. SIGGRAPH members come from many disciplines and include researchers, hardware and software systems designers, algorithm and applications developers, visualization scientists, educators, technology developers for interactive visual communications, animators and special-effects artists, graphic designers, and fine artists.

For further information about ACM and ACM SIGGRAPH, contact:

ACM Member Services
1515 Broadway, 17th floor
New York, NY 10036-5701
Phone: 1-212-626-0500
Fax: 1-212-944-1318
E-mail: acmhelp@acm.org

ACM European Service Center
108 Cowley Road
Oxford, OX4 1JF, United Kingdom
Phone: +44-1865-382388
Fax: +44-1865-381388
E-mail: acm_europe@acm.org

URL: *http://www.acm.org*

Networked Virtual Environments

Design and Implementation

Sandeep Singhal
IBM Corporation

Michael Zyda
The Naval Postgraduate School

ACM Press • SIGGRAPH Series
New York, New York

ADDISON-WESLEY

An imprint of Addison Wesley Longman, Inc.

Reading, Massachusetts • Harlow, England • Menlo Park, California
Berkeley, California • Don Mills, Ontario • Sydney
Bonn • Amsterdam • Tokyo • Mexico City

Many of the designations used by manufacturers and sellers to distinguish their products are claimed as trademarks. Where those designations appear in this book and Addison-Wesley was aware of a trademark claim, the designations have been printed in initial caps or all caps.

The authors and publisher have taken care in the preparation of this book, but make no expressed or implied warranty of any kind and assume no responsibility for errors or omissions. No liability is assumed for incidental or consequential damages in connection with or arising out of the use of the information or programs contained herein.

Library of Congress Cataloguing in Publication Data

Singhal, Sandeep.
    Networked virtual environments : design and implementation /
Sandeep Singhal, Michael Zyda.
       p.   cm.—(SIGGRAPH series)
    Includes bibliographical references and index.
    ISBN 0-201-32557-8
    1. Interactive multimedia.   2. Virtual reality.   3. Computer
networks.   I. Zyda, Michael.   II. Title.
QA76.76.I59S56   1999
006--dc21   99-31315
                                CIP

ISBN 0-201-32557-8
Text printed on recycled and acid-free paper.

1 2 3 4 5 6 7 8 9 10 — MA — 03 02 01 00 99
First printing, July 1999

Contents

Chapter 4   Communication Architectures   87

Chapter 5   Managing Dynamic Shared State   101

Preface

Networked virtual environments (net-VEs) allow multiple users to interact in real-time even though those users may be located around the world. These environments usually aim for a sense of realism and an immersive experience by incorporating realistic 3D graphics and stereo sound. Increasingly used for military and industrial team training, collaborative design and engineering, and multiplayer games, net-VEs' envisioned future commercial applications include virtual shopping malls and showrooms, on-line tradeshows and conferences, remote customer support, and distance learning. In many respects, net-VEs form the foundation for a new generation of standard applications.

In recent years, we have seen a growing interest in the design and implementation of net-VEs. Several companies are deploying interactive environments for entertainment. Other commercial applications are being prototyped, and military training systems are growing in size, scope, and complexity. The research frontier into net-VEs is moving quickly, as new research efforts have been initiated at several universities and commercial laboratories. Finally, open standards for the delivery of net-VEs over the Internet are beginning to emerge.

The net-VE developer must possess expertise in a variety of areas, including network protocol design and implementation, parallel and distributed systems, graphics and rendering, asynchronous and multi-threaded systems design and engineering, database development, and user interface design. Furthermore, net-VEs pose several problems of their own: managing consistent distributed information; guaranteeing real-time interactivity; and contending with limited network bandwidth, processing, and rendering resources. Increasing numbers of computer scientists are beginning to develop infrastructures for net-VEs, develop net-VE applications on these infrastructures, and use net-VEs in day-to-day work. Rather than starting anew, these developers and users can be more effective in their work by learning the tried-and-true techniques used by existing systems, as well as the emerging techniques being pioneered in the research lab.

This book aims to teach the design and implementation of net-VEs. It employs an "outside-in" approach that assumes that the reader has minimal experience with developing distributed applications. The book is organized into three parts. The first chapters of the book introduce net-VEs. They explore the basic challenges facing the net-VE developer and provide a historical perspective based on military, industrial, and research systems. Then, they offer a review of networking principles, with particular attention to Internet communication protocols.

The second part of the book discusses each of the components of a net-VE in detail. These chapters describe how to organize the communication infrastructure, manage distributed states, and design the system to support multiuser interactions, produce high-quality graphics, and ensure real-time response.

The third part of the book describes some of the more recent developments in the area of net-VEs. The final chapters concentrate on techniques for supporting large numbers of simultaneous users by managing limited bandwidth and computational resources. They also describe the emerging standards that enable net-VEs to be deployed on the Internet and analyze the additional considerations that Internet deployment requires. The book concludes with a discussion of the significant trends and needs in the net-VE technology area.

This book is aimed at several audiences.

- *Commercial net-VE infrastructure and application developers:* The book enables practitioners to develop new net-VE systems by building on the knowledge gained from previous efforts. It can be used both as a front-to-back tutorial and as a topical reference.

- *University students:* This book can serve as the primary text for a one-semester or one-quarter course in networking virtual environments at the advanced undergraduate or graduate level. The book also makes an excellent supplemental text for traditional graphics, networking, or distributed systems courses. In these latter courses, this book exposes students to a real-world application for the core course material and offers insight into an area that bridges several different areas of computer science.

- *Researchers:* This book provides insight into the state-of-the-art of net-VEs. The discussion can also serve as a starting point for defining and exploring new techniques. The references with each chapter cover much of the significant literature in the field.

ABOUT THE AUTHORS

Sandeep Singhal is a senior architect in IBM's Pervasive Computing Division, based in Research Triangle Park, North Carolina. He is also an Adjunct Assistant Professor on the Graduate faculty at North Carolina State University in Raleigh. Singhal's research interests include network protocol design for large-scale collaborative and real-time systems, object-oriented software engineering, and network computing for small devices. He has served on a DARPA advisory board, defining a long-term networked virtual environment research agenda, and in a National Research Council effort linking military and entertainment applications of simulation technology. Singhal holds MS and PhD degrees in computer science from Stanford University, BS degrees in computer science and mathematical sciences, and a BA in mathematics from Johns Hopkins University.

Michael Zyda is a professor in the Department of Computer Science at the Naval Postgraduate School in Monterey, California. His research interests include computer graphics; large-scale, networked 3D virtual environments; computer-generated characters; video production; and modeling and simulation. A member of the National Research Council's Committee on Virtual Reality Research and Development, Zyda also has served as Chair of the National Research Council's Computer Science and Telecommunications Committee on Modeling and Simulation: Linking Entertainment and Defense. He has consulted for the White House Office of Science and Technology Policy, Silicon Graphics International, and Paramount Digital Entertainment, among others. A graduate of the bioengineering program at the University of California at San Diego, Zyda earned an MS in computer science from the University of Massachusetts at Amherst, and a DSc in computer science from Washington University in St. Louis, Missouri.

Acknowledgments

This book could not have been possible without the willing help from lots of friends and colleagues. These wonderful people contributed technical and historical information, suggestions on the text, and even language translation assistance:

Howard Abrams, David Anderson, Guru Banavar, Bob Barton, Steve Benford, Brian Blau, Fred Brooks, Gary Brown, Abbott Brush, Don Brutzman

Michael Capps, Christer Carlsson, Al Casarez, David Cheriton, Stuart Cheshire, Bob Clover, William R. Cockayne, Danny Cohen, Donna Cox, Tom Cunningham, Jerry Cuomo, Judith Dahmann

Rudy Darken, Mark Day, Ken Duda, Nat Durlach, Jose Encarnacao, John Falby, Jim Foley, Michael Fraenkel, Tom Funkhouser, Randy Garrett, Ajei Gopal, Carmine Greco, Mark Green, Michael Greenwald

Olof Hagsand, Eric Halpern, Pat Hanrahan, John Hines, Hugh Holbrook, Kai-Mikael Jää-Aro, Charles Hughes, Marty Johnson, Rosalie Johnson, Lars Karle, Warren Katz, Yoshifumi Kitamura

Bill Lambert, Jaron Lanier, Dave Lection, Jason Leigh, Hubert Le Van Gong, Marc Levoy, Ted Lewis, Jimmy Liberato, Stewart Liles, Curt Lisle, Ming Lin, John Locke

Nadia Magnenat-Thalmann, Dinesh Manocha, Dennis McBride, Bob McGhee, Don McGregor, Mike Macedonia, Dinesh Manocha, Duncan Miller, Kevan Miller, Stu Milner, Katherine Morse, Michael Moshell, Michael Myjak, Paul Mlyniec

Nobutatsu Nakamura, Binh Nguyen, Jimmy Nguyen, Craig Partridge, John Patterson, Mark Pullen, Dave Pratt, Richard Redpath

Dan Schab, Steve Seidensticker, Carlo Sequin, Chris Shaw, Jerry Sheehan, James Shiflett, Gurminder Singh, Jonathan Stone, Steve Stone, Gary Tarolli, Daniel Thalmann, Jack Thorpe, Anthony Tomasic, Greg Troxell

Brian Upton, Andries van Dam, Dan Van Hook, Mike Ward, Kent Watsen, Adam Whitlock, Gio Wiederhold, Al Weis, Scott Williams, Don Wood, Kazy Yokota, and Matt Zelesko

We would particularly like to thank those who reviewed the manuscript and contributed generously to its improvement.

We are indebted to Helen Goldstein and the staff at Addison Wesley Longman who offered continuous encouragement, advice, and support.

Finally, this two-year project has taken us away from our duties as father, son, husband, and friend. To our respective families and friends—particularly Tyerin Dennis, Ram and Sushma Singhal, and Fred and Greta Zyda—we give a heartfelt thank you for your patience, understanding, and encouragement.

Chapter 1

The Promises and Challenges of Networked Virtual Environments

In the Iraqi desert, American tanks, planes, and infantry rehearse a military campaign against an enemy force equipped with chemical weapons. The tanks are hot and cramped, and the troops are maneuvering feverishly to avoid being killed. The battlefield seems quite real, but the combatants are not in any physical danger. Instead, the participants are actually sitting inside full-size tank and fighter simulators located in Virginia and California. Tomorrow, they will rehearse the military operation again on a slightly different desert terrain and against an enemy sporting more powerful artillery.

Meanwhile, engineering teams are designing the wing for a next-generation commercial airliner. The engineers work for contractors located in Seattle, Orlando, and Frankfurt. When the distributed team has readied their design, they contact the San Diego team, which is designing the new engines. A simulation of the engine's dynamics, executing on a supercomputer in San Diego, is connected to the wing design stored in another supercomputer in New York. Together, the engineers watch a simulation of the airplane in flight. The different teams then disconnect from each other and return to improve the designs of their respective components.

George needs to buy Christmas gifts for his family and friends, but he does not have time to go to the mall. Instead, he connects to a Web site that provides a virtual shopping mall. In this virtual mall, he can wander among a variety of department and specialty stores. Inside a shoe store, he sees shoes on display. Using his mouse, he picks up the shoes and rotates them around to see them from other angles. A salesperson walks by and offers to answer George's questions. George finally decides to buy the shoes, provides his credit card number, and arranges to have the shoes sent by overnight mail.

Ten-year-old Jeremy plugs a phone cord into his game console at his home in Dallas. He inserts the Wild Warrior cartridge and dials into an Internet service provider. Today, Jeremy will be the Ninja Warrior. He enters the game and is immediately confronted by a swarm of large reptiles and alien creatures. One of those aliens is actually being played by Lucy, an eleven-year-old girl who is playing Wild Warrior on her family PC in London. Jeremy and Lucy decide to team up against the other players, and after a few minutes of battle, they both advance to the next level of the game.

All of these scenarios describe applications of networked virtual environments. Networked virtual environments are being used for education and training, for engineering and design, for commerce, and for entertainment. Indeed, the range of applications is growing rapidly, as developers find new ways to leverage the technology to save costs, reduce time-to-market, and enhance human safety.

WHAT IS A NETWORKED VIRTUAL ENVIRONMENT?

A *networked virtual environment* (net-VE) is a software system in which multiple users interact with each other in real-time, even though those users may be located around the world. Typically, each user accesses his or her own computer workstation or console, using it to provide a user-interface to the content of a virtual environment. These environments aim to provide users with a sense of realism by incorporating realistic 3D graphics and stereo sound, to create an immersive experience. A networked virtual environment is distinguished by the following five common features.

1. *A shared sense of space:* All participants have the illusion of being located in the same place, such as in the same room, building, or terrain. That shared place represents a common location within which other interactions can take place. The place may be real or fictional. The shared space must present the same characteristics to all participants. For example, all participants should get the same sense of the temperature and weather, as well as the acoustics. Though it need not be presented graphically, the most effective net-VEs provide an immersive three-dimensional graphical representation of the shared place.

2. *A shared sense of presence:* When entering the shared place, each participant takes on a virtual persona, called an *avatar*, which includes a graphical representation, body structure model (the presence of arms, legs, antennae, tentacles, joints, and so forth), motion model (the range of motion that joints may take), physical model (height, weight, and so forth), and other characteristics. An avatar does not need to take on a human form; it may be an animal, plant, machine, alien, or any other type of figure. Upon entering the net-VE, each participant can see the other avatars that are located in the shared space, and those users can see the new participant's avatar. Similarly, when a participant leaves the net-VE, other participants should see the avatar depart. Not all participants need to be human-controlled. Net-VE participants may be synthetic entities controlled by event-driven simulation models or even by rule-based inference engines.

3. *A shared sense of time:* Participants should be able to see each other's behavior as it occurs. In other words, the net-VE should enable real-time interaction to occur.

4. *A way to communicate:* Though visualization forms the basis for an effective net-VE, most net-VEs also enable some communication among the participants—by gesture, by typed text, or by voice. This communication adds a necessary sense of realism to any simulated environment, and it is a fundamental component of engineering or training systems.

5. *A way to share:* The aforementioned elements effectively provide a high-quality video conferencing system. However, the true power of net-VEs derives from users' ability to interact realistically not only with each other but also with the virtual environment itself. In a battle simulation or game, for example, users need to shoot each other, or they might collide with each other. Users should be able to pick up, move, and manipulate items that exist in the environment, and they should be able to give items to other participants. A net-VE designer might even empower users to manipulate the environment itself by building bunkers, drawing on chalkboards, or even destroying the environment.

In summary, net-VEs provide multiple users with the ability to interact with each other, share information, and manipulate objects in the environment, through immersive graphics. The presence of multiple independent users differentiates net-VEs from standard virtual reality or gaming systems. The ability to share objects differentiates net-VEs from traditional chat rooms, and the real-time interactivity differentiates net-VEs from traditional Web browsing or electronic mail. Net-VEs are most appropriate for applications that demand the creation of *telepresence*, the illusion that other users are visible from remote locations. In these applications, users demand a sense of realism approaching that which otherwise only can be achieved by face-to-face contact.

A net-VE system consists of four basic components: (1) graphics engines and displays, (2) communication and control devices, (3) processing systems, and (4) a data network. These components work together to provide the sense of immersion among users at different sites.

Graphics Engines and Displays

Graphics engines and displays are the cornerstone of the net-VE user interface. The display provides the user with a three-dimensional window into the virtual environment, and the engine generates the images for display. Traditionally, these graphics capabilities only were available on high-end graphics workstations. However, in recent years, sufficient graphics capabilities have become available on standard PCs. Add-on high-speed graphics processors are inexpensive and give PCs rendering horsepower that rivals low-to-mid-range graphics workstations. Moreover, the standard OpenGL graphics API enables the development of portable graphics-intensive applications [OpenGL97]. At the low-end, game machines, such as the Nintendo 64 and Sony PlayStation, and arcade game consoles have also become suitable display devices for net-VEs.

Although they provide high-quality 3D imagery, traditional displays offer only limited immersion to users. After all, the user can still be easily distracted by outside light and peripheral vision. For a higher fidelity experience, net-VE systems use graphical devices that more completely envelop the user by blocking all visual input from outside the virtual environment. For example, small graphical displays are often embedded within goggles. These *head-mounted displays* (HMDs) present images directly in front of the user's eyes, and they block out almost all external light [Sutherland68]. A magnetic sensor inside the HMD detects the user's head motion and feeds that information to the attached processor. Consequently, as the user turns his or her head, the displayed graphics can reflect the changing viewpoint.

Another immersive graphical display is known as the CAVE, and it was first developed at the University of Illinois at Chicago [Cruz-Neira+93]. The CAVE is essentially a five-sided cube. The participant stands in the middle of the cube, and images are projected onto the walls in front, above, below, and on either side of the participant, utilizing full 270-degree peripheral vision. As the user travels through the virtual environment, updated images are projected onto the CAVE's walls to give the sensation of smooth motion. The CAVE display model has been adapted to a variety of derivative interfaces. For example, multiple dynamic displays are used within tank simulators and simulated military command posts to provide the illusion of immersion within the battle.

Control and Communication Devices

Users need to be able to move about, pick up and manipulate objects, and communicate with other participants in the virtual environment. These tasks are accomplished through the use of various input devices. The most common are the keyboard and mouse. Using the mouse, the user navigates through the environment by changing direction and rotation. The mouse typically is also used to control speed of travel and perform other interactions, such as shooting bullets or manipulating a shared engineering model. The keyboard provides support for typed textual communication and offers access to other less common operations.

Although the keyboard and mouse are the most common control devices, they are not always the most effective.

- On game platforms, a joystick usually takes the place of a mouse.
- For more precise manipulation tasks, a dataglove may be used. Worn on the user's hand, such a glove includes sensors that detect and capture the motion of the hand and finger joints.
- As mentioned before, magnetic sensors placed inside an HMD capture the user's viewing direction and angle.
- In full-body immersive environments such as the CAVE, motion detectors mounted in the CAVE walls can detect and measure actual body movement.
- Users can be tethered to a device that determines body motion by measuring forces created by the user's movement.

Textual communication, though inexpensive, distracts from the full immersion that net-VEs strive to achieve. In more sophisticated net-VEs, users can communicate verbally using microphones. The computer receives the audio coming from the other participants, mixes the various streams, and plays the audio through a set of speakers. The audio feedback can be quite complex, incorporating not only participants' voices but also sound effects generated by activities occurring within the virtual environment.

Processing Systems

Decreasing processor prices have driven much of the growth behind net-VE deployment; net-VEs demand a considerable amount of processing capacity. The processor unit receives events from the user's input devices and computes how those inputs change both the user's own position within the virtual environment and the location of other objects within the environment. The processor determines how and when to notify other participants of these changes. Similarly, it receives information provided by other participants about their locations and behaviors within the virtual environment. The processor models autonomous net-VE objects controlled by the local host. Finally, it animates the graphic display to maintain an up-to-date window into the virtual environment.

Historically, image generation has demanded the most resources. Indeed, given the goal of full immersion, any available processor cycles can always be allocated toward generating higher-quality graphics at faster frame rates. One of the challenges facing net-VE designers, therefore, is allocating the available processor time among the myriad tasks required to support the user's net-VE presence.

Data Network

Participants in the net-VE rely on the network to exchange information. For example, as the user moves within the virtual environment, he or she must transmit updates over the network so that other users will visualize that user in the correct location. Similarly, if a user picks up an object in the environment, other users need to be notified that the object is now being carried. The network is also used to synchronize the net-VE's shared state, including weather and smoke, time, and terrain. It also supports textual, audio, and video communication among users.

For years, net-VEs could only be used at universities or large military or industrial institutions with fast local area networks such as Ethernets or Token Ring. Because networks had limited capacity and net-VE systems did not carefully manage how they used that network capacity, net-VEs could support fewer than a dozen simultaneous users. Because Internet capacity was limited, net-VEs could not be deployed over the Internet. To support users from multiple sites, a net-VE needed to be deployed over a high-bandwidth private network such as the Defense Simulation Internet (DSI).[1]

The world of networking has changed dramatically over the past five years. Local area network capacities have increased by a factor of 100 as Ethernets have grown from supporting 10 Mbps (million bits per second) to supporting 1 Gbps (billion bits per second). Over local area networks, therefore, rudimentary net-VEs can now support hundreds of users. At the same time, modern net-VEs manage the available network capacity more carefully, so they can support several thousand simultaneous participants.

---

[1]The DSI is a private, leased-line network funded by the Defense Advanced Research Projects Agency (DARPA). It is composed of 1.5 Mbps T-1 links connected by BBN routers and using the ST-II protocol. It has been widely used for defense simulation experimentation.

Advances in communications technology have also enabled net-VEs to escape from the confines of private networks. As modem speeds have quadrupled since 1993 from 14.4 Kbps to 56 Kbps, users now can participate in net-VEs by connecting to an Internet Service Provider from home. This indicates the potential growth of net-VEs for education and customer assistance applications.

The Internet has also become a viable platform for net-VE deployment. Wide-area network capacities have increased considerably as the number of Internet users has grown. At the same time, net-VE capabilities are entering the Web browser. For example, the Virtual Reality Modeling Language (VRML) enables users to download interactive 3D models over the World Wide Web [Hartman/Wernecke96]. The Living Worlds (LW) standard adds multiuser access capabilities to these VRML models, and the Virtual Reality Transport Protocol (vrtp) offers a proposed network protocol for exchanging net-VE data [VRML-LivingWorlds, Brutzman+97]. With standard Web browsers as an execution engine for net-VEs, the Internet will increasingly become the most common location for net-VE systems.

CHALLENGES IN NET-VE DESIGN AND DEVELOPMENT

Net-VEs are notoriously difficult to implement correctly or effectively. Net-VE systems are complex because they are multiple traditional types of software rolled into a single application. Net-VEs are:

- *Distributed systems:* They must contend with all of the challenges of managing network resources, data loss, network failure, and concurrency.
- *Graphical applications:* They must maintain smooth, real-time display frame rates and carefully allocate the CPU among rendering and other tasks.
- *Interactive applications:* They must process real-time data input from users. Users should see the virtual environment as if it exists locally, even though its participants are distributed at multiple remote hosts.

Net-VE design is made more complex because these systems must work with a number of existing application services.

- Net-VEs typically must integrate with database systems that store persistent information about the virtual environment. These databases include, for example, detailed information about the environment's terrain elevation, the location of buildings and other static items in the environment, and the initial net-VE configuration.
- Net-VEs need to support user authentication and may interact with commerce and other transaction systems.
- To support reproducible engineering systems, net-VEs must be able to log events in real-time to a persistent storage; this task is complicated by the fact that the complete state of the net-VE may not actually be known at any single host in the system.

The components of a net-VE system interact in complex ways, so the designer must regard the application as a unified system. Invariably, trying to optimize one element of a net-VE can adversely impact the behavior of other components. In effect, net-VE development is a difficult balancing act of engineering tradeoffs. This section describes the forces at play within a net-VE system and indicates the range of some of the design dimensions represented by these forces. The rest of the book describes these forces in more detail and how to address them during net-VE design.

Network Bandwidth

Net-VEs rely on the data network to exchange information about the current state of the virtual environment. If one user wishes to receive detailed information about another user's activity, that information must be sent over the network; if more detail is desired, then more information must be transmitted. Similarly, as more users participate in the net-VE, the aggregate amount of information generated by the application also increases.

However, network capacity is a limited resource, so the net-VE designer must carefully determine how to allocate this capacity. For example, when a user connects to a net-VE through a modem connection that offers minimal network capacity, that user cannot reasonably expect to receive detailed real-time information about every other participant in the net-VE.

Heterogeneity

In real-world net-VEs, users do not have to access the same set of equipment. For example, while some participants may be using a graphics workstation with keyboard and mouse connected to a telephone line, others may be using fully immersive head-mounted displays with datagloves connected to a multiprocessor that is linked to an Ethernet. This idea of *heterogeneous access ports* is desirable, but it also poses several challenges.

First of all, the net-VE designer must decide whether to expose or hide the differences between the capabilities and speeds of the different participants. Network heterogeneity arises because different users may be connecting to the net-VE using networks that have different capacities. Consequently, some users are capable of receiving more information about the net-VE than others. The net-VE design can hide the heterogeneity by reducing the system to a "lowest common denominator," where the network requirements are no greater than the lowest capacity network link. Though the lowest capacity approach guarantees that all users have access to the same information, it also means that the presence of a single "bad" participant effectively destroys the net-VE experience for all the other participants. An alternative approach is to take full advantage of all the available resources. However, in choosing this option, the net-VE designer must contend with the issues of "fair play" that result when users must interact even though they have received different levels of information about the environment. This issue is particularly relevant in gaming and interactive training applications where a lack of fairness can reduce the enjoyment of the experience, or lead to unrealistic training.

Secondly, heterogeneity issues arise with regard to the graphical display, computational, and audio capabilities. For example, some users might have graphic workstations capable of rendering millions of polygons per second with texture-mapped graphics, while others might have low-end PC displays capable of rendering only a few hundred polygons per second without textures. Some machines may be able to present the audio associated with the environment, while others may lack audio capabilities. Again, the net-VE designer must decide whether to use minimal resources to ensure fairness among participants or whether to attempt to expose these differences and address the resulting fairness issues.

The interactions among user interface attributes is often complex and can be counterintuitive. For example, in military training systems, the users with limited audio and graphics capability actually have an advantage over those who have better equipment. When graphics resources are limited, the host does not have enough cycles to render all of the vegetation and camouflage contained in the scene; modeling and rendering the participants in the net-VE consumes all of the available cycles. Without being impeded by these graphics that limit visibility, users can take actions that they would not otherwise be able to perform. They can shoot at users who would not otherwise be visible. When trying to integrate heterogeneous systems, therefore, the designer must carefully control how the available resources will be allocated, to avoid impractical net-VE interactions.

Distributed Interaction

Distributed interaction is one of the defining qualities of a net-VE system. Users see each other's real-time activity and react to this information in real-time. In some systems, engineering models react dynamically to stimuli provided by system components located on other machines. To be effective, the net-VE system must present each user with the illusion that the entire environment is located on the local machine and that his or her actions are having a direct and immediate impact on the environment. The system needs to mask any artifacts that might arise because of the application's distributed nature.

Maintaining the illusion of a single system is difficult because of the messaging required to exchange information within the net-VE. For example, networks impose a noticeable delay from the time that a message is transmitted to the time that a message is actually received at its destination. Moreover, different messages may incur different delays depending on the type of network and on the locations of the source and destination hosts. Each host must therefore attempt to present a consistent real-time view of the net-VE and contend with the fact that all of the incoming information about remote users is already out-of-date when it arrives.

These network delays are particularly difficult to handle when multiple users or components interact with each other directly. For example, a net-VE must support accurate *collision detection, agreement,* and *resolution* among participants. Accurate collision detection is difficult because at any given point in time, no user has accurate information about the other users' current positions; as we have seen, the network delay means that all received information is out-of-date. It is possible, therefore, that one user might conclude, based on stale information, that a collision occurred, while, in fact, the other user actually moved to avoid the collision during the network delay period. It is therefore also possible that the users may reach entirely different conclusions about whether the collision occurred because each is receiving information with different delays. Even having agreed on whether the collision occurred, the hosts may also need to agree on the precise point of impact, as well as the physical forces involved and how the collision should affect the participants. This task becomes exponentially more complicated when the collision involves more than two objects in the net-VE.

These types of direct interactions are commonplace within net-VEs. In games, collisions arise when determining whether a bullet actually hit its intended target. Even a seemingly simple handshake involves a collision. An engineering simulation must compute the constant interactions between a vehicle and the road that it is driving on or between the airplane wing and the wind flow. These interactions include frictional forces, heat, and even acoustic information. The distributed nature of net-VEs further complicates the transmission of audio communication, because the receiver must accurately determine how to attenuate the audio based on virtual distance and dynamic environmental effects.

Real-Time System Design and Resource Management

Real-time interaction defines the process and thread architecture of the net-VE application. Many different tasks concurrently compete for use of the CPU, and unlike most systems, almost all of those tasks have hard real-time constraints. Satisfying the real-time needs of these various tasks is a challenge for the net-VE designer.

The net-VE needs to support real-time interactions with the local user. The software design must accommodate quick detection and processing of user action (from the keyboard, mouse, HMD, and so forth). Delays to this processing can lead to a sluggish, distracting user interaction experience. For instance, graphical image generation must occur at a fixed rate, say 30 frames per second; delays to this processing can yield a jerky display that reduces the quality of the net-VE immersion. Without variation, all available CPU cycles can usually be devoted toward generating higher quality images. Network packets arrive asynchronously and need to be processed as soon as they are available, because delays to packet processing cause higher error rates for rendered representations of remote participants. Finally, physics modeling and collision detection must be performed several times per second within the net-VE application.

The net-VE designer may employ many techniques for managing these tasks. One approach is to place everything into a single thread that cycles through all of the tasks in a round-robin fashion fast enough to meet all of their real-time constraints. Alternatively, the application may be segmented into multiple threads that are tuned and scheduled to balance their CPU use. Besides scheduling efficient use of the CPU, multithreaded net-VE system implementations must also manage contention to the shared data structures stored on each host. Shared locks must be used to coordinate state updates (made for user input, arriving network packets, and virtual environment modeling and simulation) and state accesses (made for image generation, transmitting network packets, and virtual modeling and simulation).

Failure Management

Distributed systems must inherently contend with the possibility that one or more of the connected hosts may crash or simply be turned off at any time. Moreover, network connections may fail or become otherwise unusable either temporarily or permanently. The possibility of failures can have significant impact on the net-VE design.

The net-VE designer must determine to what extent a failure may affect the execution of the application. Failure handling falls into the following four categories.

1. *System stop:* Failures may cause the entire net-VE to terminate if the missing resource is critical to the net-VE's execution. For example, if the system architecture uses a central server to receive and distribute all data, then that server's failure would likely prevent the net-VE from operating. System-stop failures are least desirable, in general, though they may be appropriate when maintaining accuracy and realism.

2. *System closure:* Failures may not impact the existing net-VE users, but they may prevent the arrival of new users into the net-VE. For example, failure of an authentication server would prevent new users from logging into the system. Existing users need not be affected by the absence of an authentication server because they have already authenticated to the net-VE.

3. *System hindrance:* Some failures may simply degrade the experience provided by the net-VE users. For example, the failure of a weather server would mean that the users no longer receive real-time weather updates for the virtual environment, but they may still perform their other tasks within the environment. Similarly, if a single user's host crashes, then the other users would simply see that user depart from the environment. However, this class of failures can cause a broad range of effects on the net-VE, ranging from minor annoyances to major events. For example, if a machine modeling an aircraft carrier becomes disconnected and disappears from the scene, then the airplanes located on that carrier may conclude that they should fall into the ocean.

4. *System continuance:* A failure might have almost no noticeable affect on the net-VE. This situation arises when a noncritical service, such as a logging server, fails. In these cases, the net-VE's execution may continue unaffected, though the absence of the unavailable service may impact some other function, such as recording and playback of the application. System continuance is also possible when a critical service is supported by a "hot backup" server that shadows the primary server's state and can therefore be quickly activated to replace the primary server should it fail.

System continuance is the most desirable failure model for a net-VE because it allows net-VE execution to continue without interruption. However, these semantics are also the most expensive to provide and maintain. Presence of a hot-backup server requires additional hardware and network resources, and the need to shadow the state of the primary server may also slow down the primary server's execution. At the other extreme, system stop semantics require almost no system support.

Failure handling is complicated because failures typically do not occur in isolation. When a network fails, multiple participants may simultaneously get disconnected from the net-VE. Similarly, a single host may provide multiple services on behalf of the net-VE, so when it fails, all of those services immediately become unavailable. The net-VE designer must therefore assess how resources and services will be allocated among hosts and among networks to ensure that concurrent failures impact the net-VE in well-defined ways.

Scalability

Most commonly, *scalability,* or size, of a net-VE is measured by the number of *entities* that may simultaneously participate in the system. A net-VE entity is a participating object that is separately modeled by the participating hosts. Net-VE entities may include human-controlled and computer-controlled vehicles, a terrain (and associated features such as rocks, trees, and buildings), and even logical objects such as the current weather state or an object group. Systems pose a wide range of scalability requirements, ranging from two entities for simple game systems to hundreds of thousands of entities for complex engineering and training systems. Alternative measures of scalability are the number of hosts that may simultaneously connect to the net-VE and the physical distance between participants in the net-VE.

Net-VE scalability depends on a variety of factors, including network capacity, processor capabilities, rendering speeds, and the speed and throughput of shared servers. Scalability is expensive to achieve because it requires enhancements to virtually all aspects of the net-VE system.

The complexity of a net-VE theoretically increases exponentially with the number of participating entities because of the number of possible interactions among those entities. A particular interaction may involve any combination of the entities participating in the net-VE, so that there are $2^{(number\ of\ entities)}$ possible entity-to-entity interactions. In reality, however, the number of actual interactions generally does not increase as quickly as the number of possible interactions. As a rule, an entity in a net-VE does not interact with every other entity in the net-VE. For example, in a large net-VE, we would not expect the participants to congregate in a single room, and if they do, they would rarely stand in the same part of the room. Instead, users tend to scatter into different subgroups, clusters, or teams, each located in a different part of the net-VE. These entity groups may change throughout the net-VE execution, but their very existence inherently limits the number of interactions that may occur at any one time.

Deployment and Configuration

Net-VE designers face a challenge in deploying their software to potential participants. If the net-VE client software is large and monolithic, it is inappropriate for downloading. Alternatively, the software may be designed around a small core library and components that may be dynamically downloaded depending on the changing needs of the executing net-VE. These packaging alternatives impact the software design, the choice of implementation language, and the set of supported execution platforms.

Deployment issues are made more complex if the net-VE will execute within Web browsers communicating over the Internet. In this case, the net-VE designer must ensure that:

- The environment is easily downloaded.
- Implementation of the net-VE conforms to the security bounds imposed by the available browser environments.
- The software executes and displays correctly across different browser platforms. Web browsers are notoriously inconsistent in their support for downloaded applications, and standard 3D graphics markup languages such as VRML have not yet achieved true portability across different browsers.

Successful net-VE deployment involves more than software distribution. The participants need to have access to configuration information including network addresses for sending data, the location of weather and terrain servers, security encryption keys and access codes, graphic images and computational models for different types of participants, and so forth. This configuration data usually differs for each net-VE execution and may be comparable in size to the net-VE software itself. The Net-VE designer must collect this information and make it available to all participants, either as a single distribution unit or as incrementally downloadable units.

CONCLUSION

For many years, networked virtual environments have been the product of science fiction [Stephenson92, Gibson85]. The use of cyberspace to overcome the expense of travel and overcome the physical limitations of reality has sparked the imagination of many a visionary. However, until recently, net-VEs have been experimental at best.

Faster processors, more powerful graphics hardware, and higher-capacity networks are supporting the development of networked virtual environments containing more simulation entities and more detailed models of entity appearance and behavior. Consequently, these net-VE applications are seeing increased use for multiplayer games, military and industrial training, and collaborative engineering. These applications demand that each user see a consistent virtual worldview, that users be able to interact closely with one another and with other entities in the virtual world, and that maximum realism be provided by hiding the distributed nature of the application from users.

Developing effective net-VEs involves managing the interactions among a variety of system components—including the network, processor, graphics display, user input devices, databases, and other external information servers. At the same time, the developer must support the desirable goals of heterogeneity, scalability, fault-tolerance, and easy deployability. As an engineered system, a net-VE cannot fully achieve all of these goals simultaneously. The designer must therefore determine which of these attributes takes priority in the net-VE implementation.

The rest of this book concerns the various decisions faced by the net-VE designer. When making these decisions, the designer must consider the overall behavior of the net-VE system. Rarely can a single aspect of the net-VE be changed without, in subtle ways, affecting the rest of the system. Understanding the interactions among the various system components is vital for effective net-VE development.

Net-VEs are not new. Experimental systems have been around for decades. We begin the journey into net-VE design by exploring the evolution of net-VE systems. Understanding the range of designs that have been used to implement existing real systems will be important for making effective decisions for future systems.

REFERENCES

[Brutzman+97] Brutzman, D., M. Zyda, K. Watsen, and M. Macedonia. Virtual reality transfer protocol (vrtp) design rationale. In *Proceedings of the IEEE Sixth Workshops on Enabling Technologies: Infrastructure for Collaborative*

Enterprises (WET ICE '97), 179–186. IEEE Computer Society, Cambridge, MA, June 1997.

[Cruz-Neira+93] Cruz-Neira, C., D. J. Sandin, and T. A. DeFanti. Surround-screen projection-based virtual reality: The design and implementation of the CAVE. In *SIGGRAPH 1993 Conference Proceedings.* ACM SIGGRAPH, Anaheim, July 1993.

[Gibson85] Gibson, W. *Neuromancer.* New York: Ace Books, 1985.

[Hartman/Wernecke96] Hartman, J., and J. Wernecke. *The VRML 2.0 Handbook: Building Moving Worlds on the Web.* Reading, MA: Addison-Wesley, 1996.

[OpenGL97] OpenGL Architecture Review Board. *OpenGL Reference Manual: The Official Reference Document to OpenGL, Version 1.1*, C. Frazier and R. Kempf, eds. Reading, MA: Addison-Wesley, 1997.

[Stephenson92] Stephenson, N., *Snow Crash.* New York: Bantam Spectra, 1992.

[Sutherland68] Sutherland, I. E. A head-mounted three-dimensional display. In *AFIPS Conference Proceedings*, vol. 33, I:757–764, 1968.

[VRML-LivingWorlds] VRML Living Worlds Working Group Web site: *http://www.vrml.org/WorkingGroups/living-worlds/*

Chapter 2

The Origin of Networked Virtual Environments

This chapter presents a historical overview of networked virtual environments, discussing each system that has played a major part in the origins of net-VEs, including the military heritage of this field (SIM-NET and DIS), networked games (SGI *Dogfight, Doom,* and so forth), and academic research (NPSNET, PARADISE, DIVE, BrickNet, MR Toolkit, and so forth).

We do not describe the systems in depth, but rather aim to identify the central trends, or *network software architectures* (NSAs), underlying these systems. By network software architecture, we mean the inseparable issues of what network protocol is used for the system and what software architecture supports that protocol, within the confines of available bandwidth and processor cycles. We use this term to stress the importance of solving both problems at once, rather than just focusing on defining a software architecture that ignores concerns of available bandwidth or just focusing on defining a protocol that ignores processor cycle limitations.

DEPARTMENT OF DEFENSE NETWORKED VIRTUAL ENVIRONMENTS

The Department of Defense (DoD) is the largest developer of net-VEs for use as simulation systems, and its early efforts at this are of both historic and technical interest: historic interest in that the DoD was one of the first to develop net-VEs with its SIMNET system,[1] and technical interest in that the DoD was the first to do work on large-scale net-VEs.

SIMNET

SIMNET (simulator networking) is a distributed military virtual environment originally developed for DARPA by Bolt, Beranek and Newman (BBN), Perceptronics, and Delta Graphics [Pope89]. SIMNET was begun in 1983 and delivered to the U.S. Army at the end of March 1990. The goal of the SIMNET project was to develop a "low-cost" net-VE for training small units (M1 tanks, AH-64 helicopters, command posts, and so forth) to fight as a team. SIMNET was not intended to be a 100% solution for small unit training but rather a "70% solution," with the remaining 30% requiring soldiers to get into real tanks in the field.

The two key technical challenges for the SIMNET project were (1) how to fabricate high-quality, low-cost simulators and (2) how to network them together to create a consistent, virtual battlefield [Miller/Thorpe95]. To carry out the study of these technical challenges, the SIMNET project created an 11-site testbed with from 50 to 100 simulators at each site. SIMNET could be entered from anywhere on the network using a simulator as the portal into the synthetic environment. Once that synthetic environment was entered, the "player" (or participant) could interact with others who were also online in the synthetic battlefield. Play in that synthetic environment was unscripted free play, done within the confines of whatever chain of command was imposed on the simulation participants.

---

[1]*Amaze* is thought of as the first modern networked game/virtual environment, dating from 1984 [Berglund/Cheriton85].

SIMNET Network Software Architecture

The SIMNET network software architecture has three basic components:

1. An object-event architecture
2. A notion of autonomous simulation nodes
3. An embedded set of predictive modeling algorithms called "dead reckoning" [Miller/Thorpe95]

The object-event architecture is the simplest component of the SIMNET NSA. The SIMNET object-event architecture modeled the world as a collection of objects whose interactions with each other are a collection of events. Objects are the vehicles and weapons systems that can interact across the network. A single object, say a tank, in SIMNET is usually managed by a single machine. Events in SIMNET are messages to the network indicating a change in world or object state. An example event that would be transmitted as a message might be that the object (tank) is turning right. Another event might be that the tank has fired its gun.

One of the unusual design decisions in SIMNET with respect to the object-event architecture is that the basic terrain and structures that sit on the SIMNET terrain are separate from the collection of objects. This means that for a bridge to be destroyed in SIMNET it must be reclassified as an object, an object whose (dormant) state is continually transmitted onto the network.

In SIMNET, the notion of autonomous simulation nodes means that individual players, vehicles, and weapons systems on the network are responsible for placing messages, or packets, onto the network to accurately represent their current state. Beyond transmitting these state updates and events, these autonomous nodes do not interact with the packet recipients. Packet recipients are responsible for receiving such state change information and making the appropriate changes to their local model of the world. This lack of a central server means that single point failures in the system do not take the entire simulation down. Additionally, it allows players to join and leave the simulation at any time.

This notion of autonomous nodes means that each node is responsible for one or more objects in the virtual world. Object responsibility means that the node must place packets onto the network representing the current state or any changes-in-state of its objects. Placing changes-in-state on the network means that a node must place packets onto the network whenever its objects have changed enough so that the other players should be made cognizant of the changes. Placing current state onto the network also means that a node must provide a regular "heart-beat" message, usually every 5 seconds, to keep other players informed that a particular object is alive and still in the system (and hence should be displayed). Autonomy at the nodes has some interesting implications in the SIMNET NSA. Objects for which the heartbeat is delayed disappear and reappear in displays. Objects that change frequently or rapidly in state place large numbers of packets onto the network.

The third component of the SIMNET NSA is a well-defined set of predictive modeling algorithms called "dead reckoning" algorithms. When SIMNET was first constructed in prototype, it was implemented such that each change in object state was reported immediately onto the network in the form of an update packet. With small numbers of players, this was not a large worry, but it meant that for some objects, packets were being generated as fast as the simulation control program could generate them (that is, at *frame rate*). This rate of packet generation flooded the network and overloaded the CPUs.

To reduce this packet traffic, the *objects and ghosts* paradigm was created. The idea behind this paradigm is that objects only place packets onto the network when their home node determines that the other nodes on the network are no longer able to predict their state within a certain threshold amount. When this condition occurs, a node must place a packet onto the network indicating the current state of the modeled object. This paradigm assumes that the other nodes in the system are maintaining "ghost" copies of the object in their memories and that the last reported direction, velocity, and position are sufficient to predict, within the threshold amount, where that entity is now. When a new packet is received for a "ghost" object, dead reckoning begins again with the newly received motion parameters.

When new packets are received for ghost objects, the ghost object is typically seen to move over or back slightly, depending on the allowed error threshold amount. Larger thresholds mean fewer packets on the network but larger jumps when ghosts get out of synch and their positions are corrected. Dead reckoning also makes packet loss less of a problem, as the object continues to move in the direction of its last known heading and at its last known speed. If the object is not moving wildly, this is usually valid. If the object is moving wildly, another packet is most likely right behind the lost packet, and the object will not get too far afield.

The heartbeat packet also provides updates and again provides additional position synchronization. Packet rates seen within SIMNET were 1 packet per second, on average, for slow-moving ground vehicles and 3 packets per second for air vehicles. SIMNET vehicle appearance packets include absolute position, velocity, and direction, as shown in Table 2-1.

Notice that we would expect some of the information in the packet to be relatively static. For example, the markings and capabilities information is sent repeatedly at each packet transmission. The expected data for vehicle state change, location, engine speed, velocity vector, tur-

TABLE 2-1 SIMNET Vehicle Appearance Packet Contents

Field name	Contents	Field size (in bytes)
Vehicle ID	Site Host Vehicle	6
Vehicle class	Tank Simple Static Irrelevant	1
Force ID		1
Guises	Object type: distinguished Object type: other	8
World coordinates	Location: x, y, z	24
Rotation matrix	—	36
Appearance	—	4
Markings	Text field	12
Timestamp	—	4
Capabilities	—	32
Engine speed	—	2
Stationary bit and padding	—	2
Vehicle appearance variant	Velocity vector Turret azimuth Gun elevation	24

ret azimuth, and gun elevation are all there. One novel innovation is a single bit field indicating whether or not the vehicle is stationary. This field allows vehicle ghost computations to be turned off, saving CPU cycles at the recipient nodes. In addition to vehicle appearance packets, SIMNET also has other packet definitions as part of its application layer protocol, including the event packets *fire* (a weapon has been launched), *indirect fire* (a ballistic weapon has been launched), *collision* (a vehicle has collided with an object), and *impact* (a weapon has hit an object).

The software architecture of a typical SIMNET node contains the following major modules [Miller/Thorpe95], as shown in Figure 2-1, with the connections between the modules indicating data flow:

- Network interface
- Other-vehicle state table
- Computer image-generator software
- Controls and display interface
- Own-vehicle dynamics
- Sound generation

The network interface software places object state change packets onto the network. The network interface software also collects packets from the network for processing by the node. Packets are placed onto

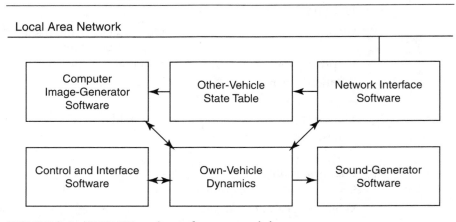

FIGURE 2-1 SIMNET major software modules

Source: From [Miller/Thorpe95]. Used with permission.

the SIMNET local area network using Ethernet multicasting, with each exercise being assigned to a different multicast address. This use of multicasting allows different exercises to coexist on the same LAN, with the hardware network interface demultiplexing the stream of packets. With this architecture, internetworking is accomplished via the use of a piece of "bridge" software (that is, a piece of software that copies the packets from the LAN and retransmits them across the wide-area T-1 link to another piece of bridge software that then multicasts the copied packets onto the second LAN).

The other-vehicle state table contains the dead reckoning information for the players ghosted by each node. The computer image generator software of SIMNET forwards the polygons to be drawn to the special purpose Delta Graphics image generator hardware. Sound generation was used to heighten the immersion of the soldier in the system.

Own-vehicle dynamics are the actual state data for the vehicles managed by a node. SIMNET's control and interface software turned human interaction into display changes and interactions and updated the own-vehicle dynamics.

SIMNET Scalability

With an exercise in March 1990, the SIMNET network software architecture proved scalable, with some 850 objects (mostly semiautomated forces) at five sites [Miller/Thorpe95]. These objects averaged 1 packet per second, with each packet about 156 bytes, for a peak requirement of 1.06 Mbps, just under the T-1 speed of the connecting links.

Important SIMNET Dates

The DARPA SIMNET program began in April 1983. The construction of a testbed with many sites with hundreds of simulators was the initial goal. The first 2 simulators at Fort Knox (out of an eventual 80 simulators that would eventually make up the Fort Knox ensemble) came online in May 1986. In May 1987, about 40 simulators were networked and nine months afterward, all 80 simulators were up and running, including tanks, personnel carriers, and a handful of helicopters and A-10 fighters. Ultimately, 11 sites (4 in Europe) and 250 simulators constituted the testbed.

Of interest, 4 simulators along with a model of the Grafenwohr tank gunnery range used for the Canadian Army Trophy competition were sent to the U.S. units in Germany to help them prepare for the competition in early 1987. The United States won for the first time in the 17-year history of the shoot-off, with the winning crews attributing their advantage to the structured use of simulation [Thorpe97].

Distributed Interactive Simulation

In September 1989 the SIMNET originating contractor, Bolt, Beranek and Newman (BBN), had defined the state of the art, by creating the SIMNET protocol to satisfy its contract with the United States government. It had not defined the network software architecture to be general purpose. It had not defined the packets that would be required to accommodate all types of simulation. In fact, it had not documented the packet formats and network software architecture sufficiently so that others could utilize it. That was not part of the contract. Non-BBN contractors who wished to interoperate with SIMNET requested copies of the SIMNET source code and a few hours of BBN engineers' time, time most often gladly provided.

Oral tradition can only accomplish so much. SIMNET's success in training tank platoons, as exemplified by the Battle of 73 Easting during Operation Desert Storm [Maguire/Reeder92], coupled with its lack of generality led to an attempt to formally generalize and extend the SIMNET protocol. This effort was called the Distributed Interactive Simulation (DIS) protocol. To facilitate the development of this protocol, a biannual conference called the Distributed Interactive Simulation Workshop was instituted. These efforts led to the first version of the IEEE standard for DIS, the IEEE 1278 standard [IEEE93].

The purpose in establishing DIS formally was to allow participation in the DIS virtual environment by any type of player, on any type of machine. This heterogeneous mix of computing and virtual environment players grew out of the thoughts then prevalent that perhaps the DoD could achieve larger simulations, with a greater variety of players, if the underlying network software architecture was nonproprietary and well-documented. To this goal, DIS was an enormous success, and that success led net-VEs from being only of DoD concern to having more widespread availability and interest.

The Distributed Interactive Simulation Network
Software Architecture

The DIS network software architecture is clearly derived from its SIMNET ancestry. DIS has the same three basic components: an object-event architecture, the notion of autonomous distributed simulation nodes, and the embedded set of predictive modeling algorithms for dead reckoning. The DIS object-event architecture is designed to cover a broader spectrum of military simulation requirements than SIMNET. For example, with DIS, seagoing vessels are part of the military virtual environment.

The core of the DIS network software architecture is the protocol data unit (PDU). Determining when each vehicle (node) of the simulation should issue a PDU is the key to this architecture. The DIS (IEEE 1278) standard defines 27 different PDUs, only 4 of which (entity state, fire, detonation, and collision) are used by nodes to interact with the virtual environment. In fact, most DIS-compliant simulations only implement those 4 PDUs, either throwing away the other 23 PDUs without comment or issuing a brief error message indicating a nonsupported PDU was received. The entity state PDU is issued for position, orientation, and velocity changes (see Table 2-2). The fire PDU is issued when a weapon has been fired. The detonation PDU is issued when a munition explodes or a vehicle crashes or dies. The collision PDU is issued when a vehicle has a collision with something against which it is doing collision detection. The remainder of the defined PDUs are for simulation control, electronic emanations, and supporting actions.

The responsibility for issuing PDUs rests with the vehicle's node in the virtual environment. A node must issue an entity state PDU when it has changed position, orientation, or velocity sufficiently such that the other nodes can no longer accurately predict the node's location via dead reckoning. A node must also issue an entity state PDU as a heartbeat if the time threshold (5 seconds) since the last entity state PDU was transmitted has been reached. A node must issue a fire PDU if it has fired a weapon. A node must issue a detonation PDU when the weapon it fired finally explodes or when the node's vehicle has died, either by crashing into something or by having been shot (death self-determination). This self-determination for a node of its own death can be misused to make oneself invincible. Detonation PDUs can also be misused to cause the mass death of other players in the virtual environment. One such example was the anecdotal Mega-Death program that collected positions of the enemy players in the virtual environment and then issued, all at once, detonation PDUs for powerful munitions next to each enemy player. Such play can only be done once, late at night, when major demonstrations are being set up—never when the Chief of Staff of the Army is present!

TABLE 2-2   Distributed Interactive Simulation Entity State PDU

Field name	Contents	Field size (in bytes)
PDU header	Protocol version, exercise ID, PDU type, protocol family, time stamp, length, padding	12
Entity ID	Site, application, entity	6
Force ID	—	1
Number of articulation parameters	—	1
Entity type	Entity kind, domain, country, category, subcategory, specific, extra	8
Alternative entity type	Entity kind, domain, country, category, subcategory, specific, extra	8
Entity linear velocity	x, y, z	12
Entity location	x, y, z	24
Entity orientation	Psi, theta, phi	12
Entity appearance	—	4
Dead reckoning parameters	Dead reckoning algorithm, other parameters, entity linear acceleration, entity angular velocity	40
Entity marking	Character set, marking	12
Capabilities	—	4
Articulation parameters	Parameter type, change, ID-attached to, parameter type, parameter value	n * 16

Source: From [IEEE93]. Used with permission.

A node must issue a collision PDU if it determines that it has collided with something against which it is checking for collisions. The implementation of collision detection is up to the individual node, and its accuracy often is quite dependent on the available CPU cycles and the skill of the DIS virtual environment implementer. It is not uncommon for DIS-based virtual environments to have no collision detection or only partial collision detection. Vehicles might be able to collide with buildings but can drive through trees (too many trees and not enough CPU cycles to check them all). It is also fairly common to see vehicles pass through each other without colliding. Moreover, no DIS virtual environment that implements collision detection does an effective job of collision response. Most collisions result in the colliding vehicles "dying" and issuing detonation PDUs. Most systems then leave the vehicles on the battlefield as smoking hulks. None models the possibilities we might actually see in the real world, such as small damage for low-speed collisions along with the concomitant elasticity of such collisions. None properly shows major damage.

Once a node has issued a PDU and placed it onto the network, it is the recipient's responsibility to receive the PDU, change the appropriate state tables, and then update the display. When an entity state PDU is received, the recipient node must update the other-vehicle state tables for that player and then the display of that player on the next display update cycle. When a fire PDU is received, the recipient must create a new vehicle in the other-vehicle state table for this munition and display the appropriate 3D icon. When a detonation PDU is received, the recipient must compute the effects of this munition, change the other-vehicle state table and its own-vehicle state table (if appropriate), and then change the display. Collision PDUs must be processed similarly. Note that it is the responsibility of the recipient node to modify its own state tables and displays. Since packets in DIS are sent via unreliable UDP broadcast, packets are sometimes lost. Hence, it is quite possible for displays and state tables to differ among different participating hosts.

An example of lost packets that is often used in the DIS community is one in which a munition is fired and then detonated near a target, where the munition is large enough to ensure a sure kill. The detonation PDU is generated by the platform that fired the munition. If the detonation PDU is not received or is ignored (unfairly) by the target, and if the target should have computed its own demise if it had received the detonation PDU, then the target vehicle has the potential to turn around and shoot at the originator of the munition. This gives the effect that objects in the simulation can shoot "from the afterlife" and has caused disputes in various DIS exercises. Disputes over such issues are typically relegated to "the fog of war" and left unresolved in the design of DIS.

Lost entity state PDUs (ESPDUs) are usually not a big problem. At most, they cause a larger jump than normal on the display when the next ESPDU arrives. Lost fire PDUs mean that a node receives a subsequent ESPDU of that munition for which no ghost entry has yet been created. This too is easily resolved. Lost collision PDUs mean that nodes may continue to display a vehicle as "live" after it has determined itself to be out of commission. This packet loss is made up at the next heartbeat from the now dead, out-of-commission vehicle.

A demonstration at the 1993 Interservice/Industry Training, Simulation, and Education Conference (I/ITSEC) showed that entity state PDUs comprised 96% of the total DIS traffic, with the remaining 4% distributed as follows: fire (4%), detonation (4%), collison (1%), logistics (0%), simulation management (0%), emission (38%), transmitter (50%), signal (0%), acoustic (2%), stealth (1%), and other (0%). The simulation contained 79 players sending PDUs, though the actual mix of vehicles involved in this exercise is not available. Air vehicles issued 1 ESPDU/second on average in that demonstration, with land vehicles averaging 0.17 ESPDUs/second. Some participants in that demonstration issued packets at frame rate, and some produced 20 ESPDUs per second [Pullen/Wood95].

The Fully Distributed, Heterogeneous Nature of DIS

DIS extended SIMNET's idea of autonomous simulation nodes. In DIS, we get more of a notion that any computer plugged into the network that reads/writes DIS PDUs and manages the state of those PDUs properly can fully participate in a DIS environment. This fully distributed, heterogeneous network software architecture means that workstation class machines can play against PC class machines. Additionally, it means that the environment can include virtual players (driven by a live human at a computer console of some sort), constructive players (computer-driven players), and live players (actual weapons systems plugged into the DIS network).

The fully distributed and heterogeneous nature of DIS has been its success. It has allowed different technologies to be utilized for DIS participation and has widened the scope of players in that world. In the various DIS demonstrations that have taken place, we have seen everything from a large 20-processor SGI Onyx machine to a single Pentium PC connected on the network. There are some concerns with this variety of platforms, however. DIS allows each node to proceed at its own speed for processing and displaying the results of PDU changes. For machines on the low-end, this might mean a frame rate of 6 frames per second and the inability to display the full set of virtual world features. This disparity sometimes has its "advantages." We have seen demonstrations where the low-end machines, the machines without the ability to texture their polygonal terrain, can clearly see the opposing forces silhouetted on the distant hillside. High-end machines with texturing do not have this "advantage." Many of these issues come under the topics of terrain fidelity and "fair fight" rules for DIS. Many long hours of DIS workshops have discussed both of these issues, thus far to no formal resolution.

Because of the fully distributed nature of DIS and its allowance of any speed processor at the node, this network software architecture raises some additional problems, most having to do with the advanced levels of modeling that the DoD would like to introduce. In particular, two types of modeling cause most of the problems—dynamic terrain and environmental effects. Dynamic terrain modeling would represent soil movement in terrain such that a participant can drive a bulldozer over the ground and the effects would be seen at all the workstations connected to the DIS environment. Unfortunately, the computations involved in dynamic terrain are large and expensive and not possible in a distributed fashion, if we allow any speed processor to participate in this distributed world.

Several proposals have been made to address this issue, including extensions to the suite of DIS packets and introduction of a terrain server for the DIS engagement. By repartitioning the problem, the latter approach puts quite a load on the network and on the CPU cycles required to process the incoming terrain PDUs. No satisfactory solution to this is available as of early 1999, although many individual studies have been done [Li/Moshell93, Li/Moshell94, Moshell+94].

Environmental effects (EE)—such as weather, smoke, dust, and other similar conditions—in the fully distributed DIS world have the same problem as dynamic terrain. Ideally, all players in the virtual world have the same world obscurants. Again, smoke and weather modeling are compute-intensive and not possible on all classes of machines that might be connected to a DIS engagement. Such modeling causes a significant load on the network and on the processor cycles required to process the EE PDUs. At best, current technology allows a display of gross smoke and weather using the fog capabilities of high-end, texture-capable SGI-class machines. PCs plugged into such networks are not yet able to display such pictures, although this is changing over time.

DIS Dead Reckoning Algorithms

Part of the DIS network software architecture is its continuance of the predictive modeling of participants via dead reckoning. The DIS standard defines 9 dead reckoning algorithms. The entity state PDU has fields for the particular dead reckoning algorithm, the entity linear acceleration, the entity angular velocity, and other parameters. A more full discussion on dead reckoning is found in Chapter 5.

DIS Scalability

While incredibly successful (with approximately 100 different systems being DIS-compliant), DIS has several limitations with its network software architecture. In order to motivate future net-VE systems, we discuss these limitations here.

From the lessons-learned perspective, one of the first things one notices about the DIS protocol is that the packets are larger than SIM-NET packets, and they consequently have the same problems as in SIMNET. The main packet used in DIS simulations, the entity state PDU, is full of data that does not change. This static information really only needs to be sent once, not in each ESPDU. With DIS as currently specified, we can even change the markings on a vehicle at frame rate if so desired! There is other constant data as well, and any redesign of packets for future net-VEs should take these factors into account.

An additional problem with DIS is that the space allocated for coordinates in the entity state PDU exceeds what is actually required. We can specify vehicle position down to subnanometer resolution with the 64-bit coordinate field. Several papers have been written on this feature, most notably, with respect to DIS [Cohen94a, Cohen94b]. In those papers, it is hypothesized that DIS packets can be redesigned, ending up only 20% of the current size.

One of the primary limitations for DIS is that it was designed for small unit engagements having fewer than 300 participants. In a heterogeneous computing environment, 300 participants are manageable with current processor clock rates and current network bandwidths. The DoD has stated explicitly, most notably in the DARPA Synthetic Theater of War (STOW) program, that it would like to be able to run real-time simulations with some 100,000 to 300,000 participants. This number represents the size of Operation Desert Storm, indicating that the DoD would like to be able to simulate an engagement just like its last large real one. There are several instances of fairly large DIS engagements, much larger than the 300 to 500 players for which DIS is designed. However, these "DIS" engagements actually modify the DIS network software architecture for their particular circumstances to achieve useful demonstrations. For example, the Real-time Information Transfer Network (RITN) experiment called STOW ED-1A sustained an exercise of some 5,000 DIS entities for 3 to 5 minutes in November 1995 [Calvin+95]. The RITN architecture was an attempt to modify the existing DIS network software architecture for large-scale simulations by utilizing multicasting to target DIS packets to particular host sets. Unfortunately, demonstrations such as this are not usually generalizable.

Some of the changes to the DIS NSA that occur in such demonstrations include delayed heartbeats (every 30 to 60 seconds instead of every 5 seconds), carefully scripted wargame scenarios (only 10% of the players moving at any one time), and packet compression and aggregation at wide area network gateway machines using large, expensive multiprocessor machines. When evaluating these systems, it is important to recognize that although some of these network optimizations may individually be of interest to future net-VE designers, the "hacked" nature of the overall system provides a poor model for net-VE design. The systems should be taken at face value, as attempts to extend the existing DIS standard, rather than as innovative attempts to achieve greater scalability.

One final comment on DIS is that its packet definition set, while broad, is definitely not general enough to allow DIS to be used across the full range of possible applications. The DIS standard does not really define "how to define" new types of information nor does it define how to modify the network software architecture to accommodate such change. Such a capability is necessary if we are going to build a network software architecture to support not only the DoD but also other interested parties. With regard to extensibility, DIS only provides a data PDU for accommodating new, previously unthought-about information. A data PDU is just a packet with a field at the top that defines what is contained inside. Data PDUs are pretty popular and have been used for supporting articulated humans [Pratt+97] and other nonstandard entities. In true DIS simulations, data PDUs are usually consumed with some risk.

NETWORKED GAMES AND DEMOS

Although the DoD has been the lead organization championing large-scale networked virtual environments with specialized image generators, on the low-end there has been dramatic parallel development in the arena of networked games and workstation demonstrations. In fact, there have been so many networked games and workstation demonstrations that we cannot possibly cover them all. In this section, we discuss a few of the more influential games and demonstrations—those that have either developed new technologies or sparked people into realizing the importance of net-VEs.

SGI *Flight* and *Dogfight*

Gary Tarolli of Silicon Graphics, Inc. (SGI) was the original programmer of the Silicon Graphics demo program, *Flight*, in the summer of 1983. *Flight* is *the* program everyone showed you if they had purchased an SGI workstation in the 1984–1992 time period.[2] As a result, his influence has been considerable in the net-VE community.

Flight was inspired by the Blue Angels air shows at Moffett Field, literally across the street from SGI's original headquarters [Tarolli97]. In that program, the user selected any one of a number of airplanes and used the keyboard of the workstation to accelerate and to steer. The primary challenge of the game was to see if you were coordinated enough to land your plane. The entire purpose of the demonstration was to show off the SGI workstation's capability to rapidly allow movement through small polygonally defined 3D virtual worlds. It was a great sales tool, a point not lost on the high-performance workstation and graphics board industry of today.

Beginning in 1984, networking was added into *Flight* in stages. The initial networked version of *Flight* actually used a serial cable between two SGI workstations and ran at something like 7 frames per second on a Motorola 68000 based workstation (about 1 MIPS with maybe 500 polygons per second graphics capability). That demonstration was then upgraded to use XNS multicasting on an Ethernet network in time for SIGGRAPH 1984. *Flight* was distributed in networked form on all

---

[2]Legend has it that every engineer at SGI was required, as their first task, to add a new feature to the simulator.

SGI workstations sometime after SIGGRAPH 1984 and could be seen in practically every SGI-outfitted lab at that time, either during breaks or after hours. In the networked *Flight* game, users could see each other's planes, although there was no other interaction between players.

Sometime after the release of the networked version of *Flight*—in early 1985 it is believed—SGI engineers modified the code of *Flight* to produce the demonstration program *Dogfight*. This modification dramatically upgraded the visibility of net-VEs, as players could now interact by shooting at each other. People spent more time in play, and many SGI administrators removed *Dogfight* from their systems as soon as the new machines were installed. It also did not help that *Dogfight* packets were transmitted at frame rate and were clogging the network. Due to this bandwidth requirement, *Dogfight* battles were initially limited to tens of players.

The main point of mentioning *Flight* and *Dogfight* is that everyone who bought an SGI saw it, inspiring many to develop their own net-VEs. We believe that networked *Flight/Dogfight* inspired the development of more net-VEs and games than SIMNET and DIS combined.[3] SGI made the source code to *Flight* and *Dogfight* freely available, and many people asked for the code just so they could learn how to read and write UDP packets.[4]

Doom

While workstation-based VEs are some of the earliest inspiration for net-VEs, the PC has taken the desire and interest for such connected worlds to the next level. On 10 December 1993, id Software released its shareware game *Doom*. The shareware giveaway of the first level of *Doom* is probably singularly responsible for the rush of startups into the business of providing online gaming networks. The posting of *Doom* caught most network administrators' eyes when their LANs started bogging down. *Doom* did no dead reckoning and flooded LANs with packets at frame rate. This networked ability to blast people in a believable 3D environment created enormous demand for further 3D

---

[3]This "games inspire research" theme is explored in [NRC97].

[4]In fact, one of the authors of this text had a kind SGI engineer (Al Casarez) read him the networking code over the phone in 1987 while that author was in Japan on a project. That code led directly to the formation of the NPSNET project.

networked games. An estimated 15 million shareware copies of *Doom* have been downloaded around the world, passed from player to player by floppy disk or online networks [idSoftware]. More than 250,000 people have registered for the full product via id's games order line.

Doom has since been ported to the Atari Jaguar, Sega 32X, Super Nintendo, Sony PlayStation, and Nintendo 64 platforms. *Doom* has received many awards (Game of the Year by both *PC Gamer* and *Computer Gaming World* and the Award for Technical Excellence from *PC Magazine*) as well as criticisms. *Doom* has been accused of many things—from being a major contributor to the moral decay of our country to being a contributor to why Fred has not yet finished his homework. *Doom II* followed in October 1994 and has sold over 1.6 million copies.

Doom's play is the archetypical shooter. You are in a 3D space, a space oozing with toxic waste and full of monsters. Played individually, *Doom* pits you against the monsters. In networked form, you play against the would-be online monsters represented by the other players. *Doom* is noisy and requires good hand-eye coordination.

Other Games

Many other games have served as inspirations to the net-VE community. On the Macintosh side, there is the 3D game *Marathon*, played across Appletalk nets, about the easiest networks to set up. *Marathon* was released in December 1994 and presold some 50,000 copies. *Marathon* has high-speed action in a 3D world, impressive graphics, and spatial sound. *Marathon* won many awards and, like *Doom*, provided tools for editing and creating additional game worlds.

Another networked Macintosh game worth mentioning is Stuart Cheshire's tank game *Bolo* [Silberman95, Bolo] played across Appletalk and, later, over IP networks. Unlike most games of the time, *Bolo* avoids broadcast protocols. Instead, the participant hosts organize themselves into a virtual ring. Game state information is therefore transmitted reliably from host to host around the ring. Though latency proves to be a problem as the number of participants grows, *Bolo* tends to successfully avoid the ire of systems administrators and has, consequently, achieved a cultlike following.

In addition to these games, there is *Amaze* from 1984 [Berglund/ Cheriton85]. There is even networked *Spacewar!* from 1961 [Pearce97]. Some claim that *Spacewar!* inspired SIMNET itself. However, we do not include much about these or other games. This is not to minimize the efforts of the developers of these other games, but rather to focus on those that provided a pointer toward modern networked VEs.

ACADEMIC NETWORKED VIRTUAL ENVIRONMENTS

Although the Department of Defense has provided leadership in funding the development of large-scale networked virtual environments, much of that technology transitioned to nowhere. Little of the SIMNET work is available other than in obscure, contractor-proprietary technical reports, reports to the funding sponsors, and the source code. The DIS work is hardly better, with much of that work being printed in the unreviewed, and hard-to-find, proceedings of the biannual DIS Workshops (now replaced by the SISO/SIW workshops). In fact, much of this lack-of-availability and lack-of-generality of technological results has fueled an enormous push by the academic community to reinvent and extend much of what the DoD did and, subsequently, to document that experience in the public literature. This experience parallels the failure of simulation graphics technology to transition its knowledge to the workstation-based VR community in the early days of VR. Much of that technology too had to be reinvented, invented, and published. For historical purposes, this section covers some of the more significant academic net-VEs.

NPSNET

The NPSNET Research Group is the longest continuing academic research effort in networked virtual environments. The focus of the group is on the complete breadth of human-computer interaction and software technology for implementing large-scale virtual environments (LSVEs) [NPSNET]. The research group focuses its efforts on developing virtual environment technology that can be useful for the DoD. The NPSNET software itself is a net-VE testbed for that research group (Figure 2-2). There have been several generations of software formally named NPSNET, as well as several precursor systems. We cover some of the most important details of those systems, primarily with respect to their network software architectures.

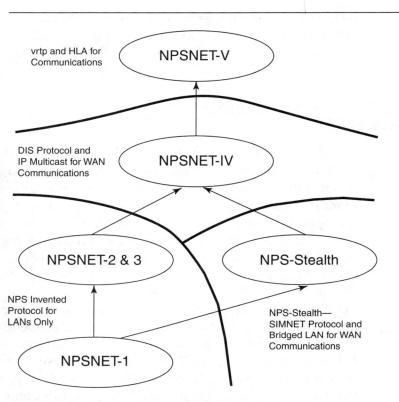

FIGURE 2-2   The evolution of NPSNET networking

Source: From [Macedonia95]. Used with permission.

Early NPS Networked Virtual Environments:
FOG-M, VEH, and MPS

The origins of the NPSNET virtual environment are an introductory computer graphics class project taught in the fall quarter 1986 at the Naval Postgraduate School. In that class, two students, Doug Smith and Dale Streyle, developed a visual simulator for the fiber-optically guided missile (FOG-M) system [Smith/Streyle87, Zyda+88]. They developed FOG-M on the Silicon Graphics, Inc. (SGI) IRIS-2400 system, a 500 polygons per second, 0.5 MIPS UNIX workstation. Smith and Streyle were true hero-coders. FOG-M was up and flying over simulated Fort Hunter-Liggett terrain at the end of the sixth week of an eleven-week quarter! The key research issue at that time was how to use such a limited graphics performance workstation to provide truly low-cost visual simulation. Initially, the NPSNET group had no idea that it should be networked.

The implementation of FOG-M came at the same time that Mike Zyda was helping Hitachi Works in Japan to solve a networking problem. Hitachi wanted to utilize 16 SGI workstations to generate a giant, high-resolution display. They planned to stack the monitors in a 4×4 grid and needed help in figuring out how to synchronize the displays, using the network as the interconnect medium. The project resulted in a nice software architecture for connecting SGI workstations. That code went home to Zyda's students waiting in Monterey.

The FOG-M virtual environment was developed using as a guide a videotape of the actual missile. The tape showed the launch of the missile, camera pointed skyward, the turn of the missile to level flight, and then the targeting of that missile on on-ground objects. The unusual technical part of the missile is its 30-kilometer rapid spooling, fiber-optic cable. This connection allows an operator to steer the missile in a manner similar to a radio-controlled model airplane (only using a really long extension cord instead of radio control). The constructed FOG-M virtual environment was modeled completely from this videotape. FOG-M even had the stopped tank on the ground as a target. Every time the NPSNET group gave the demo, the comment made was "wouldn't it be nice if the tank could be driven, too." With the networking code in hand in March 1987, the NPSNET group began the development of the FOG-M follow-on system, VEH [Oliver/Stahl87].

VEH was the target vehicle simulator. VEH and FOG-M were connected via a simple open socket that allowed the two systems to do basic UNIX read-write functions for exchange of state information. The combined systems could demonstrate a missile trying to hit a moving target vehicle. Blocking reads and writes were used to simplify the architecture. A networked demonstration was available by July 1987. The NPSNET group began to understand the importance of networking the virtual environment, as well as the need for more players.

The Moving Platform Simulator (MPS) was the NPSNET group's testbed for looking at how to achieve more players in the networked virtual environment. MPS-1, MPS-2, and MPS-3 utilized an ASCII, NPS-invented protocol and broadcasting to exchange state information [Cheeseman90, Fichten/Jennings88, Strong/Winn89, Zyda/Fichten/Jennings90, Zyda+90]. MPS was able to support as many workstations as were in the lab (5) and more.

NPSNET-1, -2, -3 and NPS-Stealth

In looking at SIMNET history, SIMNET's first networked demonstration took place in May 1986. The NPS MPS project should have known about SIMNET, but papers on SIMNET did not appear in the academic computing literature. Luckily, however, the NPSNET group learned about SIMNET early enough (late 1988) to get involved with that effort.

NPSNET-1 received its name in March 1990. The NPSNET group received funding from the U.S. Army Topographic Engineering Center to learn how to read SIMNET terrain databases. The method was to adapt and extend the MPS-developed technology and build a visual simulator on the SGI 4DGT and GTX machines. Z-buffers had just become fast enough to rely on them rather than on the painter's algorithm for hidden surface elimination. Inside of three months, NPSNET-1 debuted. NPSNET-1 again utilized an NPS-invented ASCII protocol for the exchange of information between workstations. NPSNET-1 could play among all the workstations on the local area network. NPSNET-1 did not use dead reckoning. Instead, it flooded the network with packets at frame rate.

NPSNET-1 was demonstrated live at the SIGGRAPH 1991 conference as part of the Tomorrows Realities Gallery [Zyda/Pratt91] and was the only working net-VE in that gallery. NPSNET-1 used three workstations for that demo (one 4D-VGX and two 4D 35Ts) and a local area network. The NPSNET group removed the military vehicles from the demo and replaced them with killer tomatoes, giant turkeys, and the occasional beachball (unknown object icon), so as not to offend the nonmilitary SIGGRAPH audience. It looked like a game and drew long lines of people waiting to play. The SIGGRAPH demo got the NPSNET Research Group significant ARPA funding to continue work.

After NPSNET-1, there was a split in the development efforts of the then-named NPSNET Research Group. NPSNET-2 and NPSNET-3 were utilized to explore better, faster ways to do graphics and to extend the size of the terrain databases possible. NPS-Stealth was spawned off from NPSNET-1 with the goal of developing a system capable of reading SIMNET terrain databases and SIMNET networking protocols. NPS-Stealth was operational in March 1993 and was the only workstation-based virtual environment capable of interoperating with the $350,000 per copy SIMNET system.

NPSNET-IV

In March 1993, Silicon Graphics released their Performer API for developing virtual environments and visual simulation systems. NPSNET-3 had been accepted for the Tomorrows Realities Gallery of SIGGRAPH 1993. The group decided to build NPSNET-IV after looking at the SGI Performer demos. The ARPA sponsor requested a large demo, with leased T-1 connections to the Defense Simulation Internet and five sites across the United States (Figure 2-3). NPSNET-IV was up and running about ten days before SIGGRAPH. It was DIS-compliant, and it dead reckoned. It had spatial sound too. NPSNET-IV interoperated with 50 to 60 players during that demonstration. The demonstration was highly successful, and the demonstration booth was almost always full.

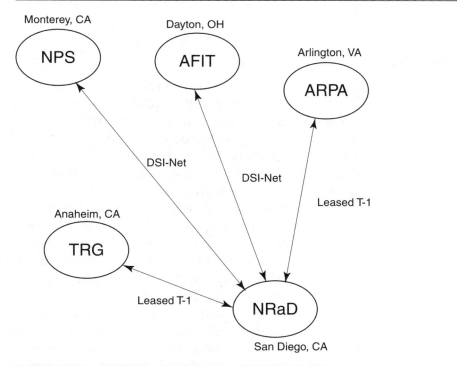

FIGURE 2-3   NPSNET connectivity at SIGGRAPH '93

Source: From [Macedonia95]. Used with permission.

Though the intent was to redesign NPSNET-IV carefully after SIG-GRAPH 1993, the NPSNET group never did, continuing to hack on NPSNET-IV until December 1996.

NPSNET-IV has many capabilities that make it one of the most ambitious virtual environments of its day. In Swiss-Army-knife-fashion, a player using NPSNET-IV can be a fully articulated human, a ground vehicle of almost any type, an air vehicle of any type, and any type of surface or subsurface vessel. A player in NPSNET-IV can walk through buildings and up stairs and ladders. An articulated human can board a ship, go up to the bridge, and drive the ship out to sea. NPSNET-IV was the first virtual environment that was Internet-capable, being able to play across the multicast backbone (MBone) of the Internet [Macedonia+95]. NPSNET-IV eventually was utilized in over 100 DoD, contractor, and university laboratories, and it has inter-operated with almost every DIS-compliant virtual environment ever constructed.

PARADISE

The Performance Architecture for Advanced Distributed Interactive Simulation Environments (PARADISE) project was initiated in 1993 by David Cheriton, Sandeep Singhal, and Hugh Holbrook of the Distrib-uted Systems Group at Stanford University [PARADISE]. Unlike most academic research projects of the period, which primarily focused on the graphical aspects of net-VE design, the PARADISE system explicitly addressed network software architecture issues facing environments containing thousands of users. The project grew out of some early experimentation by Singhal to extend the SGI *Dogfight* program with dynamic terrain capabilities (where participants could create holes in the runway and prevent others from landing) and dead reckoning.

PARADISE's designers were determined to reduce bandwidth throughout the system. The PARADISE system used IP multicast, assigning a different multicast address to each active object. However, because the early graphics-capable workstations available to the group did not support multicast at the time, they were forced to simulate mul-ticast using an application-level multicast simulator on the local area network. This configuration essentially created a mini-MBone among the nonmulticast-capable hosts on an otherwise multicast-aware net-work. Hosts transmit updates for local objects in much the same way as

SIMNET and DIS. However, to further reduce bandwidth, a hierarchy of area of interest (AOI) servers collects information subscriptions from each host. The servers monitor the positions of objects and notify hosts about which objects' multicast groups they should subscribe to.

Unlike SIMNET, PARADISE treats all objects, including terrain, uniformly as first-class entities. Each is capable of transmitting state updates. At the same time, PARADISE's designers tried to correct several of the mistakes made by DIS. For example, PARADISE recognizes that entities represent a spectrum ranging from rapidly changing objects that need to generate frequent updates to slowly changing objects that rarely need to send updates. To support rapidly changing entities, research concentrated on improved dead reckoning protocols such as Position History-Based Dead Reckoning (PHBDR) [Singhal/Cheriton95], which transmits smaller update packets and provides better accuracy when objects move wildly (the situation that causes DIS systems to transmit updates at close to frame rate). PARADISE supports multiple independent communication flows per object, with each flow enabling remote dead reckoning at a different level of accuracy [Singhal96]. PARADISE also provides techniques for combining information about groups of objects, based both on their virtual world location and on their type [Singhal/Cheriton96].

To support slowly changing entities, research focused on reliable multicast protocols to eliminate the frequent heartbeat messages present in DIS. Log-Based Receiver-Reliable Multicast [Holbrook+95] provides a lightweight reliable multicast service that includes a persistence mechanism. Latecomers to the simulation can retrieve the current state about slowly changing objects directly from a system of Logging Servers. Eric Halpern implemented a terrain server for dynamically paging terrain data over the network, effectively reducing memory and disk requirements at local hosts and enabling the introduction of dynamic terrain.

Each PARADISE entity is implemented as a composition of individual C++ modules, such as physics, appearance, collision detection, dead reckoning, and aggregation. These modules can be plugged together to form an entity, with a default implementation provided for each module type if none is specified. A Tcl interface was used to initialize and drive a PARADISE simulation. An object-oriented RPC metaphor [Zelesko/Cheriton96] was used to provide a common interface to all network interactions, including both unreliable multicast communication and reliable server transactions.

PARADISE ran on a set of four donated IBM RS/6000 workstations with basic OpenGL graphics capabilities. The system's flying helicopter demonstration could support 50 to 70 simultaneous entities, being bound by performance of the graphics hardware. The value of the PARADISE system lies in its attempt to reconsider many of the "standard" assumptions of existing net-VE systems in the context of future network capabilities and future scalability requirements. The result was a series of advances in core simulation software technology.

DIVE

The Swedish Institute of Computer Science Distributed Interactive Virtual Environment (DIVE) is another early and ongoing academic virtual environment [Carlsson/Hagsand93a, Carlsson/Hagsand93b, DIVE, Hagsand96]. DIVE uses the ISIS toolkit concept of process groups [Birman93] to simulate a large shared memory over a network.[5] A process group is a set of processes that are addressed as a single entity via multicast messaging.

DIVE uses a distributed, fully replicated database similar to SIMNET and DIS-compliant systems. However, one of DIVE's major contributions is that, unlike SIMNET and DIS, its entire database is dynamic. It has the capability to add new objects and modify the existing databases in a reliable and consistent fashion. DIVE uses reliable multicast protocols and concurrency control via a distributed locking mechanism to accomplish database updates, adding significantly to the communications costs associated with its net-VE. Because of this software architecture, it is difficult to scale DIVE beyond 16 to 32 participants. DIVE does well in situations where database changes must be guaranteed and accurate at each participant's site.

The primary application of DIVE is in solving problems of collaboration and interaction. In essence, DIVE simulates a conference room for long-distance shared interaction. Illustrations of DIVE's use show

---

[5]ISIS is a multiprocessor application environment that allows an application to be built out of large numbers of processes, employing the ISIS notions of "events," "process groups," and "tasks." ISIS is similar to the Linda toolkit in that it trades off performance in return for a simple application programming interface (API).

3D human avatars around a desktop inside of a room with video and whiteboard walls.

As is the case for most net-VEs of its day, the DIVE project did not explicitly originate as a net-VE effort [Carlsson/Jaa-Aro97]. The DIVE team originated from the programming efforts of Olof Hagsand, who developed the Multidraw system, a shared 2D drawing editor. Multidraw was demonstrated at the first MultiG workshop in late 1990. This demo program became the genesis of the Telepresence Project, which started in early 1991, with the participation of Olof Hagsand, Lennart Fahle'n, Christer Carlsson, and Magnus Andersson.

Telepresence 1 first went online in mid-April 1991. The first demonstration was a virtual clock where a viewer on one machine could watch a simple 3D clock running on another machine. Telepresence 1 ran on IBM RS/6000 workstations with GL graphics accelerators loaned from IBM Sweden. By May 1991, with the architecture in place, more advanced demos with two participants, and more elaborate environments, were constructed.

In April 1992, the team of Christer Carlsson, Lennart Fahle'n, Olof Hagsand, Magnus Andersson, Olof Stahl, Kai-Mikael Jaa-Aro, Assar Westerlund, and Marten Stenius began rebuilding the Telepresence system by changing the distribution mechanism, revamping the coordinate systems, building in automatic behaviors in objects, and throwing in every feature they could think of.[6] By summer 1992, Telepresence 2 was completed and renamed DIVE by Stephen Pope. In fact, it was DIVE 2 in the minds of the developers, even though all of their published papers refer to the system as DIVE. DIVE was ported to the Sun XGL architecture so they could have three participants in the same virtual environment.

The latest version of the system is called DIVE 3 [DIVE]. DIVE 3 uses SID, a basic communications library based on IP multicast and Scalable Reliable Multicast (SRM) [Floyd+95] as the distribution mechanism instead of ISIS, and it uses Tcl code for behaviors. Current ver-

---

[6]There is a tremendous amount to be said for exciting people about technology and turning them loose in the laboratory. The most productive efforts on the edge of technology have traditionally been where people were given free reign rather than specifications. DIVE is one of many efforts where the excitement of the participants carried them far and allowed them to make a contribution to the development of technology.

sions of DIVE 3 support subjective views, local groups for communication, and an entirely Tcl-based GUI.

BrickNet

BrickNet is the work of Gurminder Singh at the Institute of Systems Science (ISS) at the National University of Singapore. BrickNet is a virtual environment toolkit that provides support for graphical, behavioral, and network modeling of virtual worlds [Singh+94]. BrickNet allows objects to be shared by multiple virtual worlds. It does not have the replicated database model of SIMNET, DIS, and DIVE. Instead, it partitions the virtual world among the various VE clients (Figure 2-4). Requests for objects, and hence communication, are mediated by servers. Interactions on distant objects are accomplished by an object-request broker on a server, a server that knows which client owns the distant object.

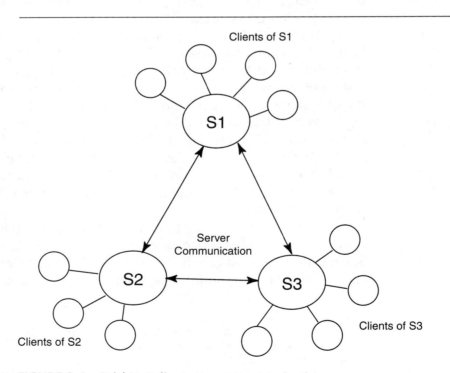

FIGURE 2-4   BrickNet client-server communication

Source: From [Singh+94]. Used with permission.

BrickNet is primarily aimed at collaborative design environments, where a complete design task is distributed over multiple client workstations. Each node in a BrickNet collaboration is responsible for its part of the design and for sharing that information with others in the collaboration. Additionally, BrickNet has been used to construct networked games, groupware systems, concurrent engineering systems, and other asynchronous, network-based graphics environments [Singh+95].

The primary contribution of BrickNet in the early net-VE arena is that it explored the client-server space and did not require each client to have a complete copy of the virtual environment database. Unfortunately, in a dynamic world, servers are bottlenecks, increasing the latency of the VE. The largest BrickNet scenario included 8 participants, although its architecture can support up to 32 players.

The BrickNet project started in early 1991 with the goal of developing a networked infrastructure to enable multiple virtual worlds—each with a different virtual world "content"—to communicate [Singh97]. In addition to reducing network load and latency, the focus was to allow VEs to share individual objects, rather than the entire content, with one another. At that time, there were no VEs that supported this "partial sharing"; most shared the complete database. BrickNet's implementation began on Sun workstations but later moved to SGI Indigo workstations. The initial implementation had a single server.

The BrickNet prototype application for performing interior design was first demonstrated in late 1991. That application could be used by a variable number of users but was demonstrated with only eight concurrent users, due to machine limitations. Singh and associates describe a four-user scenario of this application [Singh+94]. BrickNet's architecture was extended to multiple cooperating servers in 1992.

BrickNet was also extended to include behavior sharing. With that extension, the ISS team became more involved in using BrickNet for games and applications. The CyberBug game was demonstrated publicly for two months in Singapore as part of a show called MegaBugs. The public demonstration led to the formation of a spinoff company, Imagine Interactive, in June 1995, with a capitalization of 1.4 million dollars. With this spinoff, BrickNet became PC-based.

ISS began developing a new toolkit and infrastructure entitled NetEffect in 1996 [Das+97]. NetEffect is a software architecture for developing large, low-end virtual environments. NetEffect is targeted for PCs, with potentially several thousand geographically dispersed, connected users. NetEffect is being used for a major application called HistoryCity. HistoryCity, a virtual world for children based on the history of Singapore, runs on the PC, with some 5,000 copies distributed. The ISS research focus is on the architectural issues related to developing and supporting large-scale, media-rich virtual environments running on high-speed networks. Singapore is being wired with high-speed ADSL and cable networks to the home, and ISS plans to exploit this infrastructure.

MR Toolkit Peer Package

Another early effort in networked virtual environments is the Minimal Reality Toolkit Peer Package (MR-TPP), an extension of the University of Alberta's MR Toolkit [Shaw/Green93]. MR-TPP allows any number of independent applications to communicate either application-dependent data or device data to remote applications. MR-TPP allows applications to leave or join at any time.

MR-TPP is based on User Datagram Protocol (UDP) packets for network communication. Because UDP is not a reliable protocol, packets can be lost. MR-TPP, like DIS, ignores lost packets and hopes that there is sufficient redundancy in packet transmission so that losing a small percentage of packets is okay. Instead of using a heartbeat packet as in DIS, MR-TPP relies on frequent sending of packets, at the update rate of the input device, to provide the needed redundancy. The use of UDP improves network delay by a factor of ten over TCP/IP and hence is a common choice by the networked VE community. UDP also allows the networked VE to operate asynchronously.

MR-TPP has a software architecture in which local copies of shared data are maintained in a distributed fashion. For example, when a shared device changes in an MR process, it communicates that state change to the other connected MR processes via a UDP packet. On packet arrival, the information from that packet is extracted and written into a local store. Shared application-specific data are handled in a similar fashion. Programmable callbacks can be defined to allow automatic distribution of state changes in shared data.

MR-TPP maintains a complete graph connection topology, which means that the number of packets transmitted is on the order of the square of the number of participants. This limits the total number of participants to four or less because of the packet loads [Shaw/Green93]. The MR-TPP architecture does not contain any predictive modeling similar to DIS's dead reckoning.

Others

There are many other academic net-VE research efforts worth mentioning. This section has covered those that were there first or had the broadest influence on the net-VE field. We will cover some of the other systems on a per-topic basis throughout the remainder of the book.

CONCLUSION

This chapter has provided a historical context for the development of some of the central ideas in networked virtual environments, through examination of the chief contributions of the Department of Defense, SIMNET, and DIS, briefly touching on the inspirations that the entertainment and graphics demonstration community have provided. Those demonstrations provided more recognition for networked virtual environments than the Department of Defense has ever been able to achieve on its own. On the other hand, the entertainment industry has not yet achieved the scalability that the Department of Defense has achieved. Nevertheless, the commonality of purpose has inspired the possibilities of joint DoD and entertainment industry research [NRC97]. Finally, this chapter examined some of the highlights of academic virtual environments. Some of those environments are quite remarkable and contain capabilities never accomplished in DoD-directed virtual environments, environments that we will look at in more detail later.

Having discussed the landmark net-VE systems, we will now turn our attention to how net-VEs are built. To do this, we need to understand the characteristics of networks and how networks enable and restrict the design of multiuser virtual environments. The next chapter discusses network communications and protocol design for net-VEs.

REFERENCES

[Berglund/Cheriton85] Berglund, E. J., and D. R. Cheriton. *Amaze:* A multi-player computer game. *IEEE Software* 2(1):30–39, May 1985.

[Birman93] Birman, K. The process group approach to reliable distributed computing. *Communications of the ACM,* 36(12):37–53, December 1993.

[Bolo] *Bolo* Web site: *http://bolo.ncsa.uiuc.edu*

[Calvin+95] Calvin, J., J. Seeger, G. Troxel, D. Van Hook. STOW real-time information transfer and networking system architecture. In *Proceedings of the 12th DIS Workshop,* March 1995.

[Carlsson/Hagsand93a] Carlsson, C., and O. Hagsand. DIVE—A platform for multi-user virtual environments. *Computers & Graphics* 17(6):663–669, 1993.

[Carlsson/Hagsand93b] Carlsson, C., and O. Hagsand. DIVE—A multi-user virtual reality system. In *Proceedings of the IEEE Virtual Reality Annual International Symposium,* 394–400. Seattle, September 1993.

[Carlsson/Jaa-Aro97] Carlsson, C., and K-M. Jaa-Aro. Personal communication, June 30, 1997.

[Cheeseman90] Cheeseman, C. Moving platform simulator III: An enhanced high-performance real-time graphics simulator with multiple resolution display and lighting. Master's thesis, Naval Postgraduate School, Monterey, CA, June 1990.

[Cohen94a] Cohen, D. NG-DIS-PDU: The next generation of DIS-PDU (IEEE-1278). In *Proceedings of the 10th Workshop on Standards for Distributed Interactive Simulations,* 735–742, March 1994.

[Cohen94b] Cohen, D. DIS—Back to basics. In *Proceedings of the 11th Workshop on Standards for Distributed Interactive Simulations,* 603–617, September 1994.

[Das+97] Das, T. K., G. Singh, A. Mitchell, P. S. Kumar, and K. McGee. Developing social virtual worlds using NetEffect. In *Proceedings of the Sixth IEEE Workshops on Enabling Technologies: Infrastructure for Collaborative Enterprises,* 148–154. Cambridge, MA, June 1997.

[DIVE] DIVE Web site: *http://www.sics.se/dce/dive/dive.html*

[Fichten/Jennings88] Fichten, M. A., and D. H. Jennings. Meaningful real-time graphics workstation performance measurements. Joint Master's thesis, Naval Postgraduate School, Monterey, CA, December 1988 (NPS52-89-004).

[Floyd+95] Floyd, S., V. Jacobson, C. Liu, S. McCanne, and L. Zhang. A reliable multicast framework for light-weight sessions and application-level framing. In *Proceedings of SIGCOMM 1995,* 342–356. ACM SIGCOMM, Cambridge, MA, August 1995. (Published as *Computer Communications Review* 25(4), October 1995.)

[Hagsand96] Hagsand, O. Interactive multiuser VEs in the DIVE system. *IEEE Multimedia* 3(1):30–39, 1996.

[Hofer/Loper95] Hofer, R. C., and M. L. Loper. DIS today. In *Proceedings of the IEEE* 83(8):1124–1137, August 1995.

[Holbrook+95] Holbrook, H. W., S. K. Singhal, D. R. Cheriton. Log-based receiver-reliable multicast for distributed interactive simulation. In *Proceedings of SIGCOMM'95*, 328–341, ACM SIGCOMM, August 1995. (Published as *Computer Communications Review* 25(4), October 1995.)

[idSoftware] id Software Web site: *http://www.idsoftware.com*

[IEEE93] IEEE standard for information technology—protocols for distributed simulation applications: Entity information and interaction. IEEE Standard 1278-1993. New York: IEEE Computer Society, 1993.

[Li/Moshell93] Li, X., and J. M. Moshell. Modeling soil: Realtime dynamic models of soil slippage and soil manipulation. In *Proceedings of SIGGRAPH'93.* (Published as *Computer Graphics* 24(4), August 1993.)

[Li/Moshell94] Li, X., and J. M. Moshell. Realtime graphical simulation of soil slippage. *Transactions of the Society for Computer Simulation* 11(3):195–220, October 1994.

[Macedonia+95] Macedonia, M. R., D. P. Brutzman, M. J. Zyda, D. R. Pratt, P. T. Barham, J. Falby, and J. Locke. NPSNET: A multi-player 3D virtual environment over the Internet. In *Proceedings of the 1995 Symposium on Interactive 3D Graphics*. ACM SIGGRAPH, Monterey, CA, April 1995.

[Macedonia95] Macedonia, M. R. A network software architecture for large scale virtual environments. Ph.D dissertation, Naval Postgraduate School, Monterey, CA, June 1995.

[Maguire/Reeder92] Maguire/Reeder Ltd. *The Reconstruction of the Battle of 73 Easting—A DARPA Project Report.* Institute for Defense Analyses, Alexandria, VA. Videotape from DARPA, February 25, 1992.

[Miller/Thorpe95] Miller, D., and J. A. Thorpe. SIMNET: The advent of simulator networking. In *Proceedings of the IEEE* 83(8):1114–1123, August 1995.

[Moshell+94] Moshell, J. M., B. Blau, X. Li, and C. Lisle. Dynamic terrain. *Simulation* 62(1), January 1994.

[NPSNET] NPSNET Web site: *http://www.npsnet.nps.navy.mil/npsnet*

[NRC97] National Research Council. *Modeling and Simulation: Linking Entertainment and Defense.* Washington, DC: National Academy Press, September 1997.

[Oliver/Stahl87] Oliver, M. R., and D. J. Stahl, Jr. Interactive, networked, moving platform simulators. Joint Master's thesis, Naval Postgraduate School, Monterey, CA, December 1987 (NPS52-88-002).

[PARADISE] PARADISE Project Web site: *http://www.dsg.stanford.edu/paradise. html*

[Pearce97] Pearce, C. Beyond shoot your friends: A call to arms in the battle against violence. *Digital Illusion* (Clark Dodsworth, ed.), 209–228. New York: ACM Press, 1997.

[Pope89] Pope, A. The SIMNET network and protocols. *Technical Report 7102.* Cambridge, MA: BBN Systems and Technologies, July 1989.

[Pratt+97] Pratt, D. R., S. M. Pratt, P. T. Barham, R. E. Barker, M. S. Waldroup, J. F. Ehlert, and C. A. Chrislip. Humans in large-scale, networked virtual environments. *Presence: Teleoperators and Virtual Environments* 6(5):547–564, October 1997.

[Pullen/Wood95] Pullen, J. M., and D. C. Wood. Networking technology and DIS. In *Proceedings of the IEEE*, 83(8):1156–1167, August 1995.

[Shaw/Green93] Shaw, C., and M. Green. The MR toolkit peers package and experiment. In *Proceedings of the 1993 IEEE Virtual Reality Annual International Symposium*, 463–469. Seattle, September 1993.

[Silberman95] Silberman, S. O *Bolo* mio. *Netguide*, 57–60, May 1995.

[Singh97] Singh, G. Personal communication, July 25, 1997.

[Singh+94] Singh, G., L. Serra, W. Prg, et al. BrickNet: A software toolkit for network-based virtual environments. *PRESENCE: Teleoperators and Virtual Environments* 3(1):19–34, Winter 1994.

[Singh+95] Singh, G., L. Serra, W. Prg, et al. BrickNet: Sharing object behaviors on the net. In *Proceedings of the Virtual Reality Annual International Symposium* (VRAIS'95), 19–25. Los Alamitos, CA: IEEE Computer Society Press, March 1995.

[Singhal96] Singhal, S. Effective remote modeling in large-scale distributed simulation and visualization environments. Ph.D dissertation. Department of Computer Science, Stanford University, Palo Alto, August 1996.

[Singhal/Cheriton95] Singhal, S. K., and D. R. Cheriton. Exploiting position history for efficient remote rendering in networked virtual reality. *PRESENCE: Teleoperators and Virtual Environments* 4(2):169–193, Spring 1995.

[Singhal/Cheriton96] Singhal, S. K., and D. R. Cheriton. Using projection aggregations to support scalability in distributed simulation. In *Proceedings of the 16th International Conference on Distributed Computing Systems* (ICDCS), 196–206. IEEE Computer Society, May 1996.

[Smith/Streyle87] Smith, D. B., and D. Streyle. An inexpensive real-time interactive three-dimensional flight simulation system. Joint Master's thesis (NPS52-87-034), Naval Postgraduate School, Monterey, CA, June 1987.

[Strong/Winn89] Strong, R. P., and M. C. Winn. The moving platform simulator II: A networked real-time visual simulator with distributed processing and line-of-sight displays. Joint Master's thesis, Naval Postgraduate School, Monterey, CA, June 1989.

[Tarolli97] Tarolli, G., Personal communication, April 1997.

[Thorpe97] Thorpe, J., Personal communication, June 1997.

[Zelesko/Cheriton96] Zelesko, M. J., and D. R. Cheriton. Specializing object-oriented RPC for functionality and performance. In *Proceedings of the 1996 International Conference on Distributed Computing Systems* (ICDCS), Hong Kong, 175–187. Los Alamitos, CA: IEEE Computer Society, May 1996.

[Zyda/Fichten/Jennings90] Zyda, M. J., M. A. Fichten, and D. H. Jennings. Meaningful graphics workstation performance measurements. *Computers & Graphics* 14(3):519–526, 1990.

[Zyda/Pratt91] Zyda, M. J., and D. R. Pratt. NPSNET: A 3D visual simulator for virtual world exploration and experience. In Tomorrow's Realities Gallery, *Visual Proceedings of SIGGRAPH '91*, p. 30. Las Vegas, July 1991.

[Zyda+88] Zyda, M. J., R. B. McGhee, R. S. Ross, D. B. Smith, and D. G. Streyle. Flight simulators for under $100,000. *IEEE Computer Graphics & Applications* 8(1):19–27, January 1988.

[Zyda+90] Zyda, M. J., R. B. McGhee, C. M. McConkle, A. H. Nelson, and R. S. Ross. A real-time, three-dimensional moving platform visualization tool. *Computers & Graphics* 14(2):321–333, 1990.

Chapter 3

A Networking Primer

One of the distinguishing features behind a networked virtual environment (net-VE) is the presence of a *network*, a medium for exchanging data and information among the multiple hosts participating in the shared experience. The presence of a network brings up a number of issues that determine the design and implementation of a net-VE. When building a VE to run on a single machine, different components of your application can exchange information instantaneously through a function call. When exchanging information over a network, however, this information exchange is no longer instantaneous. Instead, it might take a significant fraction of a second for the information to pass from one part of your application to another. Even worse, the information might get lost on the way to its destination and, therefore, never arrive.

To enable you to learn how these and other issues affect the building of net-VEs, this chapter discusses the basic principles behind how computers exchange information over networks. It first describes the fundamental principles behind computer networking, including concepts such as bandwidth, latency, and reliability. It discusses how hosts manage the different flows of incoming information (so that your application only receives information that it should receive). It then describes the most common communication protocols and techniques in use today on the Internet, namely TCP/IP, UDP/IP, IP broadcasting using UDP, and IP multicasting. The chapter concludes with a discussion of how choices among these communication protocols govern the design of net-VE systems. Furthermore, this book's appendix provides an overview of how to write basic networking code in C, C++, and Java.

Networking is a complex field, and this chapter can only provide an introduction. To learn more, the reader is referred to one of the many books on the subject, particularly [Stevens94] and [Comer/Stevens94].

FUNDAMENTALS OF DATA TRANSFER

A computer network is much like a complex maze of roads connecting cities together. On these roads, cars navigate between their starting points and their destinations. When describing this transportation, one talks about vehicles, lanes in the road, traffic signs, and traffic jams. Just as traffic engineers have their own language for describing the road system and traffic flow through it, there is a language for describing the data flow through a computer network. We begin our discussion of networking by reviewing some of these basic concepts used to characterize the flow of computer data over networks, as shown in Figure 3-1.

Network Latency

The *network latency*, or network delay, is the amount of time required to transfer a bit of data from one point to another. When a net-VE application generates data for transmission over the network, the network latency determines when the application at the receiving host actually

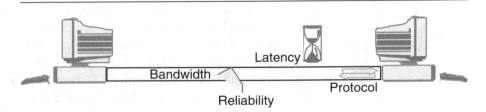

FIGURE 3-1   Network communications are characterized by latency, bandwidth, reliability, and protocol.

sees the transmitted data. This delay represents one of the biggest challenges to a net-VE designer for two reasons: (1) latency directly impacts the realism of the net-VE experience by determining how up-to-date net-VE information received over the network is and (2) because net-VE designers can do very little to reduce it.

Latency arises for many reasons. First, data transmission is governed by speed-of-light delays. Data fundamentally cannot travel faster than the speed of light, and the speed of light through transmission materials such as fiber is considerably slower than the speed of light through vacuum. This might not seem like much, but it accounts for over 21 milliseconds for transferring data from the east coast to the west coast of the United States [Cheshire96].[1] The delay is a lot more significant when data must travel up to an orbital satellite before being beamed back to Earth.

Second, delays are introduced by the endpoint computers themselves. It takes time for the data to travel through the computer's operating system and network hardware even before it reaches the network; similarly, the data must travel through network hardware and the operating system before being delivered to the application on the destination host. Latencies within modems and network hardware represent some of the most significant, though most often ignored, sources of latency in a net-VE.

Third, delays are introduced by the network itself. Typically, data cannot travel down a direct wire between the source and destination hosts. Instead, it must pass through network intersections, or *routers*, that shuffle the data from one wire to another on its way to the destination. Processing at these routers introduces its own delays to the data.

Network latency values fall into a wide range. If you are sending data along an Ethernet local area network (LAN), latency is typically under 10 milliseconds. However, if you are dialing into the Internet by a modem through the telephone system, your latency will be at least 100 milliseconds. In addition to these values, latency increases as the

---

[1]As a useful rule of thumb, speed-of-light delays account for approximately 8.25 milliseconds of delay per time zone through which the packet must travel. The speed of light is 300,000 kilometers/second (186,000 miles/second) in vacuum. However, when traveling through fiber, light travels at roughly 66% of its speed through vacuum, so the rate is only 200,000 kilometers/second (124,000 miles/second). The Earth's circumference is 44,835 kilometers (26,901 miles), which means an average of 1,868 kilometers (1,121 miles) per time zone.

destination host becomes farther from the source. Transcontinental transfers require an additional 60–150 milliseconds, and intercontinental latencies can range from 250–500 milliseconds or more.

Network Bandwidth

The *network bandwidth* is the rate at which the network can deliver data to the destination host. The available bandwidth is determined by the type of wire used to transport data, and it is also limited by the hardware used to transmit the data [Stallings96]. For example, a modem can typically handle data at the rate of between 14,400 and 56,000 bits per second (14.4–56 kilobits per second, or 14.4–56 Kbps). The phone line itself can handle a maximum of 64 Kbps. Many long-distance leased lines can support between 1 and 2 million bits per second (1–2 megabits per second, or 1–2 Mbps). A traditional Ethernet can handle 10 Mbps, and newer Ethernet technology can support 100 Mbps or even 1 billion bits per second (1 gigabit per second, or 1Gbps). The highest bandwidth fiber-optic cables can transfer data at an even faster rate, up to 10 Gbps or more.

The distinction between network bandwidth and network latency confuses many people, so it is worth reviewing the difference. Network bandwidth is a *rate* of transfer. It measures how many bits can be transported per unit of time. Another way to think of it is how many bits would pass by you per second if you stood at a particular place on the wire. On the other hand, network latency is the *delay* of transfer. It measures how many seconds one byte of data takes to travel from the source host to the destination host. It is important to remember that although bandwidth and latency both describe networks, they are not necessarily related. You can have a high-bandwidth network that offers low latency, and you can have a low-bandwidth network that demands high latency.

Network Reliability

Network reliability is a measure of how much data is lost by the network during the journey from source to destination host. This data loss can be divided into two categories, "dropping" and "corruption." Data dropping means that the data does not arrive at the destination host at all, because it has been discarded by the network. Data corruption means that the content of the data packets has been changed during transmission so that the arriving data packet is basically useless to the destination host. Networking people regard data dropping and data corruption as equivalent, because in both cases the data effectively does not arrive at the destination application in a usable form.

The most obvious cause of data loss is also the least frequent. Data might be lost as it travels along the transmission wires in the network. For example, it might be corrupted when the wires are poorly connected or are subject to electrical or magnetic interference. However, the frequency of these errors is typically measured on the order of one corrupted bit in 10^{10} or more bits. This data loss is most severe in wireless networks, where the data must be sent via radio signals, either between wireless modems or between the ground and a satellite. In these situations, the transmission medium is least controllable because it is subject to interference from competing transmissions, bad weather, or even passing airplanes.

Network designers typically include sufficient redundancy to detect data corruption. For example, each transmission usually includes a checksum value, such as a Cyclic Redundancy Check (CRC), that is computed from the data contained in the packet. The recipient attempts to recompute the checksum from the data that it receives. If the computed checksum does not match the checksum contained in the packet, then the receiver discards the corrupted data. On certain networks, data packets may also include *error-correcting codes* that include enough extra information about the data so that the recipient can even correct one-or-more bit errors in the received data.

On the other hand, the most common causes of data loss are the network routers that transfer data between transmission lines. Routers can process packets at a certain rate, but data does not tend to arrive at a steady rate. Occasionally, a burst of packets might arrive faster than the router can process them, and in these situations, the router must place the inbound data into a queue for later processing. If the burst is too big, the router might fall behind and the queues might run out of memory; the router has no choice but to catch up by discarding some of the queued data. Network reliability can vary widely. At peak times during the day, when router queues are longest, packet loss can exceed 50%. At other times, data loss can be negligible.

If the network loses data, how can we be sure that the data arrived at the destination? When reliable data delivery is desired, destination computers can send *acknowledgments* back to the source host whenever they receive data. The acknowledgment may be either a special packet or it may be included (or "piggybacked") inside another data packet transmitted by the destination computer to the source computer. These acknowledgments notify the source that the data has arrived successfully. If the source does not receive an acknowledgment within a certain time period after sending data, then it assumes that the data was lost by the network and attempts to send it again. Note that if the source does not see an acknowledgment for its transmitted data, it is still possible that the destination host received the data, because the acknowledgment itself might have been lost in transmission.

Network Protocol

A *network protocol* describes the set of "rules" that two applications use to communicate with each other. A protocol consists of the following components.

1. *Packet formats:* Each endpoint of a communication channel needs to be able to understand what the other endpoint is saying. The destination must also be able to figure out whether the packet is corrupted or invalid, so that it does not accidentally act on misinterpreted information. The packet formats describe what each type of packet "looks" like. It tells the sender what to put into the packet, and it tells the recipient how to parse the inbound packet.

2. *Packet semantics:* Reading and interpreting the packet is not enough, however. The sender and recipient need to have agreed on what the recipient can assume if it receives a particular packet and what actions it should take in response to it. For example, if a host receives an "all is okay" packet, then it does not need to take any special action, but if it receives a "Good morning" packet, it should send back a packet asking "How are you?" to the source. Just like in human communications, it is easy to hear the same words but misinterpret their meaning, so clear protocol semantics are essential in computer communications. The packet semantics of a protocol are typically described using a finite state machine (FSM) which represents the transitions involved in the protocol.

3. *Error behavior:* Related to, but distinct from, packet semantics are rules about how each endpoint should respond to various error scenarios. If a host receives a packet that is improperly formatted, should it quietly discard the packet or should it send back an error packet or should it close the connection? If a host has been asked to perform a service, what should it do if it is out of memory and cannot complete the task? What should the requester expect the state of the system to be if the task fails halfway through? Errors do happen, and without a clear definition of how each side will respond to errors, the rest of the protocol can become useless. The error conditions are typically described within the same FSM that describes the normal protocol semantics.

There are literally thousands of network protocols in use today. Each one is specialized for a particular task, ranging from downloading documents from the World Wide Web to exchanging real-time audio and video. In fact, when two applications communicate with each other, they are typically using many protocols simultaneously. There is a protocol for exchanging information between the applications, and there is another protocol for exchanging information among routers. There is even a protocol for communicating between the host and the gateway host on the LAN and yet another protocol for communicating between a modem and a dial-up server.

THE BSD SOCKETS ARCHITECTURE

Transporting data from one host to another host is only part of the networking story. In reality, things are more complex. On a particular host, one might have several applications executing concurrently and using the network. These applications may be communicating with different destinations at once, and two applications might even be talking to the same destination host or even the same destination application at the same time. (Imagine, for example, two FTP clients, using the File Transfer Protocol, to simultaneously transfer two files from a server to your client machine.) Even worse, a host might need to use several different protocols to communicate with the various routers and gateways with which it is connected.

Hosts therefore face the challenge of keeping track of all of this communication. When an application sends a packet, the host must make sure that it gets sent to the right destination, and when a host receives a packet it must make sure that it is delivered to the correct application. To achieve these two tasks, most hosts on the Internet use the Berkeley Software Distribution (BSD) Sockets network architecture to keep track of applications and network connections. The elements of this network system architecture are illustrated in Figure 3-2. The BSD architecture first gained wide acceptance in the UNIX operating system, but today it is implemented on virtually all of the major commercial operating systems. The WinSock library used on Microsoft Windows 3.1/95/NT platforms is a derivative of the BSD interfaces [Quinn/Shute95].

Sockets and Ports

Applications that communicate over the network send data over a socket. A *socket* is a software representation of the endpoint to a communication channel. Sockets can represent many different types of channels, including reliable communication with a single destination host, unreliable communication with a single destination host, unreliable communication with multiple destination hosts, or even in-memory communication with another application on the local host. Regardless of the type of communication channel, the application sees a common abstraction.

A socket identifies several pieces of information, including the following five, about a communication channel.

1. *Protocol:* How the operating systems exchange application data. The protocol implies a level of reliability by specifying whether the destination operating system will send acknowledgment packets and whether packets should be retransmitted if no acknowledgment is received.

2. *Destination host:* The destination host address(es) for packets sent on this socket. In some cases, the destination address is not stored with the socket, in which case the application must specify one whenever it sends a packet.

3. *Destination application ID, or port:* This number identifies the appropriate socket on the destination host. For each protocol, each of a host's sockets is assigned a different 16-bit integer by the operating system. By specifying the protocol along with this port number in each packet, the source host ensures that the destination host can deliver the

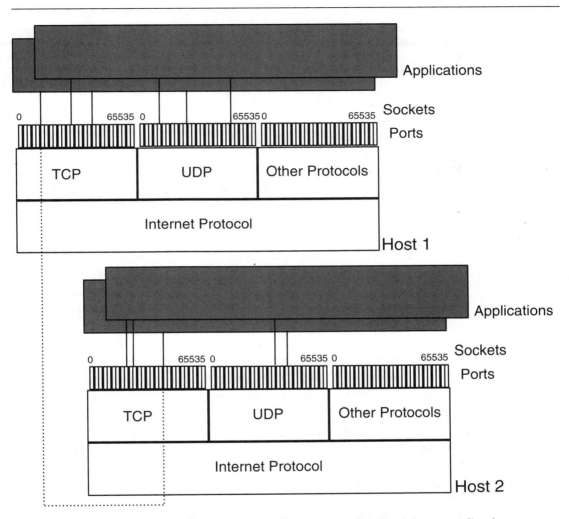

FIGURE 3-2   The BSD Sockets architecture allows multiple networking applications to coexist on a single host.

packet to the correct application. Just as with the destination host address, some sockets may not have a destination port specified, in which case it must be specified whenever the application sends a packet.

   4. *Source host:* This address identifies which host is sending the data. This information is rarely needed at the source host because there is only one choice in most cases. However, if the host has multiple Internet addresses assigned to it, it can legally specify a different source address in each data packet.

5. *Local application ID, or port:* A 16-bit integer that identifies which application is sending data along this socket. By including this port number along with the source host address in the packet, the source host ensures that the destination host will be able to send reply packets back to the sending application.

When the application sends data to a socket, the operating system has enough information to figure out how to send the data (which protocol to use), to whom to send the data (destination host address and desti-nation application port), and how to identify the sender (local host address and source application port).

The use of port numbers is one of the foundations of open network-ing on the Internet. Port numbers are like a set of post office box numbers for a communication protocol. Each application grabs a port number and by advertising that port number along with the host address, it can make sure that other applications can connect and send data to it. There are over 65,536 valid port numbers, so an operating system can support many different applications at once. Note that two communicating appli-cations do not need to (and rarely do) have the same port number. Each host assigns port numbers independently, and each packet typically includes both the source and destination port numbers.

However, if port numbers are so arbitrary, how can one application ever find another one? For example, when a Web browser visits a site, how does it know which port it should use to talk with the Web server? The answer to these questions is both simple and elegant. Port numbers 1 through 1023 are "reserved" for certain well-known applications or services known to the operating system, and ports 1024 through 49151 are "registered" for use by certain well-known application protocols. For example, port 80 is reserved for HTTP, the Hyper-Text Transport Protocol used over the World Wide Web. Port 25 is used for Simple Mail Transfer Protocol (SMTP) used for electronic mail, and port 1080 is used by SOCKS which is used by network firewall security perimeters. The reserved and registered port number assignments are managed and published by the Internet Assigned Numbers Authority (IANA).

When writing a new net-VE application protocol, one should be sure to use an unregistered port number to ensure that other hosts will not connect to it expecting to find another application or service. The easiest way to do this is to select one of the ports in the unassigned range, 49152 to 65535. However, if a net-VE is going to enjoy widespread use and needs to use a fixed port number, then one should apply for a registered port. This can be done through IANA [IANA].

The Internet Protocol

Most hosts on the Internet today use the Internet Protocol (IP) [Postel81a] to communicate with each other. IP is a low-level protocol used by hosts and routers to ensure that the packets travel from the source host to the destination host. IP hides the fact that the transmission path might include phone lines, local area networks, wide area networks, wireless radios, satellite links, or carrier pigeon. The Internet Protocol includes facilities for segmentation and reassembly (SAR), namely splitting the packets into small fragments when they traverse network links that cannot support large packets and for reassembling the packets at the other end. The IP header also includes a "Time-to-Live" (TTL) field that specifies how many network hops may transfer the packet. Each time the packet is transferred by a router, the TTL field is decremented, and if it ever hits zero, it is discarded. In this way, packets cannot accidentally be routed in infinite loops around the Internet.

Applications almost never use the Internet Protocol directly. Instead, they use one of the protocols that are written on top of IP. These higher-layer protocols provide support for application port numbers, and they also include services such as acknowledgments and retransmission. The next section discusses these protocols.

INTRODUCING THE INTERNET PROTOCOLS FOR NET-VES

The various Internet protocols take advantage of the basic services provided by IP and extend those facilities to provide services that are suitable for applications to use for transmitting their own data. The basic Internet protocols in common use today allow programmers to decide how best to balance the need for efficiency (low bandwidth, low latency) against the desire for good transmission semantics (sending to one or many destinations, transmission reliability, and so forth). In general, the more services that one desires from a protocol, the more the protocol costs in terms of efficiency and scalability. When building a net-VE, the designer must choose the right protocol for the job [Gossweiler+94].

This section discusses the common Internet protocols—TCP and UDP—along with broadcasting and multicasting. These protocols are summarized in Table 3-1, which illustrates the different service levels provided by the protocols. The following sections discuss the design decisions involved when choosing the protocol to use within a net-VE.

For reference, this book's appendix provides basic examples of how to use the network protocols in the C, C++, and Java programming languages.

TABLE 3-1   Communication Protocols and Techniques Used in Net-VEs

Protocol or technique	*Characteristics*
Transmission Control Protocol (TCP)	Point-to-point connection with reliable transmission using acknowledgment and retransmission, providing stream-based data semantics.
User Datagram Protocol (UDP)	Lightweight data transmission with "best efforts" delivery (e.g., no reliability guarantees), providing packet-based data semantics.
Internet Protocol (IP)	End-to-end connectivity between source and destination host(s) across heterogeneous transmission media, including fragmentation and Time-to-Live (TTL) services.
IP Multicasting	Efficient, "best-efforts" data transmission to multiple destination hosts whose individual identities are anonymous to the transmitter. Appropriate for the Internet and large-scale systems.
IP Broadcasting	"Best-efforts" data transmission to all hosts on a LAN. Appropriate for small LANs and low-bandwidth transmissions.

Transmission Control Protocol

The Transmission Control Protocol (TCP) [Postel81b] is the most common protocol in use in the Internet today. When layered on top of the Internet Protocol, it is more commonly referred to as TCP/IP. TCP/IP provides the application with the illusion of a simple point-to-point connection to an application running on another machine. TCP/IP appears to be reliable, because it automatically transmits acknowledgments and retransmits data. The reliability of TCP/IP is enhanced because the receiver verifies the integrity of data packets against a data checksum contained in the packet header and because the two endpoints employ a flow control procedure to ensure that the sender does not transmit packets faster than the network can transfer them or the destination host can process them. In summary, each endpoint can regard a TCP/IP connection as a bidirectional reliable stream of bytes between the two endpoints. TCP/IP automatically takes care of dividing the sent data into network packets for transmission, and it automatically extracts data from inbound packets, discards duplicate packets, and inserts the data in the correct order into the byte stream that the application reads. Finally, the protocol allows the application to detect when the other end of the connection has gone away or disconnected.

All of this function comes with a price, however. Because of its reliability and ordering semantics, TCP/IP must transmit more information to describe the data ordering, checksums to detect corruption, and acknowledgment/retransmission packets. Moreover, the receiving application cannot easily "skip ahead" in the data stream if it falls behind. It must receive and accept the entire stream in the order that it was transmitted by the other end; the TCP protocol handler may therefore arbitrarily hold, or buffer, transmitted data away from the receiving application in order to preserve the packet ordering guarantees. Consequently, though TCP/IP is useful for a large variety of applications, it is not suitable for applications that do not necessarily need the strict ordering and consistency guarantees that TCP/IP provides.

User Datagram Protocol

The User Datagram Protocol (UDP) [Postel80] is a lightweight communication protocol. It differs from TCP in three respects: connectionless transmission, best-efforts delivery, and packet-based data semantics.

UDP does not establish peer-to-peer connections. Put simply, the sender and recipient of UDP data do not keep any information about the state of the communication session between the two hosts. Such information was used by TCP to detect packet loss, request retransmissions, and dynamically adjust the rate of data transmission. With UDP, therefore, none of these features is available. Instead, UDP simply provides *best-efforts delivery*, meaning that it makes no attempt to guarantee that data is delivered reliably or in order. In effect, the data is transmitted blindly. The sender must rely on other information (such as responses from the recipient) to determine whether the recipient is still alive, whether the data arrived, and whether the recipient can keep up with the data. Finally, because the endpoints do not maintain any state information about the communication, UDP data is sent and received on a packet-by-packet basis. These *datagrams* must not be too big, because if they must be fragmented, some pieces might get lost in transit.

At first, it may appear that UDP/IP is too weak to be powerful. However, its power lies in its simplicity. Because it does not include the overhead needed to detect reliability and maintain connection-oriented semantics, UDP packets require considerably less processing at the transmitting and receiving hosts. Because UDP/IP does not maintain the illusion of a data stream, packets can be transmitted as soon as they are sent by the application instead of waiting in line behind other data in the stream; similarly, data can be delivered to the application as soon as it arrives at the receiving host instead of waiting in line behind missing data. Finally, many operating systems impose limits on how many simultaneous TCP/IP connections they can support. Because the operating system does not need to keep UDP connection information for every peer host, UDP/IP is more appropriate for large-scale distributed systems where each host communicates with many destinations simultaneously.

These characteristics reveal why UDP/IP has traditionally been the protocol of choice for large-scale networked virtual environments. In these systems, data must be sent directly to multiple recipients, and real-time data delivery is important. As you will see in chapter 5, net-VEs have adopted a number of techniques for detecting and dealing with lost data. Indeed, in many cases, lost data is not even important.

One aspect of UDP/IP can make it unsuitable for some environments. As we have seen, when a socket is receiving data on a UDP port, it will receive packets sent to it by any host, whether it is participating in the application or not. This possibility can represent a security problem for applications that do not robustly distinguish between expected and unexpected packets. For this reason, many network firewall administrators block UDP data from being sent to a protected host from outside the security perimeter [Greenwald+96]. Unless the participants' firewalls support the relatively new SOCKS version 5 protocol [SOCKS96], full Internet UDP connectivity cannot be assumed.

IP Broadcasting Using UDP

With UDP/IP, an application can direct a packet to be sent to one other application endpoint. Of course, using a single socket, one could send the same packet to multiple destinations by repeatedly calling sendto() (in C/C++) or DatagramSocket.send() (in Java). However, this approach has two disadvantages: Excessive network bandwidth is required because the same packet is sent over the network multiple times, and each host must maintain an up-to-date list of all other application endpoints who are interested in its data.

IP broadcasting [Mogul84] provides a partial solution to these issues by allowing a single transmission to be delivered to all hosts on a network; if data is transmitted using UDP/IP, then it is only delivered to applications that are receiving on a designated port at each host. This approach is particularly useful for small net-VEs. When a net-VE participant starts, it can simply start listening for data on the application's well-known port and start broadcasting its own data on that same port. It does not need to notify anyone of its presence, and, consequently, the participant can also terminate at any time. On the other hand, broadcasting is expensive because every host on the network must receive and process every broadcast packet, even if no local application is actually interested in receiving the data.[2] In addition, broadcasting cannot

---

[2]Broadcasting cannot be efficient because of the way that broadcast packets are addressed. Recall that UDP packets are encapsulated inside the IP protocol and further encapsulated into the LAN protocols such as Ethernet or Token Ring. The only information available at these latter protocol layers is the IP address destination of the packet (which gets translated into a LAN network address), not the UDP port number. Consequently, a machine cannot determine whether to discard the packet until the UDP information, including the UDP port number, is processed by the operating system. With multicast, things are better because different types of packets have different destination IP addresses. The network interface card can actually discard undesired packets by looking at the destination address.

be used for Internet-based net-VEs. For large net-VEs or Internet-based systems, IP multicasting is more appropriate (see the next section).

To send a broadcast message, the sender generates a bit mask representing the subnet of hosts that should receive the message. By carefully constructing the address, the broadcaster can control the *scope* or range of the broadcast. For example, to send a broadcast to all hosts on the 10.25.12 LAN (that is, all hosts with IP addresses 10.25.12.*), the application would direct the broadcast to the address 10.25.12.255. Using a similar approach, one can send a broadcast to all subnets within a company's network.[3] For example, if a corporate network is network 10, then sending to 10.255.255.255 causes a site-wide broadcast.

For most purposes, however, broadcast is only recommended (and is only guaranteed to work) on the local LAN. Instead of computing the appropriate broadcast address, one can simply use the address 255.255. 255.255. Packets sent to this address are guaranteed to only be delivered to the hosts on the local LAN.

IP Multicasting

IP broadcasting can only be used in a LAN environment, and even there, it is relatively expensive because each host on the LAN must receive and process the packet, even if no application on that host is actually interested in receiving that packet. IP multicasting [Deering89] is the solution to both of these concerns. It is appropriate for Internet use, as well as LAN use. It also does not impose burdens on hosts that are not interested in receiving the multicast data.

Routing

To understand multicasting, it is useful to consider a process for distributing a newspaper, as shown in Figure 3-3. Imagine that the *Daily News* needs to distribute newspapers to subscribers located around the world. The paper might be printed in Chicago, and one copy would be

---

[3]Message broadcasts to multiple LANs connected by network gateways or switches are not guaranteed to work. Local policy will determine whether a particular switch will forward broadcast packets to adjacent LANs. Therefore, it is possible, even likely, that a particular broadcast packet will only travel along the network segment that is most local to the sending host. Unfortunately, because broadcast packets are unreliable and are not acknowledged, there is no way for a sender to know automatically how far its broadcast packets have been disseminated.

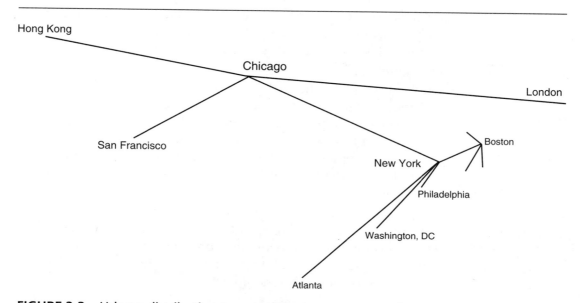

FIGURE 3-3 Using a distribution tree, multicast messages are disseminated from the source and through network links to each subscribing destination.

sent to each of four major distribution sites—say, San Francisco, New York, London, and Hong Kong. Each of these distribution sites can take the copy that it receives and make copies for a set of subdistribution sites. For example, the New York distribution site might make and send copies to Boston, Philadelphia, Washington, DC, and Atlanta. Each of these subdistribution sites makes a copy for each subscriber and sends those copies. Alternatively, a subdistribution site may send a copy to an even smaller distributor who may, in turn, have its own set of sub-scribers. The tree may have arbitrary depth or breadth, as long as all of the subscribers eventually receive their newspapers.

With the *Daily News* distribution system, the newspapers "fan out" from the publisher to the subscribers. The distribution network is like a tree, with the newspaper publisher the root, the distributors the branches, and the subscribers the leaves.

This newspaper distribution system has several important properties.

- Newspapers are only delivered to subscribers. Each distribution site makes certain that it only sends newspapers where they are wanted.

- Subscribers need to explicitly request the newspaper from their local distributors. Without such an explicit request, the distributor would never know that the subscriber is interested in receiving the newspaper.

- Duplicate copies of the newspaper are never sent down the same distribution path. For example, only one copy is sent from New York to Boston, even though the Boston distributor might represent thousands of customers. Each distributor is responsible for making new copies of the newspaper when it needs to send them down different distribution paths. In this respect, the distribution is quite efficient.

- The publisher does not need to know the identities of all of the subscribers. In fact, each distributor, including the publisher, only needs to know the identity of the appropriate subdistributors. Only the subscriber's local distributor—the paperboy or paper-girl—needs to know who should actually receive the newspapers.

This is an example of *receiver-controlled distribution*. Contrast this with direct-mail marketing, which is an example of *sender-controlled distribution*. Under such schemes, the sender unilaterally establishes a mailing list and controls the set of destinations for publications.

The newspaper distribution system is quite different from a traditional broadcast system, such as that used by radio. In a broadcast-based system, information is transmitted to all possible hosts. A host will receive the information regardless of whether the transmitter (that is, the radio station) intended the information to travel there and regardless of whether the host actually requested it. When compared with the newspaper distribution system, broadcasting consumes more communication resources, most of which are wasted.

Multicasting over networks is very similar to the newspaper distribution system described above for the *Daily News*. The network "distributors" are the multicast-capable network routers that are responsible for determining which destination networks should receive a particular multicast packet. Together, these routers construct a *multicast distribution tree* from each sender (publisher) to each recipient (subscriber). The details of how the multicast distribution tree is constructed are beyond the scope of this book, but [Maufer98] offers a good overview of the various techniques in use today.

Addressing

Each multicast distribution tree is represented by a special pseudo-IP address called a *multicast IP address* or *class D address*. IP addresses in the range 224.0.0.0 through 239.255.255.255 are designated as multicast addresses. However, the 224.*.*.*, 225.*.*.*, and 232.*.*.* addresses are currently reserved addresses assigned by the Internet Assigned Numbers Authority, and packets sent to the 239.*.*.* addresses are typically only sent to hosts within a single organization. To be safe, an Internet-based net-VE application should therefore use one or more addresses in the 226.*.*.* to 231.*.*.* or the 233.*.*.* to 238.*.*.* ranges. The sender transmits data to a multicast IP address in use by the application, and a subscriber receives the packet if it has explicitly subscribed to that address (that is, joined that multicast group).

Of course, multicast addresses are a limited resource, and it is desirable to avoid having multiple applications using the same address at the same time. Such collisions might cause each application to unexpectedly receive packets produced by the other application; these collisions can degrade the performance of the entire net-VE by causing excessive network resource consumption as well as wasted packet processing at participating hosts. Moreover, these unexpected packets may be hard to distinguish from the packets that the application actually expects to receive and may, therefore, cause erroneous application behavior.

If the net-VE will use a small number of multicast addresses on a regular basis or will be deployed commercially, the net-VE developer may want to permanently reserve a set of multicast addresses. These permanent address assignments are governed by the IANA. A form to request a permanent multicast address assignment is available from the IANA Web site [IANA].

If the application does not require a permanent address assignment, it can instead choose to use one temporarily. Of course, it is free to select one at random. However, a well-behaved multicast application should first listen to the Session Announcement Protocol (SAP) [Handley96] to learn about which multicast addresses are currently in use. SAP messages describe active multicast sessions; the format of these session descriptions is defined by the Session Description Protocol (SDP) [Handley/Jacobson97]. After selecting an unused multicast address, the net-VE should announce the address selection. Alternatively, the Session DiRectory (SDR) tool can be used to monitor the currently active multicast addresses and to announce new ones; it may be downloaded from [SDR].

At the time of this writing, the Internet Engineering Task Force (IETF) is actively exploring more robust mechanisms for managing dynamic multicast group address assignments. The reader is referred to the Multicast Address Allocation (MALLOC) workgroup for the current status of this work [MALLOC]. Some of the technical challenges behind deploying a scalable multicast address allocation scheme for the Internet are provided by [Handley98].

Scoping

When sending multicast data, an application can specify the IP Time-to-Live field to control how far multicast packets should travel. The TTL field can take on values between 0 and 255, but as shown in Table 3-2, different ranges of the TTL field are designated to represent different network scoping. Though an application can send all of its packets with a high TTL, it is generally desirable to use the scoping range that is actually necessary.

It is important to note that TTLs are only approximately honored by the multicast distribution system. Moreover, the multicast protocols impose no restrictions on which applications or hosts may send packets to a particular multicast address. As a result, a particular application might receive multicast packets transmitted by some completely unknown application located halfway around the world. As with any UDP-based application, a robust net-VE must be able to differentiate its

TABLE 3-2   TTL for Multicast Packet Distribution

TTL value	Scope of multicast
0	Only deliver to the local host
1	Only deliver on the local LAN
2–31	Only deliver to the local site (network)
32–63	Only deliver to the local region
64–127	Only deliver to the local continent
128–254	Deliver globally

Note: Although ranges 32–63 and 64–127 are defined with restricted scope, these restrictions are not reliably implemented. In practice, therefore, anything with a TTL above 32 may effectively have global scope, depending on router behavior.

own packets from those of other applications (or even from other unrelated instances of the same net-VE application being executed by a different group of users).

Overall, multicast is rapidly emerging as the recommended way to build large-scale net-VEs over the Internet. It provides desirable network efficiency while also allowing the net-VE to partition different types of data by using multiple multicast addresses. Using an application's well-known multicast address, net-VE participants can announce their presence and learn about the presence of other participants. Multicast is also an appropriate technique for discovering the availability of other net-VE resources such as terrain servers. For example, a host can transmit a "search" query to a well-known multicast address; terrain servers listen for queries sent to that address and respond appropriately. These features make multicasting desirable even for LAN-based net-VEs.

On the other hand, multicasting does have some limitations, generally related to its infancy. Although an increasing number of routers are multicast-capable, many older routers are still not capable of handling multicast subscriptions. In the meantime, multicast-aware routers communicate directly with each other, "tunneling" data past the routers that cannot handle multicast data. This Multicast Backbone, or MBone [Macedonia/Brutzman94], provides its participants with the illusion of a fully connected multicast-capable Internet even though the Internet is not fully multicast-capable. However, a host cannot participate in a multicast-based net-VE if its local router is not itself multicast-capable and connected to the MBone. Although multicast is rapidly becoming universally available, it is not quite there yet.

SELECTING A NET-VE PROTOCOL

With so many protocols available, the net-VE designer faces a difficult task in choosing among them. Each protocol offers its own combination of services and costs, and the protocol choice therefore largely depends on the particular needs of the net-VE and its underlying communications architecture. Indeed, each of the Internet protocols that we have described is in widespread use within net-VEs today. This section summarizes the strengths and limitations of the communication protocols and highlights their implications on net-VE architecture design. Table 3-3 further summarizes these protocol strengths and limitations, and Chapter 4

TABLE 3-3   Comparison of the Network Protocol Alternatives for Net-VEs

Protocol	Strengths	Limitations	Net-VE characteristics
TCP	Guaranteed packet delivery Ordered packet delivery Packet checksum checking Transmission flow control Ubiquitous, with many firewalls supporting outbound connections	Only supports point-to-point connectivity Bandwidth overhead Packets may be delayed to preserve ordering guarantees	Virtual environments having relatively small number of hosts and limited data requirements; typically used in a client-server configuration
UDP	Packet-based data transmission Low overhead Immediate delivery Nearly ubiquitous, but firewalls are often problematic	Only supports point-to-point connectivity No reliability guarantees No ordering guarantees Packet corruption possible	Virtual environments having higher data requirements; used in both client-server and peer-to-peer configurations
IP Broadcasting	Same as UDP, except simultaneous delivery to multiple hosts	Same as UDP, except delivery scope limited to local networks	Small-scale peer-to-peer net-VEs with high data requirements and time-sensitive data delivery needs
IP Multicasting	Same as IP broadcasting, except efficient Internet-wide delivery	Same as UDP, except only available from/to Internet hosts connected to the MBone	Large-scale peer-to-peer and client-server net-VEs, particularly over the Internet

discusses the different types of net-VE communication architectures in more detail.

Net-VE design does not easily reduce to simply choosing a single protocol. Net-VE designers have recently begun to see the value in using multiple protocols within a single system. The choice of protocol is determined by the type of data being transmitted, reliability and timeliness needs, and the number of destinations. Therefore, the question is not, "Which protocol should I use in my net-VE?" but is instead, "Which protocol should I use to transmit this piece of information?"

Using TCP/IP

The TCP/IP protocol provides net-VE systems with reliable data transmission between exactly two hosts. The packets are delivered in order, and checksums ensure the automatic detection of data transmission errors. The TCP protocol is also relatively easy for programmers to use because its powerful semantics free the developer from having to handle many of the housekeeping tasks commonly associated with datagram-based protocol usage. On the other hand, the point-to-point nature of TCP also limits its use within large-scale net-VEs because it is often difficult to establish and maintain connections between every pair of hosts participating in the net-VE. The TCP/IP bandwidth overhead is also considerable. Finally, to guarantee the ordering semantics, the TCP protocol handler must arbitrarily delay the delivery to the application of available data.

Based on these characteristics, TCP/IP has seen greatest use in net-VE systems having a relatively small number of participating hosts. Rather than establishing connections between every pair of hosts, net-VE designers designate one host as a *server*, and each of the other hosts establishes a single TCP/IP connection to that server. This server acts as an information clearinghouse, receiving data from each participant and passing that information to other interested participants. This client-server model can be further extended to include multiple servers that communicate with each other using a TCP/IP link.

Using UDP/IP

The UDP/IP protocol removes most of the communication overhead introduced by TCP, but it also provides a much-reduced level of service. It offers a simple best-effort delivery semantic on transmitted data packets and offers no reliability or ordering guarantees. As with TCP/IP, packets are transmitted point-to-point between two hosts. However, because UDP/IP transmission does not require the sender and receiver to establish an explicit connection, a host can easily send UDP/IP packets to multiple hosts.

Net-VEs use UDP when they must convey time-sensitive information among a larger number of hosts. In such situations, data reliability may be less critical because lost information will be replaced by an update transmitted a short time afterward. Because UDP/IP does not require an explicit connection setup, the protocol is not limited to client-server configurations. Instead, a host can transmit UDP/IP packets directly to other participating hosts in the system. However, because UDP/IP still only supports point-to-point communications, such peer-to-peer transmissions cannot easily be scaled to large net-VEs, with hundreds or thousands of participating hosts.

In many situations, a net-VE system requires some of the services normally provided by TCP/IP but cannot accept all of the overheads introduced by that protocol. In such situations, the net-VE designer must employ mechanisms within the net-VE's UDP packets to achieve similar functionality. For example, to achieve packet ordering, the source host can associate each data packet with a unique *serial number*. As long as the host increases the serial number monotonically (by using a simple counter to generate the serial numbers), then each destination host can reorder the packets from each source by inspecting the serial number contained within each packet, in combination with the source host address contained in the UDP header. Because the UDP protocol itself is unaware of these sequence numbers, the destination application receives the packets as soon as they are received by the network protocol software, and the application may choose to either process the packets immediately or wait until out-of-order packets have arrived.

Of course, the use of a serial number does not allow destination hosts to construct a common ordering of the packets arriving from different source hosts; each source host generates its own independent sequence of serial numbers. To provide global ordering capabilities, most net-VEs therefore include a timestamp within each transmitted packet. The timestamp indicates when the packet was generated and sent, and provides a common frame of reference for comparing packets from different sources. The destination host can compare timestamps in packets from multiple hosts to reconstruct a global ordering. Moreover, packet timestamps can be useful for other purposes within the net-VE. As we will see in Chapter 5, timestamps can help to maintain consistent shared state. Timestamps also help in the processing of real-time data such as streamed audio or video. Of course, any timestamp-based scheme requires the existence of a clock synchronization protocol, such as the Network Time Protocol (NTP) [Mills91].

The use of a packet serial number allows destination hosts to re-order packets in the order sent, but serial numbers do not allow the destination host to detect and recover from packets that are lost in transit over the network. Because the source assigns each packet to a unique serial number and because it typically does not transmit all packets to all destinations, a particular host can expect to see gaps in the serial numbers that it receives from a source host. A net-VE can address this limitation by using a more sophisticated method for assigning serial numbers to each packet transmission. The source host can maintain a sequence number counter for each destination host to which it transmits data. Whenever it transmits a UDP packet, the host increments the sequence number counter for the corresponding destination host and includes that sequence number in the transmitted UDP packet. Unlike a simple serial number scheme which gives a unique serial number to each data packet regardless of its destination, a sequence number scheme gives a different serial number to the data packet depending on its destination host. In this way, each destination host receives a consecutive series of sequence numbers from each source host and can therefore detect any missing packets.

To support the recovery of lost packets, the destination host can transmit acknowledgment packets to the source host. The following two approaches are possible.

1. In a *positive acknowledgment scheme,* the destination transmits packets to the source whenever it receives data. These acknowledgments include the serial number (or other ID) of the received packet. Such acknowledgments need not be sent for every packet; instead a single packet may acknowledge multiple packets at once. After transmitting a packet, the source host initiates a timer. If it does not receive a suitable acknowledgment before the timer expires, the source retransmits the packet and restarts the timer.

2. In a *negative acknowledgment scheme,* the destination host maintains a timer and transmits a negative acknowledgment packet to the source if it does not receive any packets from the source before the timer elapses. Whenever it receives a packet, it resets the timer. The negative acknowledgment scheme is more effective when the destination knows from which hosts to expect data and with what frequency. It therefore requires that each source host transmit data at a predictable rate or, in cases where that rate cannot be sustained, transmit occasional heartbeat packets that prevent the destination host's timer from expiring. (For example, the DIS protocol, described in the previous chapter, generates heartbeat packets once every five seconds.)

UDP-based flow control is a reflection of the destination application's ability to process incoming packets at the rate that they arrive. The destination host receives UDP packets and holds them for processing. If the queue of unprocessed packets exceeds some threshold level, the application may transmit a *quench* packet indicating that packets are arriving too quickly. Upon receiving such a quench packet, a host should attempt to reduce its data transmission rate to the requesting host.

As should be apparent, each of these services introduces new overhead to UDP either in terms of extra information transmitted within each data packet or in terms of extra packets transmitted. As a general rule, adding one or two services generally does not present too much of a burden, but when multiple services are required, the net-VE designer is often better off simply moving to TCP/IP, which provides these services in an integrated, efficient way.

Using IP Broadcasting

The design considerations for IP broadcasting largely parallel those for UDP/IP, with the exception that a single IP broadcast transmission delivers the packet to all hosts on a local network. This multihost delivery makes broadcasting capable of supporting relatively high data rates with the same time-sensitive delivery capabilities as UDP. Moreover, because transmissions go to all hosts at once, a host needs to maintain only a single sequence number counter, rather than one per destination host.

Because IP broadcasting can only be performed over a local network, it is only used by net-VEs whose participating hosts are located within a single network domain. Moreover, because packets are sent to multiple destinations simultaneously, net-VEs use IP broadcasting in support of peer-to-peer communication architectures. Though the bandwidth requirements for multipoint delivery are less than those for UDP/IP, IP broadcasting still consumes considerable network and computational resources, particularly because data may be received and processed by hosts that have no interest in the contained information. For that reason, IP broadcasting cannot be used effectively in net-VEs having large numbers of participating hosts.

With broadcast-based protocols (and multicast protocols, as described below), a host is subject to receiving packets from other net-VE instances, or indeed other applications, that happen to be simultaneously using the same port number (and, in the case of multicast, the same multicast group address). For example, multiple net-VEs may be running on the same network, and a particular host may receive broadcast packets from all of them. In designing the net-VE protocol, it is therefore important to distinguish and filter the packets generated by the different net-VEs (or other applications) to avoid accidentally acting on information that does not correspond to the net-VE of interest. Many solutions exist for addressing this concern, including the following four.

1. *Avoid the problem entirely:* On a managed network, it is often possible for an administrator to preassign temporary port numbers to each net-VE instance or other application that uses IP broadcast. In this way, conflicts can be avoided, although one can never avoid the possibility of misconfiguration or human error. Alternatively, these port numbers could be reserved permanently through the IANA.

2. *Detect conflict and renegotiate:* When a participating host detects a conflicting transmission, it can notify its peers and direct them to migrate the net-VE to a new port number. Though conceptually simple, this approach can prove to be quite complex, both in terms of detecting conflicting packets and in terms of ensuring that all net-VE participants successfully migrate to the new port.

3. *Use protocol and instance magic numbers:* When the net-VE starts, a designated host (or an administrator) can select a "magic number," a random number intended to uniquely distinguish the particular net-VE instance. Each transmitted net-VE packet subsequently includes this magic number at a well-known position. Upon receiving a packet, each host can inspect the contents of that location in the packet and filter those packets that do not contain the magic number. This technique relies on the assumption that other net-VE instances are unlikely to randomly select the same magic number and that packets from other protocols are unlikely to hold the magic number in the specific position.

4. *Use encryption:* When the net-VE starts, a designated host or a system administrator can select a key that hosts will use to encrypt all packets. Upon receiving a packet, the host attempts to decrypt the packet contents and simply discards any packets that do not decrypt into a well-formed protocol packet. This technique relies on the relative impossibility that different net-VE instances or other applications will generate packets that can be decrypted into valid packets with a particular encryption key.

Using IP Multicasting

IP multicasting provides the most efficient means of transmitting information among large numbers of net-VE hosts because the network restricts information delivery based on both the TTL indicated by the source host and the group subscriptions registered by potential receivers. Information only travels along networks that lead toward an interested destination host, and it never travels over a single network multiple times. Although not all hosts are connected to multicast-capable networks today, multicast is emerging as the preferred method for data transmission in large-scale net-VEs.

The toughest decision facing the net-VE designer who has chosen to deploy a multicast-based system is how to separate the information flows among different multicast groups. In the simplest configuration, a single multicast group is used for all information in the net-VE, and all participating hosts subscribe to that single multicast address. Such a system is functionally equivalent to an IP broadcast-based system; however, unlike IP broadcast, it is deployable over wide area networks. However, net-VE designers typically choose to employ several multicast groups within a single net-VE in order to segment the information transmissions and provide some level of information filtering. In this way, hosts do not have to receive all information in the net-VE and instead only need to subscribe to information that may be of local interest. Chapter 7 delves into these different models for data filtering and information interest management using multicast group management.

CONCLUSION

Networking is the defining characteristic of net-VEs, and one cannot develop net-VEs without some understanding of how computers communicate over networks. This chapter has provided a basic review of the language used to describe data transmission, and it has described the architecture behind the BSD Sockets library and Internet protocol suite. Finally, it has provided examples of how to use the network communication techniques commonly used by net-VEs: unicast TCP/IP and UDP/IP, IP broadcasting using UDP, and IP multicasting. Each communication technique provides a different level of reliability, functionality, and scalability. When building net-VEs, one must be sure to select the most appropriate protocol for the application requirements.

Networking considerations define many of the decisions faced by net-VE designers. For example, to implement a large-scale net-VE for the Internet, the designer has little choice but to use multicasting. Consequently, the net-VE must provide mechanisms for handling packet loss, receiving data out of order, selecting an agreed-upon multicast address for the application, and discarding packets sent by other applications sharing the same multicast address. Similarly, if the designer chooses to use TCP/IP and avoid these concerns, he or she must instead provide mechanisms to determine the identity of other participants, open and manage connections among those participants, and handle the possibility that data might get delayed in transit because of packet loss earlier in the data stream. In all of these cases, the design tradeoffs are often subtle and complex. The next several chapters will address how these design decisions can be made.

One of the first decisions faced by a net-VE designer is to select a communication architecture for the net-VE system. This communication architecture defines how data will flow among the participant hosts in a net-VE. As we have seen, the choice of communication architecture and of communication protocol go hand-in-hand, because certain protocols lend themselves better toward certain communication architectures. The next chapter explores the available communication architectures for net-VEs, particularly client-server and peer-to-peer systems.

REFERENCES

[Cheshire96] Cheshire, S. It's the latency, stupid. May 1996. Available from: *http://rescomp.stanford.edu/~cheshire/rants/Latency.html*

[Comer/Stevens94] Comer, D. E., and D. L. Stevens. *Internetworking with TCP/IP, vol. 1.* Upper Saddle River, NJ: Prentice Hall, 1994.

[Deering89] Deering, S. E. Host extensions for IP multicasting. Internet RFC 1112, Information Sciences Institute, Marina Del Rey, CA, August 1989. (Available at *http://info.internet.isi.edu/in-notes/rfc/files/rfc1112.txt*)

[Gossweiler+94] Gossweiler, R., R. Laferriere, M. Keller, and R. Pausch. An introductory tutorial for developing multiuser virtual environments. *PRESENCE: Teleoperators and Virtual Environments* 3(4):255–264, Fall 1994.

[Greenwald+96] Greenwald, M. B., S. K. Singhal, J. R. Stone, and D. R. Cheriton. Designing an academic firewall: Policy, practice, and experience with SURF. In *Proceedings of the Internet Society 1996 Symposium on Network and Distributed System Security*, 76–91. Internet Society/IEEE Computer Society, February 1996. (Excerpted in *On the Internet* 2(3):24–29, May/June 1996.)

[Handley96] Handley, M. SAP: Session announcement protocol. Internet Draft, Internet Engineering Task Force, November 1996. (Available at *ftp://ftp.isi.edu/confctrl/docs/draft-ietf-mmusic-sap-00.txt*)

[Handley98] Handley, M. Session directories and scalable Internet multicast address allocation. In *Proceedings of the ACM SIGCOMM 1998 Conference*, 105–116. ACM SIGCOMM, Vancouver, BC, August 1998. (Published as *Computer Communications Review* 28(4), October 1998.)

[Handley/Jacobson97] Handley, M., and V. Jacobson. SDP: Session description protocol. Internet Draft, Internet Engineering Task Force, March 1997. Available at *http://north.east.isi.edu/sdr/sdp.ps*

[IANA] Internet Assigned Numbers Authority Web site: *http://www.iana.org*

[Macedonia/Brutzman94] Macedonia, M. R., and D. P. Brutzman. MBone provides audio and video across the Internet. *IEEE Computer* 27(4):30–36, April 1994.

[MALLOC] Multicast Address Allocation workgroup Web site: *http://north.east.isi.edu/malloc/*

[Maufer98] Maufer, T. A. *Deploying IP Multicast in the Enterprise.* Upper Saddle River, NJ: Prentice Hall, 1998.

[Mills91] Mills, D. L. Internet time synchronization: The network time protocol. *IEEE Transactions on Communications* 39(10):1482–1493, October 1991.

[Mogul84] Mogul, J. Broadcasting Internet datagrams. Internet RFC 919, Information Sciences Institute, Marina Del Rey, CA, October 1984. (Available at *http://info.internet.isi.edu/in-notes/rfc/files/rfc919.txt*)

[Postel80] Postel, J. User datagram protocol. Internet RFC 768, Information Sciences Institute, Marina Del Rey, CA, August 1980. (Available at *http://info.internet.isi.edu/in-notes/rfc/files/rfc768.txt*)

[Postel81a] Postel, J. Internet protocol: DARPA Internet program protocol specification. Internet RFC 791, Information Sciences Institute, Marina Del

Rey, CA, September 1981. (Available at *http://info.internet.isi.edu/in-notes/rfc/files/rfc791.txt*)

[Postel81b] Postel, J. Transmission control protocol: DARPA Internet program protocol specification. Internet RFC 793, Information Sciences Institute, Marina Del Rey, CA, September 1981. (Available at *http://info.internet.isi.edu/in-notes/rfc/files/rfc793.txt*)

[Quinn/Shute95] Quinn, B., and D. Shute. *Windows Sockets Network Programming.* Reading, MA: Addison-Wesley, 1995.

[SDR] Session Directory Web site: *http://north.east.isi.edu/sdr/*

[SOCKS96] SOCKS protocol version 5. Internet RFC 1928, Information Sciences Institute, Marina Del Rey, CA, March 1996. (Available at *http://info.internet.isi.edu/in-notes/rfc/files/rfc1928.txt*)

[Stallings96] Stallings, W. *Data and Computer Communications,* 5th ed. Upper Saddle River, NJ: Prentice-Hall, 1996.

[Stevens94] Stevens, W. R. *TCP/IP Illustrated. Vol. 1, The Protocols.* Reading, MA: Addison-Wesley, 1994.

Chapter 4

Communication Architectures

This chapter discusses the range of communication architectures that networked virtual environments use, along with their respective advantages and disadvantages. The chapter starts with the most basic architecture involving two players and ends with peer-to-peer architectures. It discusses the limitations on the number of players, both live and autonomous, for such architectures. This chapter concentrates on basic information flow, deferring issues of state management to Chapter 5.

TWO PLAYERS ON A LAN

Figure 4-1 shows the basic two-player virtual environment on a local area network (LAN). The players are people interacting via personal computers or workstations that are on the LAN. The connections in this figure represent two different things:

1. *The logical connections,* the messages to the net-VE software along a communication pathway
2. *The physical connections,* or wires, between the workstations

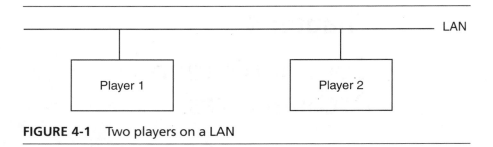

FIGURE 4-1   Two players on a LAN

Usually we discuss the communication architecture of a net-VE with respect to its logical connections, that is, how its messages flow. However, we also have to discuss the physical connections, as the wires and hardware become the limiting factor in our communication architecture design. To illustrate the limitations of wires in our communication architecture, we need to consider message sizes and frequencies.

As a baseline for communication architecture performance metrics, we utilize a Distributed Interactive Simulation (DIS) protocol data unit (PDU) [IEEE95]. That packet is 144 bytes in length and contains the information necessary to manage entity state for the various players, live and autonomous, that we expect to populate our virtual environment. That packet also contains the identification of the player that issued the packet, that player's location, the player's orientation, the player's velocity, the player's acceleration, any articulation information for the player (joint angles, turret angles, and so forth), and any special, dynamic information about the player that needs to be communicated.

We hypothesize great graphics performance for our virtual environment, 30 frames per second on each workstation. If we use NPSNET-IV DIS performance measures as our guide [Macedonia+94], we find aircraft generating 12 PDUs per second, ground vehicles generating 5 PDUs per second, weapon firing generating 3 PDUs per second, and fully articulated humans generating 30 PDUs per second (frame rate).

We also need some bandwidth metrics for our wires, and we use the most commonly available. We use 56 Kbps for modems, assuming V.90 connections are really possible on the telephone system, 10 Mbps for our Ethernet LAN (ignoring for the moment that Ethernet saturates at 70% utilization), and 1.5 Mbps for T-1 lines for WAN connections.

What does this mean for our two-player LAN? How many live and autonomous players can we put into our virtual environment before the LAN is saturated? We would also like to know how our players connect to each other on that LAN. For the number of players we can support, we need to make some more assumptions. We assume that we have sufficient processor cycles on each workstation, at least at first, to simplify our computation. We also need to assume a mix of players—for example, how many aircraft, ground vehicles, and articulated humans. For our computations, we will use the two extremes, the entities requiring the least and most bandwidth.

Therefore, for our two players on an Ethernet LAN we have 10 Mbps of available bandwidth. A PDU is 8 bits per byte times 144 bytes or 1,152 bits. This means that we have the ability to send about 8,680 packets per second on our Ethernet LAN. If we assume mayhem (kids in 3D networked videogames), all players firing once each second, we can make some statements about the outer bounds of what we can support. If we assume that our virtual environment is comprised of fully articulated humans (30 PDUs per second) firing once per second (3 PDUs per second), we can have 263 humans on such a LAN. If we assume all aircraft (12 PDUs per second) firing once per second (3 PDUs), we can have 578 aircraft. If we assume all ground vehicles (5 PDUs per second) firing once per second (3 PDUs per second), we can have 1085 ground vehicles. So, our network can support somewhere between 263 to 1,085 players, assuming away all other usage of the LAN (no Web browsing, no NFS, no e-mail . . .) and assuming we have sufficient processor cycles. Typical NPSNET-IV DIS battles maxed out at about 300 players on a LAN due to processor cycle and network limitations (other usage of the net) [Macedonia+94].

If we again assume DIS packets and our two players are connected via modem-speed lines, 56 Kbps, we have the ability to send about 48 packets per second. This gets us 1 human or 3 aircraft or 6 ground vehicles. At that point, we may wish to rethink our packet format to make it smaller or come up with a compression scheme of some sort. One scheme in [Cohen94] indicates that DIS can be accomplished with packets only 22% the size of the normal DIS PDU (say, 32 bytes instead of 144 bytes). We then have 218 packets per second with our modems and 7 articulated humans, 14 aircraft, or 27 ground vehicles.

Now that we understand the limitations of our physical connection, we can discuss the logical connection, how we send messages along the communication pathway to our net-VE. In a simple two-player LAN, we are sending messages between two machines. Those messages can be sent reliably, ordered, and slowly using a protocol such as TCP or faster via best-effort services such as UDP (see chapter 3 for a discussion of these protocols). The packets can be sent to a particular application endpoint listening to a particular socket, or the packets can be broadcast to all application endpoints listening to a socket configured for broadcast. The actual selection of how we send messages is usually determined by the importance of reliable and ordered delivery, and by the size of the net-VE in terms of players (live and autonomous). For a two-player net-VE, it hardly matters. For a two-machine net-VE where there are lots of autonomous players, we rapidly get pushed toward best-effort services and broadcast.

MULTIPLAYER CLIENT-SERVER SYSTEMS

Figure 4-2 shows the logical communication architecture for a multiplayer client-server net-VE. As stated above, the logical view shows how messages are being passed through the net-VE software. In a client-server system, each player sends packets to other players via a server. Packets are received via that same server. However, servers slow down the exchange of entity state message delivery in a net-VE. Despite being likely bottlenecks, servers do have a purpose. Servers can reduce message traffic to individual players by not sending packets to those players if the packet in question is out of the area of interest of the potential

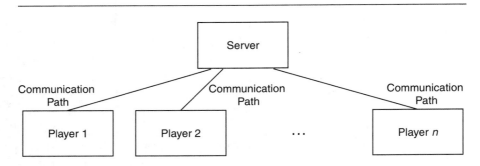

FIGURE 4-2   Multiplayer client-server—logical architecture

packet recipient. Servers can also compress multiple packets into a single message, eliminating redundant and unnecessary message flow. Servers can also convert bursty packet reception into smoother packet rates, thus delivering packets at a slower rate than they are generated by the individual players. Servers can be configured to communicate with their player clients reliably, if reliability becomes important in a net-VE, without the overhead associated with a fully connected net-VE. Client-server architectures are also preferred if there is an administrative task that must be performed, such as accounting for time spent in the net-VE on an individual basis (video game metering).

Figure 4-3 shows the physical architecture for a multiplayer client-server net-VE on a LAN. Notice that messages to the server from all players travel on the same wire. Messages back to the players from the server are also on that wire. For a server to be meaningful in this physical architecture, the server must be performing some added-value function. The server might be collecting data from each player via reliable connection and redistributing that information to players in compressed form. The server might also be doing some computation that the player machines are not capable of.

Figure 4-4 shows the physical architecture for a multiplayer client-server net-VE, where the physical links are via phone lines and modems. This physical architecture matches our logical architecture. As discussed above, the limitations of modem connections apply as long as we stick with the DIS packet model. Such an architecture can support 6 articulated humans, 14 aircraft, or 27 ground vehicles. This architecture is similar to one that might be used for an Internet game server like the Kali, TEN, and Mplayer systems described in Chapter 8, a server that can generally support between 32 and 128 players. Game servers do this by increasing the allowable net-VE errors perceived by

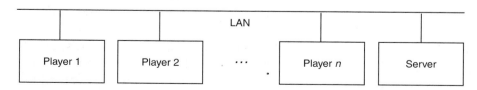

FIGURE 4-3   Multiplayer client-server—physical architecture on a LAN

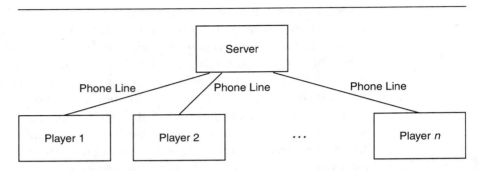

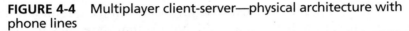

FIGURE 4-4   Multiplayer client-server—physical architecture with phone lines

each player (allowing updates to be transmitted less often by each participant) and by increasing how long the server holds data before redistributing it to clients, allowing more opportunities for compression and packet merging. Game companies are not kept to the 100 ms maximum latency expected for the DIS system. Moreover, game system servers also need to provide accounting as they dispatch entity updates.

Despite these optimizations, game companies are rapidly outgrowing dialup modems and are moving toward cable modems and DSL (Digital Subscriber Line) to the home. Cable modems have tremendous promise, with a bandwidth on the order of 10 Mbps. With cable modems, between 1,184 and 4,883 players can be supported using 32-byte PDUs and the performance specifications of DIS (that is, under 100 ms latencies). This assumes that we have sufficient graphics hardware, computational capabilities, and the ability to utilize the full network at the client end. This also assumes that we are not using any of the bandwidth for a voice or video channel, something highly likely in the future of interactive entertainment. If we add an audio and video channel, for chats with our friends on the other side of the game or for postgame discussions, we can still support between 1,117 and 4,609 players (Table 4-1).

Current DSL to the home at 1.5 Mbps can support 178 to 732 players using 32-byte PDUs and the performance specifications of DIS. If we add in an audio and video channel, we can still support between 111 and 459 players.

TABLE 4-1 Players Supportable in a DIS-like Net-VE versus Various Available Network Technologies

Technology	Minimum speed (bps)	Maximum speed (bps)	Minimum players DIS-like	Maximum players DIS-like	Minimum players game-like	Maximum players game-like	Minimum players game and video	Maximum players game and video
V.90 Modem	28,800	56,000	1	6	7	27		
DSL	384,000	1,500,000	39	163	178	732	111	459
T-1	384,000	1,500,000	39	163	178	732	111	459
Cable Modems	2,000,000	10,000,000	263	1,085	1,184	4,883	1,117	4,609
10BT	7,000,000	10,000,000	263	1,085	1,184	4,883	1,117	4,609
100BT	70,000,000	100,000,000	2,630	10,851	11,837	48,828	11,771	48,555

Source: [Dawson98]. See also Cable Modem FAQ at *http://www.cox.com/highspeed/modemfaq.html*

1. Assumptions

   a. Infinite compute cycles at each node

   b. Infinite graphics cycles at each node

   c. Network interface with infinite cycles

2. Packet Sizes

   a. Packet size for DIS-like VEs = 144 bytes, 1,152 bits

   b. Packet size for Game-like VEs = 32 bytes, 256 bits

   c. Video/audio stream (bytes/second) = 70,000 bytes, 560,000 bits (Origin—Media 100 natural video rate)

   d. Articulated humans (PDUs/second) = 30 just moving, 33 mayhem (mayhem used for minimum players)

   e. Aircraft (PDUs/second) = 12 just moving, 15 mayhem (not used but included here for completeness)

   f. Ground vehicles (PDUs/second) = 5 just moving, 8 mayhem (mayhem used for maximum players)

MULTIPLAYER CLIENT-SERVER, WITH MULTIPLE-SERVER ARCHITECTURES

Figure 4-5 shows more rationale for adopting a client-server logical architecture. This figure shows multiple servers, with each server serving a number of client players. Such an architecture allows a designer to scale beyond the processor cycle limits that a single server can achieve. In such an architecture, we might have players sharing an area of interest in the net-VE but residing on different servers, and these server-to-server connections transmit packets (world state information) that are required by these players. The Funkhouser RING system has such an architecture [Funkhouser95].

We can implement a multiple-server architecture in a number of ways. Usually the server-to-server connections are LAN or WAN speed. We need such high speed if we are going to build a net-VE that is not affected too badly by latency. If player (1,2) is going to be able to interact with player (3,1), then the wires, hardware, and software must be blazingly fast. If not, then we are going to perceive a lag in our net-VE and perhaps we will lose the illusion of the virtual environment.

The player-to-server connections with such an architecture can be implemented at LAN, cable modem, DSL, or modem speeds. The number of players we can serve to a client is similar in number to that discussed above and is detailed in Table 4-1. The net-VE scalability

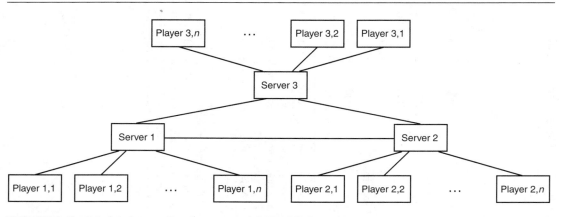

FIGURE 4-5   Multiplayer client-server with multiple servers

depends on the speed of the server-to-server connections and how many processor cycles are available at each server. Again, this also assumes high-speed computers at the client end, with sophisticated software and 3D-capable graphics hardware.

Server-to-server communication in this system is expected to be at LAN (10 Mbps or 100 Mbps) or even higher optical speeds. Packets that are transmitted from server to server will be compressed in some form. The physical architecture of the server will depend on the size of the net-VE and what financial resources are available.

PEER-TO-PEER ARCHITECTURES

In the ideal large-scale net-VE design world, we eschew servers. Servers mean that eventually we cannot scale our net-VE—that there is some finite limit to the number of players. Experience and research have shown that even if we purchase million-dollar servers, the limit on the number of players happens much faster than if a peer-to-peer, fully distributed architecture had been designed first [Calvin+95, Macedonia+95]. Our design goal is VEs that communicate peer-to-peer and are scalable within the available limits of computing resources. Peer-to-peer means that communications go directly from the sending player to the receiving player, or set of receiving players, to whom the information must be communicated.

What peer-to-peer means with respect to net-VE communication architecture is that early in the design of our net-VE we have to decide how geographically widespread our net-VE is going to grow. If our net-VE is going to exist on a LAN or on a bridged LAN (separate LANs connected by packet-copying and retransmitting gateway computers), then our communication architecture choices are pretty simple (Figure 4-6). If we wish to build a scalable net-VE on such a LAN, we either use broadcast or multicast for our packet transmission. Broadcast means that an entity state change by a player in the net-VE is placed onto the network and all machines on the LAN see the packet and must read, utilize, and discard that packet. This means a busy LAN and busy computers on the LAN, as they spend a lot of time throwing away packets.

Multicast on a LAN means that packets can be directed to machines that have subscribed to particular, agreed-upon multicast groups. Multicast packets that arrive at network interfaces that have subscribed to

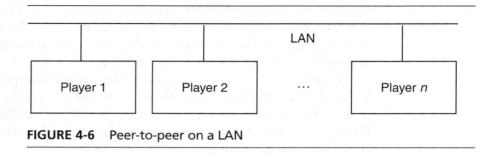

FIGURE 4-6   Peer-to-peer on a LAN

the specified multicast group are brought through the operating system kernel of the computer, where they can be read, utilized, and discarded. Multicast packets that arrive at a network interface that has not subscribed to the specified multicast group are not, in theory, passed on to the operating system kernel of the computer, and hence do not use processor cycles. Just like broadcast, multicasting floods the LAN, but it has a reduced requirement for processing at each player node in the net-VE.

For a scalable net-VE on a LAN, multicasting is the way to go. To utilize multicasting, distributed software must be developed that assigns packets to proper multicast groups. This is generally called area of interest management (AOIM) software, as shown in Figure 4-7. This layer of software assigns outgoing packets to the appropriate multicast group, receives incoming packets and propagates them to the appropriate net-VE state table in the local machine, keeps track of what groups are available (maybe by the use of a specially designated informational channel), and (possibly) even takes care of incoming and outgoing stream information (video and audio). Chapter 7 discusses multicast group assignment and AOIM software in depth, but a simple AOIM might be a geographic partition of the net-VE, with each region being assigned a multicast address (Figure 4-8) [Macedonia+95].

When we move peer-to-peer communications to a wide area network, broadcast is not an option, as most routers block broadcast packets from propagation. WAN multicasting means that our net-VE-generated packets are transmitted through routers out to wider regions of the network. Unfortunately, multicast-capable routers are not yet universally deployed. To propagate packets across such a deficient network often requires wrapping the multicast packet inside a unicast UDP packet using

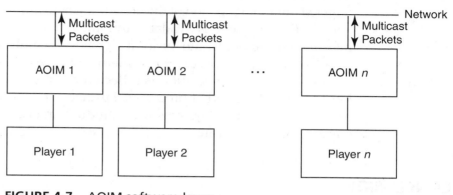

FIGURE 4-7 AOIM software layer

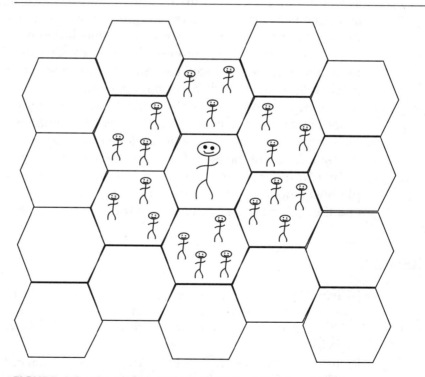

FIGURE 4-8 Spatial partitioning of the VE using AOIM

a machine designated as the multicast router. That unicast UDP packet is targeted for another region of the network, where multicasting is known and another machine is available to remove the unicast UDP packet information and put it onto the local segment as a multicast packet.

Over time, we expect that the Internet will become fully multicast-capable, and this expectation is reflected by Internet-2 and all other Next Generation Internet programs. Furthermore, the widespread use of multicast in net-VE systems will introduce an even greater need for effective AOIM software.

CONCLUSION

This chapter has looked at various communication architectures for networked virtual environments: two players on a LAN, with large numbers of autonomous entities in the system; multiplayer client-server architectures and their implementations, through a variety of available networking choices; and multiplayer, client-server architectures with multiple servers. The chapter concluded with a look at peer-to-peer architectures for large-scale net-VEs. Chapter 7 examines, in more detail, some advanced communication architecture issues, particularly large-scale area-of-interest management.

We next turn to one of the central issues defining net-VE design, shared state management. Indeed, shared information—where multiple users can see each other and interact in a shared environment—is the foundation of the net-VE experience. The choice of communication architecture defines how that shared state is maintained across multiple hosts, how up-to-date that information can be kept at each host, and the scalability characteristics of the resulting system.

REFERENCES

[Calvin+95] Calvin, J., J. Seeger, G. Troxel, D. Van Hook. STOW real-time information transfer and networking system architecture. In *Proceedings of the 12th Workshop on Standards for Distributed Interactive Simulations*. Orlando, FL, March 1995.

[Cohen94] Cohen, D. NG-DIS-PDU: The next generation of DIS-PDU (IEEE-1278) (94-87). In *Proceedings of the 10th Workshop on Standards for Distributed Interactive Simulations*, 735–742. Orlando, FL, March 1994.

[Dawson98] Dawson, F. XDSL market blooming. *Interactive Week* 5(39):28–29, October 12, 1998.

[Funkhouser95] Funkhouser, T. A. RING: A client-server system for multi-user virtual environments. In *Proceedings of the 1995 SIGGRAPH Symposium on Interactive 3D Graphics*, 85–92. ACM SIGGRAPH, Monterey, CA, April 1995. (Available from *http://www.cs.princeton.edu/~funk/symp95.ps.gz*)

[IEEE95] Institute for Electrical and Electronics Engineers. IEEE Standard for Distributed Interactive Simulation—Application Protocols. IEEE Std 1278.1—1995. Piscataway, NJ: IEEE Standards Press, September 1995.

[Macedonia+94] Macedonia, M. R., M. J. Zyda, D. R. Pratt, P. T. Barham, and S. Zeswitz. NPSNET: A network software architecture for large scale virtual environments. *PRESENCE: Teleoperators and Virtual Environments* 3(4): 265–287, Fall 1994.

[Macedonia+95] Macedonia, M. R., M. J. Zyda, D. R. Pratt, D. P. Brutzman, and P. T. Barham. Exploiting reality with multicast groups. *IEEE Computer Graphics & Applications*, 38–45, September 1995.

Chapter 5
Managing Dynamic Shared State

The fundamental goal of a networked virtual environment is to provide users with the illusion that they are all seeing the same things and interacting with each other within that virtual space. In a multiplayer shooting game, for example, you want to see the current location of the other players so that you can aim your gun. When you shoot your gun, the other players need to see your bullet's current position so that they can try to evade it. Finally, to determine whether the bullet actually hit someone, you and the target need to agree on both the bullet's position and the target's position.

As we build a net-VE, a key consideration is how to make sure that the participating hosts keep a consistent view of this dynamic shared state. *Dynamic shared state* constitutes the changing information that multiple machines must maintain about the net-VE. Dynamic shared state in a net-VE includes, for example, information about what and who is currently participating in the VE, their relative locations, and their current behaviors.

However, the dynamic shared state can be far more complex than simple position information. For example, hosts in a net-VE might share detailed information about the current weather conditions in the environment. If snow is falling in one area of the world, then everyone should know how fast it is falling, how large the flakes are, and so forth. In a virtual world, shared state may also involve the direction and force of gravity. If the world contains entities that change their shape dynamically, then shared information involves the current geometry of each entity, its color, reflectivity, and so on. In a highly dynamic environment, almost all information about the world may change and, therefore, needs to be shared.

Accurate dynamic shared state is fundamental to creating realistic environments. Shared state information is the unifying force that makes these environments truly "multiuser." Without dynamic shared state, each user works independently and loses the illusion of being located in the same place and time as other users. The dynamic shared state provides the common context that makes the virtual environment into a collaborative or competitive experience. In fact, many people equate the building of a net-VE with the problem of managing dynamic shared state.

As we see in this chapter, maintaining dynamic shared state is one of the hardest challenges facing the net-VE developer. The developer must make difficult tradeoffs between the available network and computational resources, on the one hand, and the desired realism of the VE experience, on the other hand. After describing these tradeoffs, this chapter discusses the three basic approaches to maintaining dynamic shared state: (1) shared repositories, (2) frequent broadcast, and (3) state prediction. For the sake of illustration, we focus on the maintenance of position of entities in the VE; however, these techniques apply equally well for the maintenance of other shared state information such as entity orientation, entity structure, weather, and terrain structure.

THE CONSISTENCY-THROUGHPUT TRADEOFF

In many cases, each piece of shared information in the net-VE is produced at one host and must be "mirrored" to other participants by transmitting it over the network. For example, suppose that Joe is moving around the VE. His machine keeps track of his current position and sends it over the network so that other users know Joe's location. Now, suppose that Joe is currently located at position (10,20) in the VE, as shown in Figure 5-1. Joe's host transmits this information across the

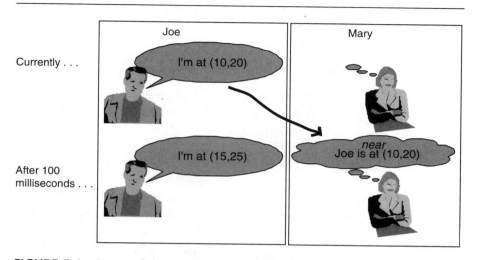

FIGURE 5-1 Network latency makes it difficult for shared state to be kept consistent at different hosts.

network, and Mary's host receives the message 100 ms later because of the network latency. Now, Mary perceives Joe's current location to be at (10,20). However, during the 100 ms that the message took to arrive, Joe may have already moved to a new location, say (15,25). In other words, by the time the information arrives at Mary's machine, it is already obsolete. Mary really can only guess that Joe is located somewhere *near* (10,20).

Our story of Joe and Mary provides an example of the difficulty that net-VE developers face when managing dynamic shared state. In fact, this scenario illustrates the fundamental rule about net-VE shared state:

> It is impossible to allow dynamic shared state to change frequently and guarantee that all hosts simultaneously access identical versions of that state.

This statement is known as the *Consistency-Throughput Tradeoff* faced by net-VE designers. Put simply, it means that the net-VE can either be a dynamic world in which information changes frequently or be a consistent world in which all hosts maintain identical information. The net-VE cannot support both dynamic behavior and absolute consistency.

Proof of the Tradeoff

The reasoning behind the Consistency-Throughput Tradeoff is quite straightforward. To guarantee absolute consistency among hosts, the data source must wait until everybody has received the information before it may proceed with its computations (or, in particular, update the shared state again). That delay includes transmission time and network latency for the original message, waiting for acknowledgments that the remote hosts have received the data, and possible retransmission in case the data was lost by the network. Because the source must wait for this consistency to be achieved, it can only generate data updates at a limited rate. In other words, to ensure absolute state consistency, the source must reduce its update rate to allow time for the communication protocol to reliably disseminate the state updates to the remote hosts.

In our previous example, Joe would not be able to move to a new location until he is sure that Mary has received the current position update. As shown in Figure 5-2, without any packet losses, this delay is at least 200 ms, consisting of 100 ms for the update to be transmitted from Joe to Mary and another 100 ms for an acknowledgment packet to be transmitted from Mary back to Joe. Thus, in an environment with absolute consistency, the delay limits Joe's update rate to five per second. As we shall see in chapter 6, this update rate is typically too slow for interactive net-VE systems.

Conversely, when a state change is generated at a particular host, there is a necessary delay before other hosts learn of the change; this delay consists of the network latency for transmitting the update over the network. Consequently, if the shared state is updated often enough, then the shared state might be updated while previous update messages are still in transit to remote hosts. As a result, some hosts may see a new state value while others still see older values being disseminated by the state consistency protocol. Put another way, because of the inherent transmission delay in state update distribution, one cannot update the shared state frequently and still ensure that all remote hosts have already received all previous state updates.

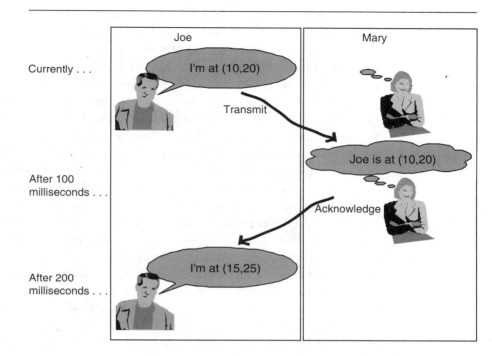

FIGURE 5-2   Ensuring dynamic state consistency across multiple hosts reduces the rate at which the data may change.

Design Implications of the Tradeoff

So far, we have framed the Consistency-Throughput Tradeoff as a network latency issue: After updating shared state, the source must decide whether to wait and ensure that all hosts have received the update or whether to proceed with future updates and risk that the current update has not yet arrived at some or all hosts. To better understand the implications of the tradeoff, let us consider an alternative formulation of the tradeoff in terms of network bandwidth:

Available network bandwidth must be allocated between messages for updating the dynamic shared state and messages for maintaining a consistent view of that dynamic shared state among participants in the net-VE.

To support a highly dynamic shared state, hosts must transmit more frequent data updates. To guarantee consistent views of the shared state, hosts must exchange acknowledgments and retransmit lost state updates. The Consistency-Throughput Tradeoff tells us that we must allocate our available bandwidth between these two uses.

Table 5-1 summarizes how the Consistency-Throughput Tradeoff affects the characteristics of net-VE systems. One end of the tradeoff spectrum contains systems that attempt to guarantee information consistency at all hosts. In these systems, all users see identical snapshots of the VE (though possibly from different vantage points). To ensure information consistency, packet losses must be detected and update retransmission must occur. To do this, each host must either know the identity of all other participating hosts in the net-VE or a central server must be used as a clearinghouse for updates and acknowledgments. The transmitter must wait for acknowledgments from all hosts, so if one of the hosts is connected to a slow or unreliable network link, then it slows down the net-VE performance for all participants. Furthermore, if someone starts up a heavy data transfer, then the net-VE's speed may be temporarily affected by the network congestion. This class of systems therefore has the advantage of ensuring accurate views of the net-VE but requires consistent network performance.

The other end of the tradeoff spectrum shown in Table 5-1 contains systems that strive to maximize the potential rate of shared state

TABLE 5-1   Spectrum of Dynamic Shared State Management Determined by the Consistency-Throughput Tradeoff

System characteristic	Absolute consistency	High update rate
View consistency	Identical at all hosts	Determined by data received at each host
Dynamic data support	Low: Limited by consistency protocol	High: Limited only by available bandwidth
Network infrastructure requirements	Low latency, high reliability, limited variability	Heterogeneous network possible
Number of participants supported	Low	Potentially high

updates. To achieve this throughput, the net-VE must tolerate some inconsistency in the shared state updates seen by each host. Each host generates a view of the VE based on the shared state updates that it has actually received. It is therefore possible that at any given time, no two hosts will see identical views of the VE. Simulation designers who choose this point in the tradeoff spectrum work to minimize the effects of these inconsistencies on the user's overall shared world experience. Because hosts process data independently, these systems can run over a network environment exhibiting more variable latency and reliability. This class of systems therefore has the advantage of supporting more users over a shared heterogeneous network but forces the VE designer and user to contend with potential data inconsistencies.

Three basic techniques for maintaining shared state are in common use.

1. *Centralized information repositories* represent one extreme of the tradeoff spectrum.
2. *Dead reckoning* represents the other extreme.
3. *Frequent state regeneration* represents a third approach, an intermediate between the two extremes.

We discuss each of these approaches in the following sections.

MAINTAINING SHARED STATE INSIDE CENTRALIZED REPOSITORIES

Centralized repositories allow the net-VE developer to ensure that all hosts display identical views of the VE by making sure that all hosts see the same values for the shared state values at all times. As shown in Figure 5-3, the centralized repository contains the current value of all of the shared state used in the net-VE. It is protected by locks to guarantee that writes to the repository are made in a particular order and that all hosts see those updates in the same order. Whenever a host needs to access a piece of shared state, it reads the value from the repository. To increase the speed of reading shared data, each host may cache and reuse previously read values; however, when the state is updated in the repository, the writer is responsible for ensuring that the caches are invalidated at all of the other hosts.

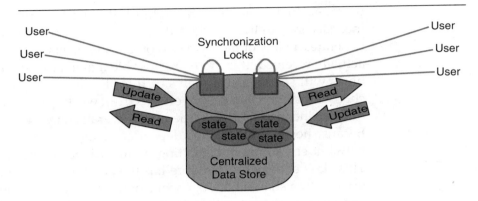

FIGURE 5-3   A centralized data store holds the net-VE shared state information and ensures that all users simultaneously see consistent information.

A File Repository

The simplest implementation of a centralized repository is a directory containing files that hold the shared state. For example, we can create a file for each user in the net-VE. By placing these files in a shared file system such as NFS [Callaghan/Pawlowski/Staubach95] or AFS [Campbell98], we can allow multiple hosts to access the shared state. Whenever a host needs to access some shared state, it simply locates the file(s) containing that information and reads the file data. With such a file repository in place, each host uses the following algorithm whenever it needs to generate a graphical view of the VE for the local user:

```
for all files in the directory
    open the file in read-only mode
    read the user position, orientation, and other state from the file
    close the file
draw the scene from the local user's point of view using the
                            state collected from the files
```

The host may even need to read the file containing information about the local user because that user might be remotely controlled by another host. For example, if the local user can be carried piggyback by another user, then the local host may not be able to retrieve that user's up-to-date position from the local memory. Of course, if users can only be controlled at their local hosts, then you can always skip your own file in the repository directory.

When a host needs to update the location of a user in the VE, it must simply update the file containing that state in the repository directory. For example, when a user moves, the local host follows the following steps:

```
open the file corresponding to the user in write-only mode
write the new position, orientation, and other state to the file
close the file
```

Naturally, our repository directory can contain files representing more than just user information. For example, suppose that the net-VE contains a ball that anyone can see or move. We can create a file ball in the repository directory that contains the ball's current location. When a user wishes to move the ball, the host simply updates the ball file. Clearly, we could also have files describing the current weather in the VE, the game's current leader, or any other dynamic information that we want all participants to be able to access.

Now, what happens when two hosts want to update information about our ball at the same time? Clearly, we cannot have two hosts simultaneously writing into the same file, because the resulting data is likely to contain partial information from each of the two writers. Fortunately for us, most shared file systems take care of serializing write-access to shared files. NFS and AFS both maintain lock information for each file, and only one writer may hold that lock at a time. Our simple data repository therefore works because no host caches any (possibly out-of-date) information in memory. Instead, each host always reads data directly from the repository, thereby ensuring that it accesses the most up-to-date information available, including updates made by other hosts during the intervening period since it last retrieved that information.

Although our centralized file repository is fully functional, it has a few problems. First, performance is slow. Opening a remote file is a slow procedure, so hosts face a considerable delay in gathering information from the repository before rendering each graphics frame. Similarly, a user's speed of motion is limited because the local host must continually open, update, and close a remote file. Second, the system does not easily support many users. For each user, we have to add a file to the repository directory. As we add more files, the file system takes longer to open each one, and it takes longer to cycle through all of the files and retrieve all of the available information needed to generate each frame. We can do better.

A Repository in Server Memory

Instead of storing all of the VE's shared state in files, we can write a server process that simulates the behavior of a distributed file system. A net-VE client can query the server for the value of any of the shared state, and the client may also initiate a write to any of the shared state. Each host participating in the net-VE maintains a TCP/IP connection to the server process and uses that connection to perform read and write operations on the shared state.

Access to shared state through a server process is noticeably faster than access in the shared file system implementation for several reasons.

1. The server can keep the current shared state in memory, rather than having to access disk whenever a read request arrives.

2. The client no longer has to perform explicit open and close operations on each file or unit of shared state; in the shared file system implementation, each data access costs two extra network round-trips to open and close the file.

3. Because the server process can arbitrate among incoming requests, clients do not explicitly need to request locks when writing data. The server can choose to queue consecutive writes or even to discard writes that will be immediately supplanted by other pending writes.

4. The server may support batched operations, allowing the client to initiate multiple reads or writes in a single request, thereby further reducing the number of network roundtrips and potentially supporting atomic transactions on the central data store.

On the other hand, the server does introduce some new problems.

1. If the server crashes, we will lose the current VE state, unless it is written to disk on every update.

2. Maintaining a persistent TCP/IP connection to each client consumes considerable operating system resources at the server host. In fact, the operating system may even limit the number of TCP/IP

sockets that may be open simultaneously, effectively limiting the number of clients that may participate in the net-VE.

It should be clear, however, that these penalties are far outweighed by the performance benefits provided by a server-based repository. Indeed, the simplicity of a server repository, together with the reasonable performance that it provides, has led to its popularity for supporting small to medium-sized net-VEs.

The Networked VR project [Nakamura+94] from NEC Research Laboratories provides a real-world example of such a server-based repository. The server (referred to as a "dialogue manager") permits clients to query for the current state of entities in the VE. The NEC system carries this architecture one step further, however, as shown in Figure 5-4. For each client, the server maintains a separate FIFO queue of events that the client can retrieve at its own pace. For example, this FIFO queue might contain messages notifying the client about new users who have entered the VE or existing users who have departed the VE. The FIFO might also be used to deliver incremental updates to the shared state (for example, the geometry of a user's avatar) when transmitting the entire state is too expensive and the timing of the changes is not important to remote users.

Although the VE state is stored in a single location, the requirement of absolute consistency at all clients is relaxed somewhat when "even-

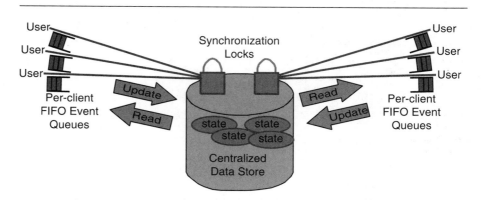

FIGURE 5-4   The NEC Networked VR project adds per-client FIFO queues to support "eventual consistency" state update delivery. Similar queues are used by Shastra to enable client-side state caching.

tual" consistency is sufficient. Although every client does not necessarily have identical information about who is currently inside the VE, this information is not particularly time-sensitive; the system works because all hosts will eventually have received the correct information as they read from their respective FIFO queues.

The centralized repositories that we have seen so far allow clients to "pull" information whenever they need it. The problem with this approach is that the client must make a request to the central state repository whenever it needs to access data. These requests can cause unnecessary delays because they are performed even if the state data has not changed since it was last retrieved. We can solve this problem by having each client maintain a local cache of the current net-VE state so that it can access that information immediately (that is, from the local cache) upon demand. In this case, the server must "push" information to the clients whenever the data is updated. The push updates keep the client-side caches consistent with the true VE state stored in the central repository.

The Shastra system [Anupam/Bajaj94], developed at Purdue University, uses a central server (called a "session manager") of this type to support collaborative design applications. Whenever a client updates data, the server pushes the update out to each client over a reliable, ordered TCP/IP stream. Because any user may modify the state of any design entity, the session manager prevents multiple clients from simultaneously modifying the same data. Instead, clients must explicitly request and obtain a lock on the particular entity before updating it. A client may hold that lock to make a series of exclusive updates to the associated entity. The session manager uses a round-robin token-passing scheme to ensure that all clients get an equal opportunity to make shared state updates. Otherwise, a fast client would be able to initiate more requests on the server and therefore block out other clients.

Virtual Repositories

In both the file system and the server process approaches, we guaranteed absolute consistency by keeping the net-VE state in a single location (that is, on a single disk or in a single application process). By caching data at each client, the Shastra system moved one step closer toward reducing the bottleneck of accessing a centralized data store. However, although each client did not continually access the central repository, it was still needed to provide a universal ordering of state updates and to ensure that the updates were disseminated to all interested clients.

We can eliminate the centralized repository altogether by placing this burden on a distributed consistency protocol. Using such a protocol, the participating hosts can exchange messages directly with each other to disseminate state updates, ensure that all hosts receive those updates, and determine a common global ordering for those updates. This consistency protocol might be implemented as a library that is linked into the net-VE application.

As shown in Figure 5-5, we can think of this protocol-based consistency mechanism as providing a "virtual" centralized repository. Although the state information is not physically managed at any one central host, every participating host has an identical sense of what shared state that central repository would contain, were it to exist. Indeed, though all state information is accessed from local caches, these caches behave as if they were shadowing a central repository.

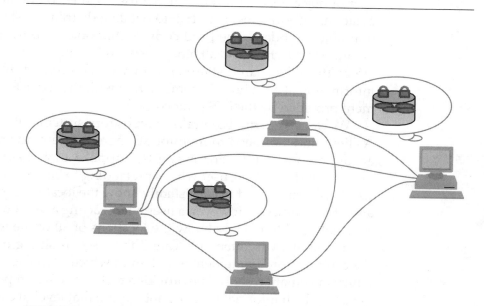

FIGURE 5-5 A consistency protocol can establish a "virtual" central state repository by ensuring reliable message delivery, effective message dissemination, and global message ordering.

Making the central repository virtual offers a number of advantages to the net-VE implementation. First, distribution eliminates the performance bottleneck introduced by accessing the single-host central repository. For example, if the server became loaded, then the entire net-VE would suffer, even if all of the clients had excess computing capacity. Second, distribution eliminates the bandwidth bottleneck at the central repository host. Because all state updates must flow to and from the central repository, its network link is most likely to become saturated. Finally, distribution permits better fault tolerance. With single-host centralized repositories, failure of the repository host would cause the net-VE to become inoperable until the machine recovered. With virtual repositories, the system can recover from single (or even multiple) host failures.

Early versions of the DIVE virtual reality system [Carlsson/Hagsand93], for example, used a distributed data management model by relying on the ISIS communications library [Birman/Marzullo92] developed at Cornell University to provide reliable, in-order delivery of network data. DIVE allows a user to see, move, and interact with any user or object inside the VE. When a user wishes to update an object's position, his local host uses ISIS to obtain a distributed shared lock on that object, updates the local copy of that object's position, reliably broadcasts the change to all other hosts, and finally releases the lock. In effect, the VE's shared state repository is represented by the cached information at each host, in combination with the consistency management provided by the ISIS protocol suite.

We can take virtual centralized repository systems one step further. A client may not need to monitor all shared state in the net-VE with absolute consistency. For example, suppose that the VE contains humans and insects. A user who is pretending to be an insect in the VE would probably need to consistently know the location of other insects and of the humans. However, a user who is acting as a human in the VE may not need to reliably know the locations of all of the insects. After all, in real life, you often only care if the insect is sitting on your arm! We can therefore implement a system in which each client can decide which information should be provided to it in a shared repository fashion and which information does not require that level of consistency.

In the BrickNet toolkit [Singh+94], for example, data subscribers inform a central server of their consistency requirements for each piece of information. That consistency can range from reliable, in-order (central repository) consistency to unreliable, possibly unordered delivery of updates. Hosts transmit information to the central server but do not wait until that information has been transferred to the other users. Instead, the server ensures that the data is forwarded to receivers according to their particular consistency requirements.

Advantages and Drawbacks to Centralized Repositories

Table 5-2 summarizes the broad range of centralized repository approaches for net-VE systems. Centralized repositories may be implemented by placing the store at a common server host or by creating a virtual store using a communication protocol to ensure consistency. These systems offer a variety of performance characteristics for information update and access. Finally, these systems offer a variety of failure characteristics, including systems with a single point of failure whose loss destroys all dynamic information about the net-VE, systems

TABLE 5-2   Evolution of Central Repository Approaches for Shared State Management

Technique	Examples	Characteristics
File system—pull	NFS, AFS	Simplest to program Highest consistency Slow data updates and access Automatic persistence
Central server—pull	Networked VR (NEC)	Faster data updates and access "Eventual" consistency No persistence in FIFO queues
Central server—push	Shastra	Immediate data access Slower updates
Virtual central repository	DIVE with ISIS	Better fault tolerance (no server to crash) Immediate data access Greater protocol overhead
Client consistency selection	BrickNet	Greater complexity Better management of bandwidth resources Potential data inconsistencies

that maintain persistent state so that the net-VE can resume when that central host recovers, and systems that can continue despite any single host crash.

However, despite their variation, centralized repository systems do share several common characteristics. First, they provide us with an easy programming model. The net-VE developer can access information at any time, ignoring the existence of the network. The actual location of the state information, whether it is in a local cache or at a remote server, can be hidden from the rest of the net-VE application, except, of course, for the response time of the function call.

Second, centralized repositories generally guarantee information consistency, meaning that all net-VE clients access identical information. This consistency further aids the simplicity of net-VE development because the designer does not need to worry about how to mask short-term inaccuracies in the information presented to the user.

Third, centralized repository systems do not impose any notion of data "ownership." In other words, any host is able to update any piece of shared state by simply writing to the repository. This flexibility is valuable in interactive net-VEs in which the user's primary goal is to manipulate shared entities in the world, as was the case with the Shastra system for collaborative design. Of course, if the user updates are not coordinated (through human conversation, for instance), the net-VE must contend with the potential for update conflicts. Typically, therefore, for consistency, security, and performance reasons, some basic locking and access control is usually provided through the centralized repository.

Fourth, data access and update operations require an unpredictable amount of time to complete. For example, data access may return almost immediately (by reading from the local cache) or incur a network roundtrip to access the data from the centralized repository located on another host. The updating host must wait for the update to be propagated to the centralized repository before proceeding with its processing. In some systems, this repository update involves multiple network roundtrip messages, either to update every host or to obtain and release a shared lock on the state being updated. In all of these cases, the system depends on the network's response time, which may be highly variable, particularly on the Internet. This variable response time can cause clients to see a nonsteady frame rate.

Finally, these systems require considerable communications overhead. Reliable data delivery requires acknowledgments and possible data retransmission. Communication protocols that support virtual repositories must exchange control messages to agree on a common ordering for updates. In "push" systems, updates are disseminated to all hosts, regardless of whether those hosts actually need that update.

All of these characteristics have several implications for net-VEs based on centralized repository infrastructures. Their ease-of-use and tight semantics make them the most popular approach for maintaining shared state. At the same time, the slow speed and high communications overhead mean that they can only support a limited number of simultaneous users—on the order of 50 or 100. Additional users either overload the server or the communications network. Finally, the aggressive communications among hosts to maintain absolute consistency means that each client's performance is closely linked to the performance of the other hosts. For example, if one host has a slow processor, then it might take longer to acknowledge "push"-style data updates from the net-VE server. This delay means that the information generator must wait longer before proceeding with its own processing.

REDUCING COUPLING THROUGH FREQUENT STATE REGENERATION

Many net-VEs cannot afford the communications and processor overhead required to support absolute consistency through a centralized repository. Furthermore, many net-VEs do not require that level of consistency. For example, in a flight simulator, I might not notice a slight inaccuracy in your airplane's position on my display, as long as the error is limited and temporary. In fact, in this application, a user would probably value smooth motion more than absolute accuracy.

In such situations that do not require absolute consistency, the net-VE developer can replace the distributed consistency protocol with a more aggressive state update notification system. In such a system, the sending host makes no assumptions about what state information is cached or available to other hosts. Instead, each host uses *frequent state regeneration* to maintain the shared state at other hosts. Each transmitted update contains a full description of the entity's state, whether or not it has changed, so that receivers can frequently capture the entire state of the entity. The "owner" of each piece of state information transmits these current state values using *blind broadcasts* that are sent asynchronously and unreliably at some regular interval to everyone participating in the net-VE. For example, in our flight simulator application, my host would regularly broadcast the current position and orientation of my airplane to the other players, possibly ten times per second.

```
/* Repeat at some fixed frequency per second */
for my local airplane and all objects owned by my host
    broadcast the current location, orientation,
                            and other state of the object
```

Receivers do not transmit acknowledgment packets, no assurance is made that each broadcast is received by the destination hosts, and no protocol is used to achieve a global ordering of updates.

Each client simply maintains a cache of the most recent update received for each piece of shared state. Because each transmission describes the complete state information about the net-VE entity, it is sufficient to replace all information being kept in receivers' caches. To render the scene, each client simply queries its local cache.

```
for all entities in the scene
    read the local state information cache for that entity
draw the scene from the local user's point of view using the
                            state collected from the cache
```

Although an update might not be received (or may arrive only after some significant delay), the net-VE designer assumes that a high transmission frequency will make such inconsistencies relatively unnoticeable to the users. For example, if the source is transmitting data 25 times per second, then a lost packet will only affect the receiver's display for about 40 ms, which should be almost imperceptible to humans [Arthur+93, Escobar+94]. In fact, even with a moderate level of packet loss in the network, blind broadcast systems can typically deliver more updates per second than shared database systems because each update incurs lower overhead.

Explicit Entity Ownership

As we have seen, blind broadcasting sacrifices absolute consistency, and it also reduces some of the flexibility that centralized repositories offer to net-VE designers. In most of the centralized repository systems that we have seen, any host could modify information about any entity in the VE. The centralized repository guaranteed that everyone saw the updates reliably and in the same order. However, with frequent state regeneration systems, we must ensure that multiple hosts do not attempt to update an entity at the same time, because we cannot guarantee how those updates will be received and processed at each host.

For example, suppose that two users, Joe and Mary, both try to move a ball at the same time. Each host would transmit an update for the ball's position. Now, some hosts might receive Joe's update before Mary's update, and others might receive Mary's before Joe's. Consequently, some hosts will display the ball in the position set by Mary, while others will display the ball in the position set by Joe. Unless Joe and Mary agree on who actually picked up the ball, each will continue to update the ball's position independently, and remote users will see the ball oscillate between Joe's position and Mary's position, depending on whose update is the most recently received.

To solve this potential conflict, we must ensure that each piece of shared state can only be updated by one host at a time. To do this, we assign *ownership* of each piece of state to exactly one host. The host that owns state information takes responsibility for periodically broadcasting the value of that state. A host cannot broadcast updates to a state's value unless it owns that state.

State ownership is similar to the locks in our shared file repository implementation. However, while the shared repository lock enabled the host to make one update to the state, shared state ownership allows a host to update the state value any number of times, until ownership is transferred to another host.

Typically, each user's own character representation, or *avatar*, is owned by that user, while locks on other entities are managed using a *lock manager* server at a designated host in the net-VE system. Clients query the server to obtain ownership for a shared entity and contact the server to release ownership. The server ensures that each entity has only one owner at a time, and if no client owns an entity, then the server assumes the ownership. The lock manager might also provide facilities for recovering locks owned by failed hosts by imposing an automatic timeout, or "lease" [Gray/Cheriton89], on the lock. The lock manager may also enforce fair ownership of an entity lock among the different hosts.

Returning to our example, before updating the position of the ball, Joe and Mary both issue ownership requests to the lock manager server, as shown in Figure 5-6. Based on a lock arbitration policy (for

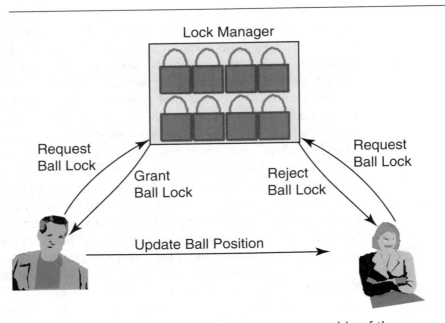

FIGURE 5-6   A lock manager server arbitrates ownership of the state of nonuser entities in the net-VE.

example, FIFO, round-robin, user priorities, and so on), the lock manager grants the lock to one of the users (in this case, Joe). Joe is then free to update the ball's position until he either relinquishes the lock through a message to the lock manager or until he is notified by the lock manager that the lock has been revoked.

Now, suppose that Mary wishes to move the ball, which is currently owned by Joe. Mary has two options: (1) proxy update or (2) ownership transfer. In the *proxy update* approach, which is illustrated in Figure 5-7(a), Mary sends Joe a private message containing the desired new location for the ball. Upon receiving the update request, Joe decides whether to accept the update, and if he does, he begins to broadcast the new location value (as provided by Mary). In this way, Joe serves as a proxy for handling all changes to the ball state, even though the updates may originate at any host. The proxy update approach incurs an extra message cost on each nonowner update. It is

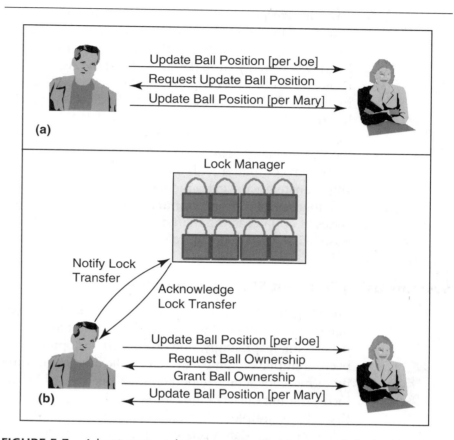

FIGURE 5-7 A host may update an entity that is currently locked by another host by either (a) using the current lock owner as a proxy or (b) requesting a lock transfer.

most suitable when nonowner state updates are rare or when many hosts desire to update the state.

As its name implies, *ownership transfer* refers to the transfer of state ownership from one host to another. An ownership transfer may be performed in many different ways. In one method, shown in Figure 5-7(b), Mary sends Joe a private message requesting ownership of the ball's location. If granted, then Joe notifies the lock manager of the change, and then responds to Mary with a message confirming the transfer. Mary now takes responsibility for periodically broadcasting the ball's location and is free to update that state. In alternative lock transfer schemes, such as those used by current implementations of the Defense Department High Level Architecture [DMSO98] and the Aggregate Level Simulation Protocol (ALSP) [Feineman+95], Mary would issue her lock transfer request to the lock manager, which adjudicates the lock transfer. Regardless of the lock transfer scheme, it is important to note that the lock manager owns the lock information at all times. In the case of host failures, the lock manager defines the current lock ownership state.

When compared with the ownership proxy approach, lock ownership transfer incurs extra message overhead to transfer lock ownership. It is therefore most appropriate when a single host is going to make a series of updates to the shared state and there is little contention among hosts wishing to make updates.

Systems Using Frequent State Regeneration

The frequent state regeneration approach has been used in a number of net-VEs that demand real-time interaction among a small number of users. Not surprisingly, one of the early adopters of the approach has been multiplayer games. In that application environment, the popularity of frequent state regeneration has been aided by the relative ease of incorporating the technique into existing single-user game implementations. For example, it is relatively easy to add a single network send() call after every state update and to add a simple thread that reads updates from the network and incorporates them into the local state cache. For developers seeking a quick way to enable their VEs to support multiple users, state regeneration has proven to be the perfect solution.

The flight simulator *Dogfight*, shipped with Silicon Graphics workstations, represents one of the most long-standing uses of the technique in a net-VE game. In this multiplayer net-VE, each player attempts to shoot down opponents' planes. On each frame, each host simply broadcasts the complete data structure describing the local player (player name, plane type, position, orientation, speed, state of landing gear, and so on). Remote hosts collect these data structures into a local cache and use them to render the scene for the local user. If one of the data structures is not updated within a particular timeout period, then the associated player is assumed to be dead, their data structure is deleted from the local cache, and the user is no longer drawn on the display. Remote hosts recognize new players when an update arrives for a previously unseen player name.

In a similar fashion, the basic state regeneration technique has become the foundation for a new generation of PC-based multiplayer games such as *Doom*, *Diablo*, and *Interstate 76*. A demonstration at the 1993 IMAGINA conference supported two players, located 200 miles apart, manipulating a world containing 100 shared entities at 10 updates per second [Quéau93].

State regeneration has been used to support more critical net-VE applications. For example, in a prototype Japanese system to support intravascular telesurgery [Arai+96], the dynamic shared state consists of the position of the surgical catheter device and an appropriate camera position for the doctor. The patient site blindly broadcasts this information over a dedicated 155 Mbps ATM link. At the doctor's site, the view is reconstructed using the dynamic shared state read from the local cache and static information about the location of the patient. In this case, frame-rate updates were appropriate, given the availability of a dedicated high-bandwidth link and the need for high data consistency within a medical application.

Blind broadcasts have been used to support net-VEs that create the illusion of video conferencing. However, instead of transmitting 15 Hz to 30 Hz camera frames, which require considerable network bandwidth, a system developed by ATR Communication Systems Research Laboratories in Japan tries to generate realistic images of the teleconference using shared state from a net-VE [Nagashima+91, Xu+90]. In this case, the shared state information is the dynamic position of each participant's head and the dynamic structure of each participant's facial features (eyes, mouth, wrinkles, and so forth). This "virtual space" teleconferencing system is designed to operate over low-bandwidth lines.

Before the conference starts, multiple photographs of each speaker are taken, and those images are processed to construct a prototype wiremesh model of that person's face. These prototypes are exchanged. During the teleconference, real-time images of the speaker are processed to determine the current physical location of facial features such as the tip of the chin, corner of the eyes, nose position, and so forth.[1] This location

---

[1]In more recent versions of the system [Ohya+93], each speaker wears pieces of blue tape to highlight these facial features. The tape significantly reduces the image processing requirements at the local host, thereby enabling a faster broadcast rate.

information is blindly broadcast over the network. Remote hosts use this location information to anchor corresponding points on the wire-frame model before applying a texture map and displaying the image. Each speaker's state typically consists of 11 facial points, 4 body points, and 10 points on a hand-held dataglove. Using a 1,000-node wire-frame facial model, the teleconference renders 10 frames per second.

Reducing the Broadcast Scope

Under a frequent state regeneration system, each host sends updates to all participants in the net-VE. However, broadcasting typically causes hosts to receive lots of extraneous information. For example, suppose that Joe is inside a building in the net-VE. While blindly broadcasting his position, Joe sends frequent position updates to Mary, even if she is outside the building and, therefore, cannot see Joe at all. Delivery of this extra information requires extra network bandwidth, and Mary consumes CPU cycles to receive and parse the update packets sent by Joe. Therefore, it would be more efficient to avoid sending unnecessary updates.

There are many ways to eliminate these extra updates, and here we will sample those that have been used in conjunction with state regeneration. Details about more sophisticated multicast and area of interest techniques can be found in Chapter 7.

One basic approach to eliminating extra traffic is to filter the updates before they get sent to inappropriate recipients. For example, we want to block Joe's broadcast message before it gets sent to Mary's host. To do this, we must address the question of where this filtering can be done. Clearly, if each player is responsible for filtering their own data, then each player must somehow gather enough information to determine who does not need to receive these broadcast updates.

The RING system [Funkhouser95], developed at Bell Labs, handles this filtering by sending all updates to a central server. The server tracks the current location of each entity, and it can determine which users would not be interested in a particular update. The server forwards updates only to users who can "see" the entity.

To reduce the broadcast message overhead, the VEOS System [Bricken/Coco94] from the University of Washington uses a so-called epidemic approach for distributing frame-rate updates. VEOS hosts are organized hierarchically. At the end of each iteration of a host's event loop, a communications daemon sends updated state information to the neighbors in the host hierarchy. Each recipient places the state information into an outbound queue, which is processed during its next event-loop cycle. The host hierarchy and event queues enable the updates to propagate hop-by-hop among all of the participating hosts in the net-VE. If a host receives an update for an entity whose previous update has not yet been propagated, it discards the old update. As a result, each host only propagates the most recent update available.

Advantages and Drawbacks of Frequent State Regeneration

As we have seen, state regeneration is popular among developers trying to add multiuser capabilities to existing single-user applications. The technique requires almost no code changes, and it can be implemented easily by developers not concerned with optimizing network performance. Furthermore, blind broadcasting does not require the deployment of a server, consistency protocol, or (in most cases) a lock manager.

By relaxing some of the tight state consistency requirements supported by centralized repository systems, net-VE designers can deploy environments supporting larger numbers of users. For example, because state regeneration messages are transmitted asynchronously without regard to how or where those updates are delivered, each host can continue with its local processing without being affected by network latency or remote host performance. Without having to wait for lock acquisition, release, or update acknowledgments, the sender typically can exhibit better interactive behavior with the user as well as a higher frame rate.

However, frequent broadcasts are not perfect, by any means. The most obvious limitation is the considerable network bandwidth utilization, particularly in net-VE systems with many hosts. Most users on the Internet today are connected by low-bandwidth dialup modems providing a maximum of 56 Kbps. As we saw in Chapter 4, with DIS packets, such a line can only sustain 48 packets per second without compression. At 10 updates per second per user, such a net-VE can only support four or five users.

A second problem with frequent broadcasting is network latency. By the time an update arrives at a particular receiver, it may be several hundred milliseconds old, and the source may have already placed a new update in transit. Latencies of 250 ms are not uncommon over wide area networks. Users who must rely on that information to make decisions are frequently annoyed when their decisions turn out to be based on incorrect data. Many game players have complained about the lag in the network, as they try to shoot at opponents who never seem to be where they appear. This latency becomes more critical when dealing with medical applications and immersive environments that might cause simulator sickness.

Closely related to the issue of network latency is the issue of network jitter. *Jitter* refers to the variation in network latency from one packet to the next. Because of network jitter, updates typically are not received at a steady rate, even if they were transmitted at fixed intervals. Because arriving state information is simply copied into the local state cache when it arrives, users will perceive that entities are not getting updated smoothly. Remote entities appear jerky on the display.

Finally, even if network jitter were eliminated, frequent state regeneration still assumes that all hosts are broadcasting at the same rate, equal to their display frame rates. Each host should update the state of local and remote entities at the same rate, in order to reduce the perception that some entities are physically located over the network. After all, one of the goals of net-VEs is to present the illusion of a single-host environment. However, in reality, different hosts do not run at the same frame rates. They might have different display hardware or CPUs, or they might simply do different amounts of local computation. As a result of these variations, we cannot guarantee that remote updates will be sent at the speed desired by local display. The user will undoubtedly notice those differences, and consequently, the net-VE cannot fully mask the distinction between local and remote entities.

In summary, when the net-VE does not require the absolute consistency provided by centralized repository systems, frequent state regeneration can support more users because network bandwidth and delay no longer lie in the critical path of the application's event loop. This effectively gives more autonomy to the sending hosts. However, the basic constraints of network bandwidth and latency are still visible to the end-user, who can notice the difference between an entity owned at the local host and entities owned at remote hosts. To relax these constraints, we also need to provide additional autonomy to the data receivers.

DEAD RECKONING OF SHARED STATE

In the techniques considered so far, hosts simply display information that they have received over the network, either synchronously by querying the centralized database or asynchronously from the state regeneration broadcasts. The idea behind our third shared state maintenance technique is to transmit state update packets less frequently and instead use information contained in those updates to *approximate* the true shared state. In between updates, each host predicts the position, velocity, acceleration, and other state of the entities based on locally cached information. Unlike the two previous techniques, each host is expected to construct an up-to-date approximation of the VE based on whatever information it has locally available.

For example, suppose that we are generating frames 30 times per second but only receive update packets 1 time per second. As shown in Figure 5-8, we learn that a ball is located at position (4,5) at time 3 and is traveling with velocity (3,2). At time 3.5, we can estimate that the ball is located at (5.5,6). Of course, the ball might not actually be at (5.5,6) at time 3.5 (for example, perhaps it accelerated in a different direction), but until we receive more accurate information about the ball's true location, we use the estimated position information.

These state prediction techniques are known as *dead reckoning protocols*. They represent the other extreme of the design space defined by the Consistency-Throughput Tradeoff. By using prediction, dead

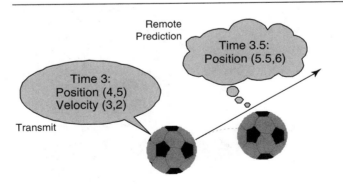

FIGURE 5-8 Prediction can be used to estimate the current state of a remote object.

reckoning protocols sacrifice accuracy of the shared state, but they allow us to reduce message traffic and therefore support net-VEs with more participants.

Prediction and Convergence

A dead reckoning protocol consists of two elements: a prediction technique and a convergence technique. *Prediction* is the way the entity's current state is computed based on previously received update packets. For example, in the example above, the prediction algorithm estimated that the ball was at position (5.5,6) at time 3.5 and at position (7,7) at time 4 (see Figure 5-9).

However, as we observed, the prediction is just an estimate of the ball's true location. Suppose, for example, that we receive a new update at time 4 showing that the ball is actually located at (6,2) and traveling with velocity (3,1). The current displayed position of (7,7) is therefore

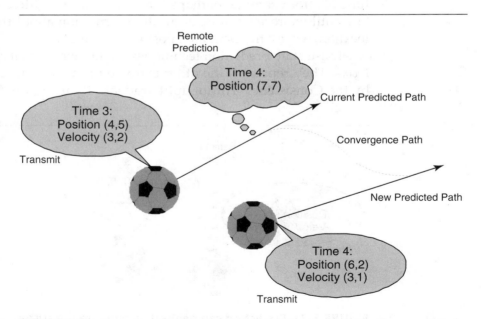

FIGURE 5-9   Convergence is used to correct inaccuracies in the predicted (and displayed) position and smoothly move the object toward its new predicted path.

incorrect; furthermore, our predictions for the ball's future position will change in light of the new velocity information. We must therefore move the ball from its previously computed location and predicted trajectory to its revised location and predicted trajectory.

The *convergence* technique defines how we correct the ball's position and trajectory. For example, we can move the ball to location (8,9) and subsequently follow the newly predicted path. However, "jumping" to the new location presents the user with an unnatural animation of remote entities. Instead, we can attempt to gradually correct the ball's displayed position over the next several frames until it matches our updated predicted trajectory.

Prediction Using Derivative Polynomials

The most common dead reckoning protocols use *derivative polynomials* to predict an entity's future position. A derivative polynomial is formed by constructing a formula involving various derivatives of the entity's current position. Recall from physics that the first derivative of position is velocity, the second derivative is acceleration, and the third derivative is jerk. We can use these values to estimate the object's position.

The simplest derivative polynomial is a zero-order polynomial, which uses the object's instantaneous position but does not use any derivative information. The position prediction is as follows:

```
predicted position after t seconds = position
```

The zero-order polynomial reduces to nothing more than the state regeneration technique, where the state is simply copied from the update packet into the host's local state cache. As we see, state regeneration therefore is actually a degenerate form of dead reckoning.

The first nondegenerate derivative polynomial has order one, meaning that it takes advantage of the first derivative of position, namely velocity. Because velocity gives us some indication of the object's behavior over time, first-order prediction gives us a significant improvement over the zero-order case—that is, state regeneration. The simple distance formula gives us this position prediction:

```
predicted position after t seconds = position + velocity x t
```

The state update packet must provide the object's current position and instantaneous velocity. It is the polynomial that we used previously in our ball example.

Early systems, such as the *Amaze* multiplayer game [Berglund/Cheriton85] developed at Stanford University, used first-order polynomial prediction. In this LAN-based shoot-'em-up game, players broadcast their position and velocity roughly once per second. In *Amaze*, remote hosts ignored the effects of network latency. For example, suppose that a packet is transmitted at time 3. When a remote host receives the update, it treats the position in the packet as the object's current position, even though the information is slightly out-of-date because of network transmission delay. This simplification is barely noticeable to users because the LAN environment has minimal latency. For the same reasons, the *Amaze* system did not use a convergence algorithm, opting instead to "jump" each displayed user to the new position.

We can usually obtain better position prediction by incorporating more derivatives into the update packet. Second-order polynomials include the object's acceleration:

```
predicted position after t seconds = position + velocity
                         x t + 1/2 x acceleration x t2
```

Naturally, the state update packet must provide the object's position, velocity, and acceleration. Second-order polynomial prediction is the most popular prediction technique in net-VEs today. It is easy to understand and program, is fast to compute, and provides relatively good predictions of entity position. For example, second-order prediction is the cornerstone for the DIS protocol, IEEE standard 1278, which is in widespread use in military net-VEs [IEEE95].

Hybrid Polynomial Prediction

The choice of derivative polynomial order need not be an absolute one. For example, whenever we receive an update packet, the remote host can dynamically choose between a first-order and a second-order prediction polynomial. Why might it want to do this? The first-order polynomial requires fewer computational operations, so it enables better overall performance when the entity is undergoing only a minimal acceleration. Furthermore, there are many situations in which the object's position can be more accurately predicted by ignoring the acceleration information. For example, when the object's acceleration changes frequently, we are better off ignoring the acceleration estimate than taking the chance of producing a prediction that will be inaccurate because of an acceleration change that occurs before we receive the next update packet.

The Position History-Based Dead Reckoning (PHBDR) protocol developed by Singhal and Cheriton for the Stanford PARADISE net-VE system, represents an example of a hybrid approach that dynamically chooses between first-order and second-order derivative polynomials [Singhal/Cheriton95]. Whenever a packet arrives, the protocol evaluates the object's motion over the three most recent position updates. If there has been minimal acceleration or if the acceleration has been substantial, then the protocol selects a first-order derivative polynomial. Threshold cutoff values must be provided for each entity and are used to define the bounds of both minimal and substantial acceleration. The acceleration behavior is also used to select an appropriate convergence algorithm.

The PHBDR protocol takes the nontraditional approach of entirely ignoring instantaneous derivative information. Update packets only contain the object's most recent position. Remote hosts estimate the instantaneous velocity and acceleration by averaging the position samples provided by the most recent update packets received. This approach has the advantage of eliminating up to two-thirds of the required network bandwidth by avoiding the transmission of derivative data. Moreover, it has the counterintuitive effect of *improving* prediction accuracy in many cases. As we will see, instantaneous velocity and acceleration samples can be inaccurate or misleading. The use of long-term velocity and acceleration averages allows the PHBDR to produce predictions based on more long-term, stable information.

Limitations of Derivative Polynomials

So far, we have considered derivative polynomials of order zero, one, and two, as well as a hybrid technique. Naturally, we could continue the progression ad infinitum, adding more terms to the derivative polynomial by transmitting higher-order derivatives. Why not do this? After all, so far, more polynomial terms have generally provided us with better prediction accuracy. However, it turns out that more terms rarely improve the quality of the position prediction, as shown in Figure 5-10, and in many cases, more terms make things worse.

As we move toward higher-order polynomials, we must transmit more information within each update packet. Remember that the goal behind using dead reckoning and prediction is to reduce the bandwidth. In other words, for every additional derivative that we transmit,

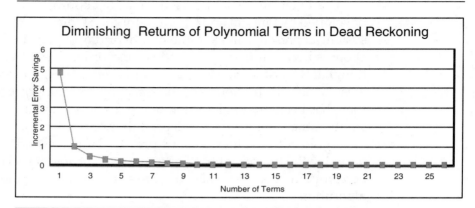

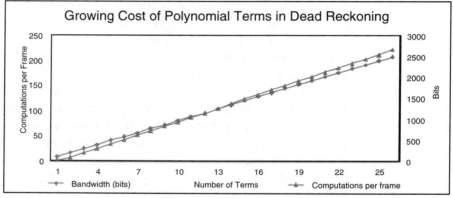

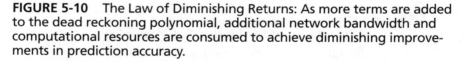

FIGURE 5-10   The Law of Diminishing Returns: As more terms are added to the dead reckoning polynomial, additional network bandwidth and computational resources are consumed to achieve diminishing improvements in prediction accuracy.

we start getting less bang (bandwidth reduction) for the buck (decision to accept state inaccuracy). After a certain point, we are better off using state regeneration.

Furthermore, as we add more terms to the polynomial, the computational complexity of the algorithm increases. We need to update our position prediction for each entity on each frame, and each additional term requires an extra floating point addition and multiplication on each frame (for a total of six extra operations per frame—two for each dimension—for each entity being dead reckoned). This overhead may not seem like much, but it can become important if the number of entities or the frame rate is high.

There is also another, more subtle reason for avoiding higher-order derivatives. If you study the second-order polynomial equation, you will notice that over time, the equation is more sensitive to the acceleration term than it is to the velocity term. In other words, increasing the acceleration by 10% will impact the position more than would increasing the initial velocity by 10%. This trend carries forward with ever higher-order polynomials, where, for example, the jerk affects predicted position more than either velocity or acceleration. In other words, if we are going to rely on high-order derivatives to predict position, we must be certain that the derivative information is accurate, because otherwise, the inaccurate values for the higher derivatives might actually make our prediction considerably worse.

As it turns out, it is harder to get accurate instantaneous information about higher-order derivatives. First, a user typically only controls an object's velocity and acceleration (think about how you drive a car or fly an airplane in real life), so that is how computers typically model those entities. Higher-order derivatives must therefore be estimated or computed from acceleration changes over time. Second, because humans are controlling the acceleration, trying to define the jerk (change in acceleration) amounts to trying to predict a human's behavior. Of course, we have almost no chance of doing a good job of that prediction. Third, the numerical values of higher-order derivatives tend to change more rapidly than the values of lower-order derivatives. They can completely change as a result of air resistance, human muscle tension, collisions, and so forth. Therefore, we conclude that because high-order derivative information is hard to capture and inherently inaccurate, and because inaccurate values of these derivatives can negatively impact the quality of the remote state modeling, high-order derivatives should generally be avoided when designing a net-VE dead reckoning system [Singhal96].

Our exploration of derivative polynomials illustrates the Law of Diminishing Returns—namely, that more effort typically provides progressively less impact on the overall effectiveness of a particular technique. As that happens, it pays to look for some other system bottleneck that we can effectively optimize.[2] We have seen this principle before. After devising virtual centralized repositories to eliminate the server bottleneck, we found that the next fundamental bottleneck was the consistency requirement itself. Similarly, after using multicast to reduce the scope of blind broadcasting of state regeneration updates, we discovered that the next fundamental bottleneck was the dependence of the destination hosts on frequent updates from the source hosts.

Now, instead of adding more derivatives, let us again apply this principle, to understand what other aspect of state prediction we might improve. There are two potential areas. First, the receiver does not have enough information about the actual entity being modeled, so it cannot use derivative information to effectively represent the entity's true behavior. Second, as each host transmits its updates at a fixed rate, it imposes no limit on how inaccurate the state prediction might become between updates at remote hosts. Recent net-VEs have attempted to address these two concerns directly.

Object-Specialized Prediction

One of the problems behind derivative polynomials is that they do not take into account any information about what the entity is currently doing, what the entity is capable of doing, and who is controlling the entity. Recent net-VEs have attempted to incorporate such information into their dead reckoning protocols in an attempt to generate more accurate predictions of entity position. Needless to say, this kind of specialization requires that separate dead reckoning protocols be used for each entity in the net-VE. For many applications, managing a wide variety of dead reckoning protocols is expensive, both in terms of code size and complexity. However, in cases where accurate prediction is vital, specialization is a desirable technique to employ.

For example, Katz and Graham have optimized a dead reckoning protocol to handle aircraft making military flight maneuvers [Katz/Graham94]. In these configurations, the aircraft typically moves in spiral or circular paths (that is, with a constant acceleration vector relative to its body coordinates). Consequently, given information about the air-

---

[2]The Law of Diminishing Returns is also known as Amdahl's Law: System performance is principally determined by the primary bottleneck. Optimizing nonbottleneck components of a system produces steadily decreasing value to overall system performance.

craft's constant acceleration and instant velocity, a remote host can accurately compute the airplane's position trajectory. Moreover, it turns out that in these maneuvers, the plane's orientation angle, or "angle of attack," is determined solely by its forward velocity and acceleration, as shown in Figure 5-11. In other words, physics of flight restrict the angle that the plane may follow. Therefore, the *phugoid scheme* for motion prediction does not require orientation information to be transmitted in update packets. Instead, aircraft orientation is computed from the position information.

Just as the phugoid scheme accounts for how physical laws apply to aircraft in flight, so do similar laws apply to land-based entities. For example, in many net-VEs, we want to ensure that land-based entities always be placed on the ground terrain. The NPSNET system, developed at the Naval Postgraduate School, specializes its dead reckoning algorithm to handle ground-based tanks [Pratt93]. Update packets provide the object's position and velocity to support a first-order derivative polynomial for motion prediction. However, instead of providing this information in three dimensions, update packets only specify two dimensions. An "align-to-ground" flag in the packet causes remote hosts to adjust the object's height and orientation to ensure that it always travels smoothly along the ground.

The MIT Media Lab used another specialized protocol to remotely predict the position of drumsticks as they were played above a sensor pad [Friedman+92]. A computer generated the sound of a drum whenever the sensor pad was touched by a drumstick. Because of the notice-

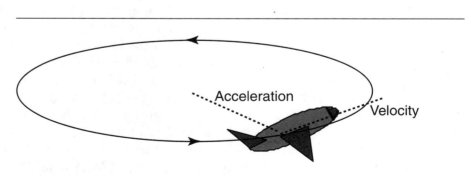

FIGURE 5-11   The phugoid scheme automatically computes an aircraft's orientation from its velocity and acceleration.

able communications latency between the sensor pad and the sound-generating computer, the computer needed to predict the position of the drumsticks. It received the updated drumstick position 30 times per second from the motion sensor attached to the drumsticks and used a derivative polynomial to approximate the drumstick position between those updates. As we have seen, however, derivative-based polynomials do not effectively handle situations where the velocity and acceleration may change suddenly. Not surprisingly, the computer occasionally would mispredict a drum hit because drummers regularly move the sticks downward toward the drum and then change direction before actually hitting the drum's surface. To counter this effect, the dead reckoning protocol included an "emergency" message that caused the computer to disregard its current prediction whenever a sudden change in the drumstick behavior was detected by the motion tracker.

This application shows how the dead reckoning protocol has been carefully tuned to the particular entities being modeled. For example, the emergency message was introduced to deal explicitly with a recognized human pattern for drumstick control. Moreover, to decide when to transmit the emergency message, the source needed to determine what constituted a sudden change in the drumstick behavior. This required a carefully tuned model for human muscle behavior to avoid capturing instantaneous muscle twitches.

One more object-specific state prediction technique is of note. In many situations, remote hosts do not need to model the precise behavior of the entity, as long as the entity's overall behavior is accurately represented. In many net-VE systems, for example, if an entity starts dancing, then remote users may be primarily interested in seeing the dancing behavior rather than seeing the precise footwork being performed by the source. Similarly, if something is on fire, then the precise movement of the flames is less critical to synchronize than the overall presence of the flames themselves. In each of these situations, remote hosts simply need to receive notification (by means of an update packet) of the high-level state change, but these hosts are free to locally simulate the precise behavior represented by that state. These types of scripted events were used in the Improv system [Perlin/Goldberg96]. They are also common in Internet-based multiuser environments based on the proposed Living Worlds API [VRML-LivingWorlds], as will be discussed in Chapter 8.

The idea of state prediction has been around for many years and has been used in applications as diverse as predicting ship movements based on periodic radar sweeps, predicting the location of the user of a head-mounted display (HMD) in light of the latencies between the sensor readings and the image generator, and predicting the appropriate value for an analog sensor based on (possibly inaccurate) previous readings. Each of these applications has led to its own specialized dead reckoning algorithms. However, in-depth discussion of these algorithms is beyond the scope of this book.[3] It is more important to recognize that customization of the state prediction algorithm is possible, and even necessary, based on the particular information being modeled. In other words, pick the *right* tool for the job.

Convergence Algorithms

Recall that a dead reckoning algorithm consists of two parts: prediction and convergence. Prediction allows us to estimate the future value of the shared state based on current or past behavior. Convergence tells us what to do when we receive updated information to correct our inexact prediction. A good convergence algorithm allows us to correct our predicted state quickly but without creating noticeable visual distortion to the user.

The simplest form of convergence is zero-order, or snap, convergence. The idea behind this technique is to immediately correct the prediction without regard to the visual distortion. For example, suppose that at time 4.5, we believe that the current position is (8.5,8). We now receive an update providing information about the state at time 4, and based on this new information, we now predict that the position at time 4.5 should really be (7.5,2.5). Using a snap convergence algorithm, we would simply move the entity to its new location—that is, (7.5,2.5), jumping from the currently displayed location—(8.5,8).

Though snap convergence is simple to understand and implement, it does not provide the best visual display. A better approach involves a slower convergence to the new prediction. For example, with linear

---

[3][Singhal96] details a number of these other application-specific customizations for state prediction.

convergence, we pick a future *convergence point* along the new predicted path. We then display the entity as if it travels in a straight line between its current displayed position and the convergence path. An example of linear convergence is shown in Figure 5-12, which is similar to Figure 5-9 with the addition of network latency. Suppose that the new predicted location at time 5 is (9,3). During the period from 4.5 to 5, the entity would move in a straight line from its current displayed location (8.5,8) to the convergence point (9,3). After reaching the convergence point, the entity would follow the new predicted path until the prediction is updated again. The interval between the current time and the convergence point (from 4.5 to 5 in this example) is known as the *convergence period*.

Linear convergence gives us continuity along the visual path, meaning that the user does not see the entity jump to a new position. However, the motion is not necessarily smooth, because the entity may

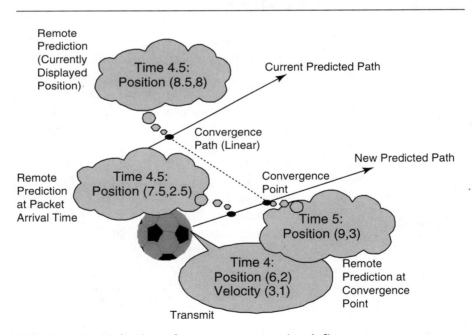

FIGURE 5-12   Selection of a convergence point defines a convergence period between update packet arrival and completion of the convergence process.

appear to make a sudden change in direction as it turns to follow the convergence path and then turns again to follow the new predicted path. By applying more sophisticated curve-fitting techniques, we can do better. For example, as shown in Figure 5-13, we might construct a quadratic curve joining a point 1 second ago along the current predicted path, the current predicted position, and the convergence point. This quadratic ensures that the entity moves more smoothly from the current position to the convergence path. However, this approach still leaves us with a lack of smoothness when the entity transitions from the convergence path to the new predicted path at the convergence point. We can address this problem by using a *cubic spline*.

The idea behind a cubic spline is to build a third-order curve connecting a point 1 second ago along the current predicted path, the current displayed position, the convergence point, and a point 1 second after the convergence point on the new predicted path. By sacrificing the computational complexity of a third-order convergence equation, we achieve a smooth transition into and out of the convergence path. In fact, we can

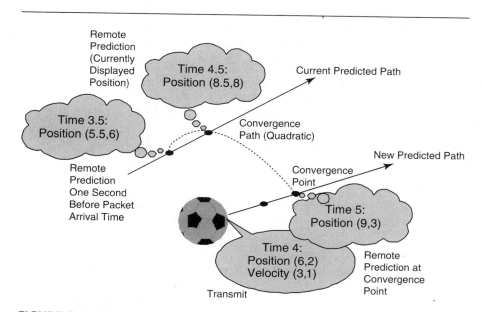

FIGURE 5-13 Quadratic convergence provides a smoother transition path to the new predicted path.

generalize an even smoother spline by adding more points to the spline, including future points along the current prediction path and points prior to the convergence point along the new prediction path.

As with most aspects of net-VE design, the convergence algorithm trades off visual accuracy against computational complexity. Smoother motion requires more computation in the form of a more complex equation for points along the convergence path. Hybrid algorithms such as PHBDR attempt to dynamically manage this tradeoff by selecting between linear and quadratic convergence algorithms, based on what appears to be necessary at the current time. For example, if the prediction error is not significant, PHBDR reverts to linear convergence to minimize computational overhead on the basis that quadratic convergence would not provide a significant visual improvement.

Addressing Consistency-Throughput through Nonregular Transmissions

Up to this point, we have assumed that updates are transmitted at regular intervals for both blind broadcasting and dead reckoning. However, once we introduce known prediction algorithms at remote hosts, we no longer need to be so rigid about when updates are actually transmitted. By taking advantage of knowledge about the computations at remote hosts, a source host can actually reduce the required state update rate.

Let us consider an example. Suppose that you are blindfolded and need to travel across the room. I tell you which direction to go, and you start proceeding. Rather than reorienting you every second, it would seem reasonable for me to correct your direction only when it looks as though you are heading in the wrong direction. In other words, as long as you are moving within some error bound, I will let you continue along your current path without interference.

We can apply the same principle to enable nonregular update packet transmission. The source host can model the prediction algorithm being used by the remote hosts, as shown in Figure 5-14. Instead of transmitting updates at a regular interval, the host only needs to transmit updates when there is a significant divergence (as defined by an error threshold) between the object's actual position and the remote host's predicted position. This update approach has been used by a variety of systems, including the U.S. Army's SIMNET system for tank battles, the DIS standard for net-VEs, NPSNET, and PARADISE.

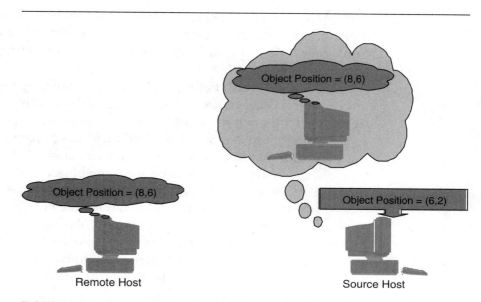

FIGURE 5-14 By modeling the prediction algorithm, the source host can avoid transmitting update packets until the remote prediction error exceeds a threshold.

This nonregular update generation technique offers several advantages to net-VE systems. First, if the prediction algorithm is reasonably accurate, then source host state prediction can potentially significantly reduce update rates. Nonregular updates allow us to avoid transmitting updates when the remote host is maintaining a reasonably accurate view of the object's state. Regular update approaches, on the other hand, must always transmit an update regardless of the remote modeling accuracy. Second, nonregular updates allow us to make guarantees about the overall accuracy of the remote state information. By transmitting an update whenever the remote state exceeds an error bound, we are sure that the remote state never becomes too erroneous. (With regular updates, we cannot make any such accuracy guarantees.) Third, the nonregular updates allow the source host to dynamically balance its network transmission resources based on the current situation in the net-VE. For instance, if bandwidth is limited, the source host might temporarily increase the error threshold on entities that reside within wide open space and simultaneously reduce the error threshold on entities that are located close to remote entities in the net-VE. In summary, nonregular updates provide a way to dynamically adapt the Consistency-Throughput Tradeoff based on the changing consistency demands of the net-VE.

One detail is worth noting about the nonregular update technique. If the prediction algorithm is really good, or if the entity is not moving significantly, the source might never transmit any updates. This is undesirable because new participants will never receive any initial state. It is also undesirable because recipients cannot tell the difference between receiving no updates because the object's behavior has not changed, receiving no updates because the network has failed, or receiving no updates because the entity has left the net-VE.

To address these two concerns, nonregular update systems typically place a timeout on their packet transmissions. In effect, if it has not transmitted an update within a particular timeout period, the source automatically generates one. The timeout periods are typically relatively long, at least 5 seconds. With this timeout, hosts can distinguish network and host failures (indicated by receiving no messages from the entity for some period of time) from normal operations (indicated by receiving at least occasional update packets from the entity). They can therefore take appropriate action to alert the user that certain information might be inaccurate because of these failures.

Advantages and Limitations of Dead Reckoning

Dead reckoning at remote hosts typically reduces bandwidth requirements because update packets can be transmitted at lower-than-framerate frequencies. Because hosts receive updates about remote entities at a slower rate than updates about local entities (whose models are driven by user input, rather than incoming packets), receivers must use prediction and convergence to seamlessly integrate remote and local entities on the display. Each host performs this dead reckoning independently, so it can provide a smooth rendering for the local user based on the periodic update packets.

On the other hand, dead reckoning does introduce several limitations. First, dead reckoning does not guarantee that all hosts share identical state about each entity. Instead, dead reckoning protocols require hosts to tolerate and adapt to potential discrepancies. Second, simulations that rely on dead reckoning protocols are usually more complex to develop, maintain, and evaluate. The application developer must be aware of the network's behavior and typically tailors the simulation software and algorithms to operate within a wide area network environment. For example, because the prediction of entity position and orientation is imperfect, collision detection requires a distributed agreement protocol. To avoid presenting a jerky view of the entity's position on the display, the host must also apply some smoothing or convergence algorithm to correct the extrapolated model after a new update arrives. Third, unlike centralized state repositories and blind broadcasting, dead reckoning algorithms must often be customized based on the behavior of the objects being modeled. It is possible to achieve good performance in most cases with adaptive protocols such as PHBDR, but highly precise remote modeling must rely on customization.

In summary, dead reckoning is most appropriate when bandwidth is limited, computational cycles are available, or the net-VE contains many participants. It is less applicable when precision and consistency are vital net-VE characteristics.

CONCLUSION

This chapter has discussed the issue of maintaining shared state among hosts in a net-VE. As we have seen, shared state is a complex issue, and we have only scratched the surface. Selecting an appropriate shared state maintenance technique is an engineering task that must balance a variety of issues, including bandwidth, computation, latency, data consistency, and reproducibility.

Shared state maintenance is governed by the Consistency-Throughput Tradeoff, which, given a bandwidth constraint, imposes physical limits on how consistent state can be among hosts in the net-VE. Essentially, shared state maintenance is a matter of selecting an appropriate point along the tradeoff spectrum.

We have discussed three broad types of shared state maintenance.

1. *Centralized repository:* Uses a centralized or distributed database to store the net-VE's current state. The repository provides highly consistent state maintenance at the expense of high bandwidth, slow throughput, and tight interdependencies among participating hosts.

2. *Frequent state regeneration:* Transmits updates on a regular basis using blind broadcasting. Sacrifices absolute consistency in favor of eventual consistency while reducing the interdependencies among participating hosts.

3. *Dead reckoning:* Transmits nonregular updates and uses prediction and convergence to manage state at remote hosts. Provides weakly consistent state maintenance (with bounded error) in order to minimize bandwidth and maximize host autonomy.

Although we have discussed shared state in the context of entity position (the most common type of shared state in a net-VE), these principles apply to almost any other type of information maintained in the net-VE. We have now covered the system architecture of a net-VE and the basic elements of communication and shared state maintenance. As discussed, a net-VE host must perform many different tasks, including rendering the graphical display, managing dynamic state information, and sending and receiving network packets. Each of these tasks has different real-time performance requirements and imposes different burdens on the CPU and other host resources. In the next chapter, we will turn our attention to how the different elements of net-VE software can be implemented efficiently into a single system.

REFERENCES

[Anupam/Bajaj94] Anupam, V., and C. Bajaj. Distributed and collaborative visualization. *IEEE Multimedia* 1(2):39–49, Summer 1994.

[Arai+96] Arai, F., M. Tanimoto, T. Futuda, et al. Distributed virtual environment for intravascular tele-surgery using multimedia telecommunication. In *Proceedings of the 1996 Virtual Reality Annual International Symposium (VRAIS)*, 79–85. IEEE Neural Networks Council, Santa Clara, CA, March 1996.

[Arthur+93] Arthur, K., K. Booth, and C. Ware. Evaluating 3D task performance for fish tank virtual worlds. *ACM Transactions on Information Systems* 11(3):239–265, July 1993.

[Berglund/Cheriton85] Berglund, E., and D. Cheriton. Amaze: A multiplayer computer game. *IEEE Software* 2(1):30–39, May 1985.

[Birman/Marzullo92] Birman, K., and K. Marzullo. The ISIS distributed programming toolkit and the META distributed operating system: A brief overview. *Mission Critical Operating Systems*, 32–35, A. Agrawala, K. Gordon, and P. Hwang, eds. Amsterdam: IOS Press, 1992.

[Bricken/Coco94] Bricken, W., and G. Coco. The VEOS project. *PRESENCE: Teleoperators and Virtual Environments* 3(2):111–129, Spring 1994.

[Callaghan+95] Callaghan, B., B. Pawlowski, and P. Staubach. NFS version 3 protocol specification. Request for Comments (RFC) 1813. Information Sciences Institute, Marina del Rey, CA, June 1995.

[Campbell98] Campbell, R. *Managing AFS: The Andrew File System*. Upper Saddle River, NJ: Prentice-Hall, 1998.

[Carlsson/Hagsand93] Carlsson, C., and O. Hagsand. DIVE—A platform for multi-user virtual environments. *Computers & Graphics* 17(6):663–669, November–December 1993.

[DMSO98] Defense Modeling and Simulation Office. *U.S. Department of Defense High Level Architecture Interface Specification*, Version 1.3, April 1998. (Available from *http://hla.dmso.mil*)

[Escobar+94] Escobar, J., C. Partridge, and D. Deutsch. Flow synchronization protocol. *ACM/IEEE Transactions on Networking* 2(2):111–121, April 1994.

[Feineman+95] Feineman, L., G. Miller, D. Prochnow, R. Weatherly, A. Wilson, and A. Zabek. Aggregate level simulation protocol (ALSP) project 1994 annual report. Technical Report MTR-95W0000017, The Mitre Corporation, McLean, VA, March 1995.

[Friedman+92] Friedman, M., T. Starner, and A. Pentland. Device synchronization using an optimal linear filter. In *Proceedings of the 1992 Symposium on Interactive 3D Graphics*, 57–62. ACM SIGGRAPH, Cambridge, MA, March 1992. (Published as *Computer Graphics* 26 Special Issue.)

[Funkhouser95] Funkhouser, T. RING: A client-server system for multi-user virtual environments. In *Proceedings of the 1995 Virtual Reality Annual International Symposium* (VRAIS), 85–92. ACM SIGGRAPH, Seattle, April 1995.

[Gray/Cheriton89] Gray, C. G., and D. R. Cheriton. Leases: An efficient fault-tolerant mechanism for file cache consistency. In *Proceedings of the 12th Symposium on Operating Systems Principles*, 202–210. ACM SIGOPS, Litchfield Park, AZ, December 1989.

[IEEE95] Institute for Electrical and Electronics Engineers. IEEE standard for distributed interactive simulation—Application protocols. IEEE Standard 1278.1—1995. Piscataway, NJ: IEEE Standards Press, September 1995.

[Katz/Graham94] Katz, A., and K. Graham. Dead reckoning for airplanes in coordinated flight. In *Proceedings of the Tenth Workshop on Standards for the Interoperability of Defense Simulations*, II:5–13. Orlando, FL, March 1994. (Published as Technical Report IST-CR-94-01, Institute for Simulation and Training, University of Central Florida, Orlando, FL.)

[Nagashima+91] Nagashima, Y., H. Agawa, and F. Kishino. 3D face model reproduction method using multi view images. *Visual Communications and Image Processing '91: Image Processing,* I:566–573. International Society for Optical Engineering (SPIE), Boston, November 1991. (Published as *Proceedings of the SPIE* 1606, Part 1.)

[Nakamura+94] Nakamura, N., K. Nemoto, and K. Shinohara. Distributed virtual reality system for cooperative work. *NEC Research and Development* 35(4):403–409, October 1994.

[Ohya+93] Ohya, J., Y. Kitamura, H. Takemura, et al. Real-time reproduction of 3D human images in virtual space teleconferencing. In *Proceedings of the 1993 Virtual Reality Annual International Symposium* (VRAIS), 408–414. IEEE Neural Networks Council, Seattle, September 1993.

[Perlin/Goldberg96] Perlin, K., and T. Goldberg. Improv: A system for scripting interactive actors in virtual worlds. In *SIGGRAPH 1996 Conference Proceedings.* ACM SIGGRAPH, New Orleans, August 1996. (Published as *Computer Graphics* 30, Annual Conference Series Special Issue.)

[Pratt93] Pratt, D. A software architecture for the construction and management of real-time virtual worlds. Ph.D dissertation, Department of Computer Science, Naval Postgraduate School, Monterey, CA, June 1993.

[Quéau93] Quéau, P. Televirtuality: The merging of telecommunications and virtual reality. *Computers & Graphics* 17(6):691–693, November–December 1993.

[Singh+94] Singh, G., L. Serra, W. Prg, and H. Ng. BrickNet: A software toolkit for network-based virtual worlds. *PRESENCE: Teleoperators and Virtual Environments* 3(1):19–34, Winter 1994.

[Singhal96] Singhal, S. Effective remote modeling in large-scale distributed simulation and visualization environments. Ph.D dissertation. Department of Computer Science, Stanford University, Palo Alto, August 1996.

[Singhal/Cheriton95] Singhal, S., and D. Cheriton. Exploiting position history for efficient remote rendering in networked virtual reality. *PRESENCE: Teleoperators and Virtual Environments* 4(2):169–193, Spring 1995.

[VRML-LivingWorlds] VRML Living Worlds Web site: *http://www.vrml.org/WorkingGroups/living-worlds/*

[Xu+90] Xu, G., H. Agawa, Y. Nagashima, et al. Three-dimensional face modeling for virtual space teleconferencing systems. *Transactions of the Institute of Electronics, Information and Communication Engineers* (IEICE), E73(10): 1753–1761, October 1990.

Chapter 6
Systems Design

This chapter discusses the fundamental software architecture issues in the development of networked virtual environments. Issues include thread allocation and management within VEs, real-time rendering, real-time collision detection and response, and computational resource management.

ONE THREAD, MULTIPLE THREADS

This section discusses some possible processing architectures for net-VEs. We start with the basics—what single-threaded net-VEs look like and why we do not usually program them that way. We then look at multithreaded task-driven structures.

With One Thread . . .

In the simplest instantiation of a net-VE, a single-thread (process) software architecture such as that depicted in Figure 6-1 is usual. There are always lots of initializations (database reads, initial control parameters sent to input devices, network sockets opened, graphics windows

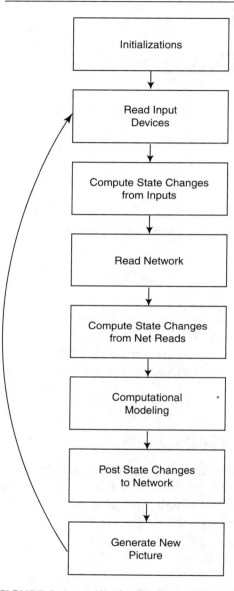

FIGURE 6-1   A single-thread net-VE

opened, and so forth). Initializations tend to be the hardest part, often requiring reuse of the most sample code during the development process. Once initializations have been performed, most single-thread VEs then enter a cycle as depicted in the figure. This cycle, generally referred to as the main *event loop*, is executed until the net-VE program terminates.

During this event loop cycle, the program reads the input devices, computes state changes from those input devices, reads the network, computes state changes from the network reads, performs some computational modeling for the virtual world, posts those state changes to the network, and then finally draws a new display frame. Developing such a program is quite simple, and if the entire cycle can be traversed completely in less than 100 ms, then we do not have to do much in the way of rearchitecting the VE software to improve performance. A 100 ms cycle time is the maximum amount of time we can reasonably allow before lag (or delay) in the system shows up as lack of smoothness: we cannot control the objects, or our viewpoint, in the virtual world smoothly [Wloka95] and the graphical rendering no longer appears smooth. To understand how lag creeps into the system, we need to look at the various components of the cycle, as shown in the figure.

There is a tremendous potential for introduction of lag in the *read input devices* block of the diagram. The current state of the VE art is that input devices such as motion trackers are usually connected to the workstation by a simple serial port running at 9,600 baud or, if you are lucky, 38,400 baud (Figure 6-2). The steps involved in getting the data from the input device to the net-VE application program are shown in Figure 6-3. The usual sequence of steps involves a command sent from

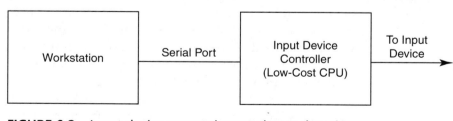

FIGURE 6-2   Input device connections to the workstation

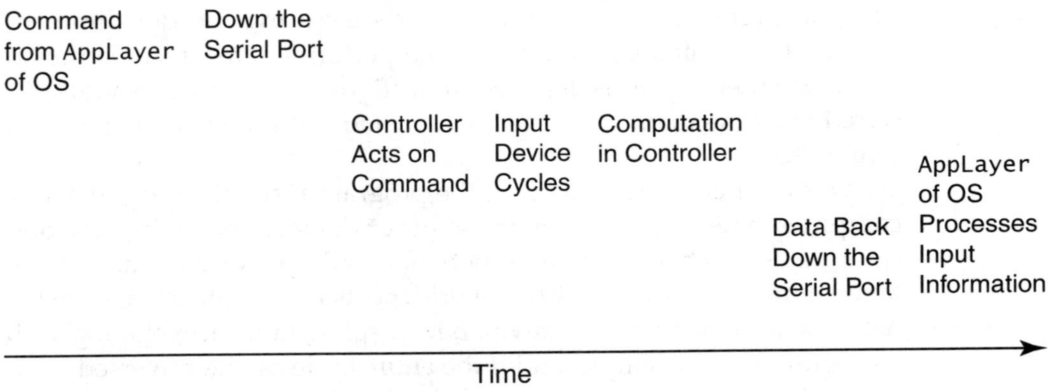

Command   Down the
from AppLayer   Serial Port
of OS

                    Controller   Input   Computation
                    Acts on   Device   in Controller
                    Command   Cycles   AppLayer
                                                               of OS
                                                  Data Back   Processes
                                                  Down the   Input
                                                  Serial Port Information

                                                                        →
                              Time

FIGURE 6-3   Sources for lag when retrieving an input from a device on a serial port.

the net-VE application program down the serial port to the controller
for the input device. That controller, usually a low-cost CPU, queries
the input device and receives back a set of values indicating the current
state of the device. The controller usually converts the device's state
into an externally meaningful format and sends that data back through
the serial port to the workstation. The workstation application receives
that information, processes it into the state tables of the VE, and then is
able to proceed to the next block of the single-thread net-VE processing.

The time required in the *compute state changes from inputs* block of
the diagram depends upon the sophistication of the processing required. Usually this set of computations is not that large and therefore
is not a bottleneck. This block determines any changes in virtual world
state and updates the corresponding state table values. Some examples
of world state changes determined at this step might include updating
the local user position based on input device movement, updating the
viewpoint position based on head tracker movement, and so forth.
Once those computations have been performed, the VE program is
then able to move to the next block of Figure 6-1.

In its simplest form, the *read network* block queries the network to retrieve any data that may have arrived from other net-VE hosts. This
query is usually performed in a "no-wait" fashion. "No wait" here

means that if no data has arrived, then the query should return right away. This query is often performed by invoking a `select()` function call on the network sockets currently in use by the net-VE application. Once the network data has been read and returned, the VE program then moves onto the next block. Reading data from the network through the operating system kernel is usually a rather expensive and slow operation because it typically involves numerous data copy operations among memory buffers as the packet is processed by the protocol stack.

The *compute state changes from net reads* block is where the packets or protocol data units (PDUs) read from the network are processed. This means that the data is extracted from the packet and modifications are made to the local state tables for the net-VE. Computations are usually performed to determine if any of the information read from the network has caused any fundamental changes to the state of the virtual environment maintained by the thread. Changes that we might see at this step include updates to networked player positions and configurations, with such updates being read from the packet and recorded in the local state tables.

The *computational modeling* block of Figure 6-1 is as expensive in terms of time as the virtual world model requires. In the simplest net-VEs, this block might not exist. In more ambitious VEs, this block could be computing the physical modeling, the collision detection and response, or any other relevant computationally expensive operations.

The *post state changes to the network* block formats data for placement onto the network and then sends that data through the kernel of the operating system. The type of data we send out includes changes to the position and configuration of any of the local players whose state is maintained on our local machine. Again, this is not fast; traversing operating system kernels seldom is.

The final block in the cycle is *generate new picture*. The time required by that block depends on the complexity of the picture to be displayed and on how much of the graphics display generation the CPU must process. If the host is a low-cost workstation, then there might not be any graphics hardware that can run in parallel with the CPU. In that case, we must devote a fairly large amount of CPU time for drawing the graphics frame.

Now, if we prototype our virtual environment in this single-thread fashion and there is any complexity to our computations, to our graphics, or to any of the other blocks of our VE program, then chances are that we will miss our 100 ms budget for the cycle of Figure 6-1. If we exceed 100 ms, the VE feels sluggish, does not respond well to control inputs, and exhibits a slow or jerky graphical display. If users are wearing head-mounted displays, then this is an excellent way for them to become quite sick. If users are staring at a monitor, the system basically becomes unusable.

There are several approaches to these problems. One is to decrease the computational requirements of the net-VE by decreasing the complexity of the world terrain, reducing the number of entities in the world, or simplifying the modeling attempted on each of those entities. That approach allows you to continue to use the same workstation, albeit on a less complex VE. A second approach is to buy a computer with a faster processor and clock rate. But even that approach has its limitations because a faster CPU cannot overcome the bottlenecks introduced by network hardware I/O, data copying in memory, and the serial bus access. Therefore, the usual approach for solving this performance problem is to rewrite the VE application using multiple threads so that a single bottleneck does not starve the entire cycle: the VE can continue computing when individual threads become blocked. For example, when *read input devices* causes a block while waiting for the device to respond, we can put that thread to sleep and allow others to utilize the processor. Of course, this requires that there be some clear way for us to break our virtual environment down into multiple threads, threads that can be performed in parallel. This rewrite of the VE into multiple threads can help our performance even if we have a single processor machine. Rehosting to a multiprocessor machine is an additional optimization we can perform once we have rewritten the application into a multithreaded system.

With Multiple Threads . . .

Multiple threads are the answer for getting complex VEs to run in real-time, faster than 100 ms per cycle. Of course, the performance benefits of multiple threads can only be achieved if the system of threads is properly balanced. Properly balanced means partitioning takes full advantage of available processor cycles and memory. This partitioning task is an art form for the well-versed systems programmer.

If we take Figure 6-1 and redraw it, partitioning the set of blocks into subsystems that can be worked on in parallel, we achieve an architecture as shown in Figure 6-4. The *input subsystem* contains the *read input devices* and *compute state changes from inputs* blocks. That subsystem could be implemented using several threads if there are several input devices that can be read in parallel. For our example though, we assume that there is only one input device and it is managed by the input subsystem, a single thread.

One of the important aspects of the input subsystem is that the speed of the cycle through the thread does not depend on threads in other subsystems. This means that fast input devices are not slowed by the rest of the blocks as they would be if Figure 6-1 were the architecture. This also means that slow input devices do not slow down any of the other blocks either. However, the input subsystem thread itself still

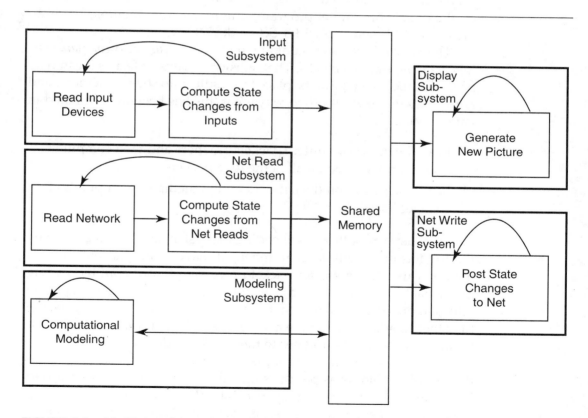

FIGURE 6-4   Multiple subsystems, multiple threads for the virtual world

has to wait until the input device has been read before it can compute state changes from that input device's status and post those state changes to the shared memory.

Shared memory is the key to why we can partition our VE software into multiple subsystems and threads. Shared memory is where we write the results of computation performed by our subsystems so that other subsystems can then read those results. Shared memory can be read and written in parallel by each of the subsystems' threads as long as the data written is temporarily protected from being read from the shared memory during the write operation. We protect shared memory with semaphores or some similar locking and synchronization mechanism, building a protocol for reading and writing the shared memory. The protocol tells other threads when it is okay to read parts of the shared memory and when it is okay to write. For further information on the details of parallel programming in a shared memory environment, see [El-Rewini/Lewis98, Schneider97].

The *net read subsystem* contains the *read network* and *compute state changes from net reads* blocks. That subsystem runs as fast as it can read packets, process the packets, place the results into shared memory, and return. There are at least two ways that this has been implemented in various VEs.

1. Read the network until no packets are there and then compute state changes based on all of the read packets.
2. Read one packet off the network and immediately compute state changes based on it.

In a nonbusy VE, both ways of coding the system are equivalent. When the VE gets busy, with large numbers of players and packets, the first method can achieve greater packet processing throughput by reading many packets at once and discarding packets that contain duplicate information, or information that is made obsolete by later packets. On the other hand, the technique also results in large positional jumps for networked players, as updates to their state are delayed.

Again, it is critical to decouple the network read processing from the rest of the blocks as per the single thread version. Single-threaded VEs with large numbers of players exhibit the same display jumps and often exhibit display freezes while processing large numbers of packets. An additional benefit of putting the net read subsystem into a separate thread is that a blocking read of the network can be performed rather than a no wait, nonblocking I/O call. This reduces calls through the operating system's kernel and allows the thread to be put to sleep when there are no packets to read, hence freeing the processor.

The *modeling subsystem* contains the *computational modeling* block. That block of the VE performs the predictive modeling of objects resident on other machines, computes the physics relevant to the objects resident on the local machine, and computes any other mathematical modeling necessary to maintain the state of the virtual environment. The computational modeling performed can be as extensive and complex as there are available processor cycles. The modeling subsystem can be highly parallelized if the computation is complex and parallelism is possible. The computational modeling can even be accomplished on a different computer entirely, with the communication to shared memory being accomplished across the network itself, again with a private protocol developed for that purpose.

The modeling subsystem can be implemented in a variety of ways that provide seemingly real-time updates to the virtual environment's state, even if the computation itself cannot be performed at that rate. The modeling subsystem could be comprised of two threads, one a dead reckoning thread and the other the actual computation thread. If the actual computation requires more than 100 ms, then we use a simplified dead reckoning thread's results until the actual computation thread completes. The utilization of dead reckoning and actual thread pairs can provide the appearance of a real-time system. Utilizing the proper convergence algorithm can minimize the differences between the dead reckoned and actual computation state.

The *display subsystem* contains the *generate new picture* block. That subsystem reads the state of the VE from the shared memory partition and then generates the proper display. In its simplest form, this is a single thread that just draws the entire set of data for the virtual world, sending the complete set of transformed 3D models down the graphics pipeline. In the more usual form, the implementation utilizes more than one thread. The classic multithreaded version of this subsystem is typified by the Silicon Graphics Performer Toolkit [Rohlf/Helman94], where this subsystem is implemented using four threads: app, cull, draw, and timer. *App* is where the VE computes the view volume, the view point, and view direction for the VE, as well as any other application-dependent modeling. *Cull* is the thread that throws most of the 3D model away, minimizing as effectively as possible the totality of polygons sent through the graphics pipeline. *Draw* is the thread that finally draws the visible polygons and sends them through the graphics pipeline. Each of these threads operates in parallel, working on a different frame of the sequence of frames that comprise the VE's animation. The *timer* thread synchronizes the frames. Again, a multi-threaded implementation of the display subsystem assumes availability of sufficient processor resources. Single processor VEs utilizing Performer are sometimes slowed down by the overhead for managing the multiple threads.

The *net write subsystem* contains the *post state changes to the net* block. That subsystem reads the state of the world as contained in the shared memory and sends packets to the network, if any changes need to be posted. The ability of this subsystem to minimize packets actually sent onto the network is one of the key components toward achieving scalability for the net-VE. The simplest implementation has this thread sending packets to the network as fast as the thread can run. The more complex implementations use techniques such as predictive modeling—as recorded in the shared memory—to determine if participants on other machines can predict (that is, dead reckon) the location of the local participant without receiving an update packet. Even more complex implementations perform area of interest management, sending output packets only to the appropriate multicast group concerned with the state change information. Area of interest management is more fully discussed in chapter 7.

IMPORTANT SUBSYSTEMS

In discussing the utility of multiple threads, we described some of the high-level processing that occurs in each of the subsystems. The delicate task in programming such a system of parallel threads is how to allocate computation among the threads to get the most parallel computation possible with the available processing resources. For some of the subsystems of Figure 6-4, we have some understanding of what needs to be done to minimize computational demands. This section explores these subsystems in more depth, to increase the likelihood that our VE system performs well within our human-computer interaction performance requirements.

Real-Time Rendering: Polygon Culling and Level-of-Detail Processing

Limitations in the performance of graphics hardware represent the key problem in the implementation of any virtual environment. In Figure 6-4, we show the display subsystem with the label "Generate new picture." In the simplest case, the display subsystem would just send the complete set of polygons representing the virtual environment through the pipeline of the graphics workstation. Unfortunately, most virtual worlds are too complex and the graphics hardware capabilities are too meager to be able to do this. To understand why this is so, take a look at Table 6-1, which shows the performance of representative graphics hardware speeds (polygons per second) at different update rates (frames per second).

Something that runs at the speed of the Nintendo 64, about 100,000 polygons per second, allows us about 3,333 polygons in our picture if

TABLE 6-1 Graphics Performance in Terms of Polygons per Frame

Polygons per second	Polygons per frame		
	10 frames/second	20 frames/second	30 frames/second
100,000	10,000	5,000	3,333
200,000	20,000	10,000	6,666
500,000	50,000	25,000	16,666
1M	100,000	50,000	33,333
2M	200,000	100,000	66,666
3M	300,000	150,000	100,000
4M	400,000	200,000	133,333
10M	1M	500,000	333,333
20M	2M	1M	666,666
50M	5M	2.5M	1,666,666
100M	10M	5M	3,333,333
200M	20M	10M	6,666,666

we wish to run at 30 pictures (frames) per second (fps). Thirty fps is our preferred update rate and allows us to move through our 3D virtual world quite nicely, as long as our world consists of fewer than 3,333 polygons. The question then arises, "Is 3,333 a lot of polygons?" The answer to such a question depends on the particular application. If we are designing a video game and are happy to live with 3D characters that are somewhat angular in appearance and lack some of the detail and personality possible, then we might require 300 to 400 polygons to represent each character. If we throw that character into a room with a staircase, some paintings on the wall, and really very little detailing—similar to Mario on the Nintendo 64—then we have about 3,000 polygons. Add one more character as complex as Mario and we have spent our polygon budget.

Some of the available PC graphics cards, or the Silicon Graphics O2 workstation, offer about 500,000 polygons/second, or about 16,666 polygons available for each picture in our sequence of animated frames. An Intergraph TDZ 3D has 1.2 million polygons per second or about 40,000 polygons per picture, and an SGI Reality Engine Monster has 80 million polygons per second or about 2.6 million polygons per picture. Consequently, if money is no object, a considerable level of polygon performance can always be bought. However, in the end, we always have the potential to build worlds that are far more complicated than the available graphics hardware. In fact, this is the usual case. So what can we do?

Polygon Culling

The usual solution is to cull, or throw away polygons, using the processor to determine which polygons do not need to be drawn (Figure 6-5). The processor must make those decisions using available, otherwise idle, processor cycles and in a time that is faster than just sending all the polygons through the graphics pipeline. Much work has gone into developing techniques for culling.

An excellent starting point for understanding culling is the 1976 paper by Jim Clark [Clark76]. Figure 6-6, which is derived from the Clark paper, shows a tree with the top node being the complete world. The tree is defined such that we subdivide the complete world, available at the top node, into separate spatial volumes or regions. For buildings, this would mean that each floor of the building is repre-

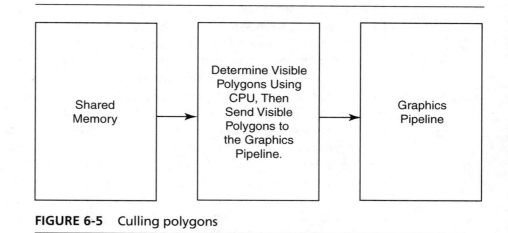

FIGURE 6-5 Culling polygons

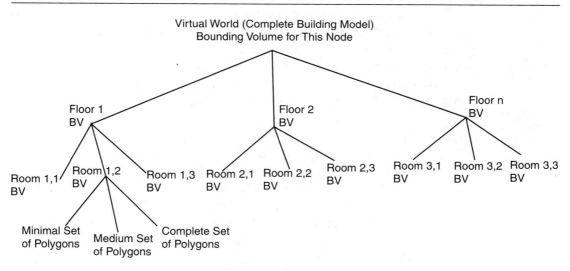

FIGURE 6-6 Hierarchical data structure for rapid polygon culling

Source: Derived from [Clark76]. Used with permission.

sented as a node underneath the world node and that farther down the tree, individual rooms on each floor have their own nodes as well.

Each node is associated with a *bounding volume* for the information below it in the tree. The idea behind the bounding volume is that the bounding volume is a small amount of data that we can check against the *view volume*, the region that is visible on the screen. If we find that the bounding volume is within the view volume, we know that we must draw some (or all) of the data farther down that branch of the tree. If we find that the bounding volume is outside of the view volume, then we know that we do not have to traverse farther down that branch of the tree. With such a tree, we can rapidly throw away large parts of our complete world model, particularly those parts that do not contribute to the final display. We then send to the graphics pipeline only those parts of the model that actually belong in the picture. We can take advantage of this technique as long as the time to compute whether we must traverse lower in the tree is less than just sending all remaining polygons underneath the node to the graphics pipeline.

Polygon culling has received a tremendous amount of study and is probably worthy of its own monograph. Two excellent overview papers are [Mine/Weber96] and [Funkhouser+96]. Mine and Weber cover the UNC Walkthrough project, and Funkhouser covers the Berkeley Walk-through project. The goal of each of these projects is to solve the polygon culling problem for building walkthrough applications.

University of North Carolina, Chapel Hill, Walkthrough Project

The UNC Walkthrough project has been documented in excellent detail [Airey+90, Brooks86, Mine/Weber96], and discussion of the project is beyond the scope of this book. The polygon culling work is based on the computation of "potentially visible sets" (PVS) of polygons. The PVS computation subdivides the building model into cells (volumes) of polygons and then computes which cells can be seen from other cells based on holes or portals in the cell boundaries [Mine/Weber96]. Only those polygons in cells that can possibly be seen from the viewer's cell are considered during the rendering phase and many are further elimi-nated depending on the viewer's location and orientation within the particular cell.

The data structure used for this work is the Binary Space Partition-ing (BSP) tree [Fuchs+83, Fuchs+80]. Large planar surfaces (walls of the building) are used to subdivide the model in the construction of the BSP tree (Figures 6-7 and 6-8). Using the location of the viewer and the equation of the partitioning plane, it is easy to determine which side of the BSP to traverse in selecting the set of polygons to display. Once the traversal reaches the leaf nodes of the tree (the cell containing the

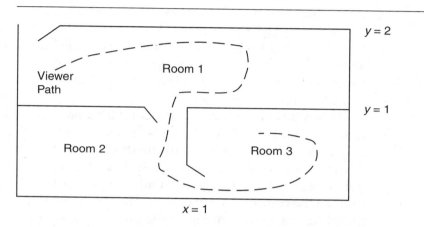

FIGURE 6-7 Building floor plan and walkthrough pathway

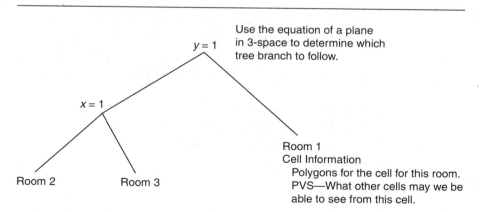

FIGURE 6-8 Binary space partitioning tree for the building floor plan

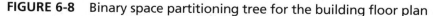

viewer), the PVS information for the cell is then used to determine which polygons to consider for display.

University of California, Berkeley, Walkthrough Project

The Funkhouser, Teller, and Sequin (FT&S) system utilizes a variant of the k-D tree to subdivide their building model [Funkhouser+92]. That data structure contains a hierarchy of visibility information, a hierarchy that rather rapidly narrows down the amount of data that must be sent through the graphics pipeline. The model is subdivided along splitting planes selected from the floors and walls of the building model. Cells are therefore composed from the boundaries of the splitting planes. Portals—the doors and windows along shared cell boundaries—are identified in the data structure.

When traversing the data structure for a particular viewer, the first task is to locate which cell contains the viewpoint location. In that cell is a set of *cell-to-object* visibility information that lists all of the objects visible from any viewpoint in that cell. This is a large number of objects, not all of which are visible from all viewpoints, but it is still a smaller set than the complete set of objects. The *eye-to-cell* visibility is then computed for the view volume of the viewer, the set of cells partially or completely visible to the viewer. The eye-to-cell visibility computation only considers the cells represented by the smaller set of objects contained in the cell-to-object list. The third step is the computation of the *eye-to-object* visibility. This is the set of objects actually visible to the viewer. That set is computed by intersecting the cell-to-object and eye-to-cell sets. The final step in the FT&S culling procedure is to determine which level-of-detail set to send through the graphics pipeline, as discussed below. For a more complete description of the polygon culling procedure, the reader is directed to the original papers.

Polygon Culling Wrapup

Both the UNC and the Berkeley walkthrough work are effective at providing data structures that allow real-time walkthroughs of large building structures. There are also other researchers with significant culling work [Green95, Zhang+97]. An inclusive, though brief, survey is to be found in [Zhang+97], and the interested reader is directed there.

Much of the hierarchical polygon culling work contains limitations. Much of the data structure work assumes that the underlying 3D model of the large building does not change. If we find that our application requires that the underlying 3D environment must change, then we must also be able to rebuild the data structure rapidly or separate out the parts that must be changed. Bruce Naylor [Naylor95] has done this to great effect with tree merging for the BSP tree. His demonstrations at the 1995 Symposium on Interactive 3D Graphics included a real-time demonstration of drilling through walls and blast effects.

The final issue is: How many threads should we use for culling in our VE architecture? The basic answer is one thread for the traversal of the hierarchical data structure and as many threads as you can effectively use to compute and maintain the data structure. However, the end answer really depends on the complexity of the 3D model and the performance requirements for the culling process. Such issues are therefore specific to each constructed net-VE system.

Levels of Detail

Figure 6-9 shows another area discussed in the 1976 Clark paper, that of levels of detail [Clark76]. Once a bounding volume's set of polygons is determined to be in view and therefore should be drawn, then another

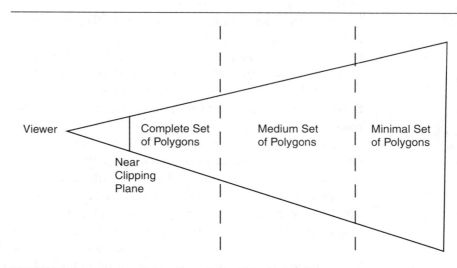

FIGURE 6-9   Levels of detail and the view volume

computation must be made, that of how many pixels will the final set of polygons actually cover on the screen. After all, why should we bother to draw a large number of polygons if they will only cover a handful of pixels? This means that once we are at a leaf of our tree with a draw decision, we should then decide on how much to draw. This is called the level-of-detail, or LOD, decision. The LOD decision presupposes that there are multiple sets of polygons to choose from: one choice is to draw the complete set of polygons at the leaf node (object is close to the viewer), while another choice might be to draw half the polygons (object is at a medium distance from the viewer), and yet another choice might be to draw only one-fifth of the polygons (object is far from the viewer), as shown in Figure 6-9 (side view of view volume).

We use three sets of polygons as an example for the LOD decision, but the truth is that there might be many different levels of polygonal model options available, depending on how far the object is located from the viewer. In fact, if the object is created from a framework that allows real-time generation of different level-of-detail models, then the level of detail can be dynamically customized according to the object's size on the display. Again, the LOD decision has to be made in the time remaining after we have completed culling and in an amount of time that is again faster than just sending the complete set of polygons through the graphics pipeline.

Now the computation as to which LOD set to draw is not too difficult. It is a function of the (virtual) distance from the viewer to the object being viewed. Moreover, the viewer should not be presented with high resolution objects that suddenly pop into lower resolution while still close to the viewer and vice versa. To support smooth transitions between different LODs, many systems blend the different object resolutions during the transition.

The hard part in getting LOD models to work is obtaining the lower resolution sets of polygons to display. In the earliest days of virtual environment creation, VEs were quite often built without LOD processing at all or with LOD models that had been hand generated. The hand generated sets would usually start with the complete set of polygons and delete some of the smaller, nonessential polygons at each lower level of resolution. Smooth surfaces would be resampled at lower resolution to construct a medium distant LOD model. The lowest resolution LOD model would be made in a similar fashion. Most early

VEs that used LODs computed at most three sets of LOD models. Sometimes the lowest resolution LOD model would just be a rectangular box surrounding the volume that contained the model. It would be colored according to the color of the largest surfaces in the model. For some VEs this simple modeling technique actually worked, assuming the object modeled by the box was also roughly rectangular in shape. However, this does not work well for objects such as airplanes where the bounding volume is much, much larger than the space the airplane really consumes. In order to work effectively, such systems need to match more closely the final pixel coverage of the high resolution models with that of the lower resolution models.

In more recent VEs, much work has gone into providing continuous solutions to the LOD model creation problem. Cohen [Cohen+96] develops simplification envelopes that allow the generation of minimal approximations that are guaranteed to be within a settable tolerance of the original set of polygons. Hoppe [Hoppe96a, Hoppe96b] develops progressive meshes that are optimized using an energy function to minimize the distance of the mesh from the original polygonal object. DeHaemer [DeHaemer/Zyda91] combines polygons until they fit within a set error tolerance. Turk [Turk92] focuses on triangular mesh decimation to reduce the total number of polygons from the original representation.

Some of these solutions are definitely non-real-time and require that a set of LODs be precomputed. The Cohen work appears to be quite capable of running in real-time, however, and its demonstrated results are quite spectacular for very large models. Again, the determination of whether any particular LOD generation algorithm runs in real-time depends on the available processor cycles and whether the computation performed is faster than just sending the remaining polygons through the graphics pipeline. The nature of this constraint shifts as technology changes. As we move from SGI workstations to Windows NT boxes, we may have to revisit past performance levels and architectures.

Real-Time Collision Detection and Response

Solving the real-time rendering problem is only part of the effort in building a compelling virtual environment. After all, what is a 3D world that we can look at and walk through but cannot touch? To be able to touch and transform a particular piece of geometry in our virtual environment, we need to be able to determine if our hand occupies the same space as the object. We need to be able to determine what object we are holding and where we are touching it. To be able to walk through the virtual world, we need to be able to determine where the floor is under our feet. For these operations, we need effective collision detection. Moreover, we need to be able to do these collision determinations in real-time.

Once we have determined that we have collided with (touched, grasped, stood on, and so forth) a particular object in our world, we then need to take some action in response to the collision or generate a message to communicate the collision to other hosts in the net-VE. If we grab an object, we may need to tell our system to attach that object to the hand that grabbed it. If we land on a stair, we need to tell our system the new ground level for our articulated avatar.

In the early days of VEs, collision detection was ignored. There are many old videotapes where cows walk through trees and avatars fly through building walls. Obviously, the illusion of presence—so sought after by the VR community—breaks down if we walk through walls. Fortunately, collision detection has been well studied: There is prior work in the literature of computer graphics, robotics, computational geometry, computer animation, physically based modeling, and virtual environments. Before examining some of the more important work on collision detection, we first discuss why collision detection is so challenging.

In its simplest form, collision detection might mean that we have an avatar for our hand in the virtual world, that avatar being driven by a dataglove, and we wish to grab an object in the world, the object having its own avatar. If we boil this down, we need to take the collection of polygons that represent our hand and determine if there is an intersection in space with the polygons of *any* object in our VE. It is that "any object condition" that is difficult to handle if our world is complex. With large worlds composed of large numbers of polygons, this is not a fast test to perform. We can achieve reasonable performance if somehow we arrange our world so that we can test the bounding volume of our hand against the bounding volume of gross objects, with a hierarchical data structure allowing us to rapidly throw away most of the world objects that we need to test against. Hopefully, the hierarchical data structure we utilize is the same one developed for culling.

Assuming that we have reduced our collision search space to something tractable, we now know the name of the object (or objects) with which our hand intersects. Maybe that is enough information for now, and we can go immediately to our collision response software. However, we typically need to know more. We need to know where on the object our hand intersects and the precise contact points. Again, we hope that there is a further hierarchy in the object's polygons that allows us to rapidly discard most of the object before we have to test individual polygons against individual polygons.

With this as background, it becomes clear why many early VEs avoided the question completely and listed the ability to fly through the VE walls as a "feature." Some declared victory if a user could grab a single object. Virtually none allowed you to grab a tool and carve on the walls, changing the virtual world.

Real-Time Collision Detection Solutions

The available collision detection literature is quite large, with much of it non-real-time [Cameron97, Cohen+95, Dobkin90, Garcia-Alonso+94, Gilbert+88, Gottschalk+96, Hubbard96, Hudson+97, Lin, Lin/Gottschalk98, Lin+98, Pratt93, Zyda+93]. In her survey of the field, Ming Lin characterizes the differing approaches to collision detection as geometric reasoning, bounding volume hierarchy, spatial representation, numerical methods, analytical methods, and hybrid [Lin/Gottschalk98]. Additionally, Lin indicates that algorithm design tends to be model representation dependent, with the major split being polygonal models (structured convex, structured nonconvex, and polygon soups) and nonpolygonal models (constructive solid geometry, implicit surfaces, and parametric surfaces).

For virtual environments we focus on two types of collision detection because of current graphics capabilities and real-time performance needs: polygonal models and hybrid approaches. In virtual environments, the hybrid approaches tend to be divided into fast-approximate and fast-accurate collision detection. As illustration, the following subsections examine two such collision detection systems.

Fast, Approximate Collision Detection—NPSNET

Fast, approximate collision detection is what we do if we are building a virtual environment where the precise location of our collision is unimportant, where the only important thing is that we recognize that a collision has occurred. NPSNET-2 through NPSNET-IV have such a collision detection capability [Pratt93, Zyda+93]. In NPSNET, moving objects (Jeeps, tanks, helicopters, people) can collide with each other and with fixed, static objects (trees, buildings, walls, and so on). Upon collision over a certain speed, the only thing that happens in NPSNET is that the moving object dies; the moving object simply ceases moving. No attempt is made to do more sophisticated physics, such as damage assessment or directional change. All interaction between moving and static objects is taken care of by the collision detection mechanism of NPSNET.

Collision detection in NPSNET is segmented into two separate parts: (1) moving object (ownship) against static objects, and (2) moving object (ownship) against moving objects (other players). *Ownship* refers to the local player in the virtual environment. When the ownship collides with a static object or a moving object, it is up to the ownship to report that collision to the network so that other players in the virtual world know a collision has occurred. It is also up to the ownship to accurately report that it has died as a result of that collision.

Ownship–Static Object Collisions: Ownship collision detection against static objects occurs as soon as a vehicle is moved and its position is updated. There are many static objects in a typical world, so NPSNET must first reduce the set of static objects that must be considered for collision against the ownship. The first part of the process is to check if the ownship is below a threshold elevation, the elevation of the highest static object in the grid square underneath the ownship. If the ownship is higher, then no collision can be occurring, and further collision detection determination between the ownship and static objects is not done. If the ownship is below that elevation, then further collision computation is necessary.

The NPSNET world is subdivided into grids. All static objects in the NPSNET world are attached to the terrain, with a linked list maintained at each grid square of the static objects covering that square. NPSNET then only needs to run through that short linked list of static objects to determine if there are any collisions. It does this level of collision detection by using bounding cylinders around each moving and static object and computing the two-dimensional distances between the ownship and all of the static objects in the grid square. If the two-dimensional distance is less than the sum of the ownship's and the static object's radii, we almost have a collision determination.

The final check is to see if the ownship's ground elevation is less than the height of the static object. If that condition is met, a collision has occurred between the ownship and the static object, and NPSNET then uses the speed of the ownship to determine its fate. NPSNET issues a message to the network indicating that a collision has occurred and the resolution of that collision (a DIS detonation PDU, if the ownship has died, or an entity state PDU with a velocity of zero, if the ownship is still alive but has stopped because of the collision).

Ownship–Moving Object Collisions: When collision detection between the ownship and static objects has finished without a collision, NPSNET then examines whether any collisions have occurred between the ownship and any moving objects. Again, the first thing that has to be done is to reduce the collision comparison space. We do not want to compare our ownship against the potentially 500 other moving objects in the NPSNET world.

NPSNET accomplishes this by again using the NPSNET grids. Each grid square has a linked list of moving objects. The ownship checks that linked list and the linked lists of neighboring grid squares.[1] If there are moving objects on any of those lists, then further computation is performed. This second computation is to compute the three-dimensional distance between the bounding spheres of the ownship and each moving object on the linked lists. If the distance is less than the combined radii of the ownship and the moving object, then we almost have a collision determination. A final check is to cast a ray from the ownship's origin to the moving object's origin.[2] That ray is assumed to pass through the colliding polygons of the objects. Using a modified ray tracing procedure, the ray is checked for intersection against all of the polygons of each object.

---

[1]With the size of the grid squares used, a moving object would have to be traveling faster than 1,000 kilometers per hour before this collision comparison space check would fail [Zyda+93].

[2]The origin for an object in NPSNET is a coordinate inside of the object, usually the point around which the object was constructed. It is also the center of the bounding sphere for the object.

Since NPSNET only uses low-polygon-count objects, less than 200 polygons each, this is not too computationally horrible. Two distances are then computed. One distance is from the ownship's origin to the point of intersection on the ownship. The second distance is computed from the moving object's origin to the point of intersection on the moving object. If the sum of the two distances exceeds the distance between the two origins, then there is a collision and the objects interpenetrate. NPSNET then issues a message to the network, indicating that a collision has occurred and the resolution of that collision (DIS detonation PDU, if the ownship has died, or an entity state PDU with a velocity of zero, if the ownship is still alive but has stopped because of the collision). It is up to the machine managing the colliding moving object to also perform collision detection and issue companion PDUs.

Fast, Accurate Collision Detection—I-COLLIDE, RAPID, and V-COLLIDE
Ming Lin of the University of North Carolina has developed a number of hybrid algorithms for fast and accurate collision detection between general polygonal models in dynamically changing, large-scale environments (hundreds of thousands of polygons at interactive rates) [Cohen+95, Gottschalk+96, Hudson+97, Lin+98, Lin/Gottschalk98, Lin]. Lin's work is hybrid in that it unifies several techniques, exploiting temporal and spatial coherence and utilizing locality and hierarchical data structures. We examine her system here as a representative collision detection algorithm.

Like the NPSNET collision detection system, Lin's algorithm begins by looking at how to reduce the collision comparison space from the complete set of objects to a smaller set [Lin+98]. It uses a "sweep and prune" algorithm for this step [Cohen+95]. The sweep and prune algorithm assumes that we have an axially aligned 3D bounding box for each object in the environment. The algorithm sorts the bounding boxes of the objects to determine if there are overlaps (potential collisions). It takes advantage of the fact that for two 3D bounding boxes to collide, their projections onto the x, y, and z axes must overlap [Lin+98]. Overlap is an easy check as all we have to do is look for interval overlap for each of the three axes to determine 3D bounding box overlap (and hence potential collision). The sweep and prune algorithm maintains a list of intervals for each bounding box for each dimension. By sorting the interval lists, the algorithm can determine which intervals overlap and then, if there is overlap in all three dimensions, which bounding boxes overlap. The sweep and prune algorithm takes advantage of temporal and geometric coherence for this sort and gets away with an $O(N)$ insertion sort, where N is the number of objects. Temporal and geometric coherence means that objects are expected to have not moved far between computation frames of the virtual environment, a reasonable expectation.

Once Lin's algorithm has determined that a pair of objects' bounding boxes overlap, the algorithm then checks whether their convex hulls also overlap.[3] The convex hull overlap computation determines the closest feature pairs and whether those features overlap. It then checks to see if the overlapping features are part of the original model or artifacts introduced as part of the convex hull computation. If the overlapping features are part of the original objects, then we have collision. The actual area of collision is then computed through the use of an oriented bounding box hierarchy (OBBTree), which is well explained in [Gottschalk+96] and [Lin+98].

Lin's algorithm has been utilized to excellent effect, with very low collision detection times reported—on the order of 4.2 ms average for two complex 140,000 polygon objects. The reader is referred to Lin's Web site [Lin] for the collision detection code and her papers.

Collision Detection Summary

Our intention has not been to be comprehensive about various collision detection algorithms. We merely wanted to show some of the complexity involved in one of the most important threads in any net-VE. Complexity means processor cycles are required. Collision detection gives us additional rationale as to why multiple threads are required for developing net-VEs.

Net-VEs and Collision Detection

Net-VEs have unique problems with respect to collision detection, some of which were alluded to above in describing the NPSNET solu-

---

[3]A *convex hull* is essentially the minimal bounding volume of an object. Imagine taking an inflated balloon, placing the object inside the balloon, and releasing the air. The resulting balloon shape, wrapped around the object, represents the convex hull. For more information on convex hulls, see [Preparata/Shamos85].

tion to collision detection. "Who determines collision in a net-VE?" is an important question. With NPSNET and all DIS-compliant VEs, it is the object that has collided, the ownship, that makes this determination. This can go wrong in many ways. DIS VEs have no requirement to utilize the same collision detection algorithm. This means that two objects colliding can have different determinations of what happened. One can decide that it has died in a collision. The other can decide that the collision did not happen at all. Such issues of fair play are hard to enforce in a net-VE unless a standard is provided for collision detection, a standard that is adhered to by all objects in the VE.

Additional collision detection problems that net-VEs can have are collisions that happen in between time steps and collisions that happen for dead-reckoned objects but not for the actual objects. Collisions in between time steps occur when the objects are moving fast and the time steps between frames in the simulation are too large. Most net-VEs periodically compute object positions and use those object locations for collision detection. To catch collisions between time steps necessitates changing the way collision detection is done; the path (a volume really) in time and space that our possibly colliding objects have taken since the last time step must be checked. This increases the computational complexity of our net-VE, and it is still an inexact determination because it assumes that the objects were simultaneously located at all points along that path. Most systems simply choose to ignore these collisions entirely, allowing the occasional rapid crossing of paths by objects in the net-VE.

If we do wish to detect collisions that happen between time steps and if we have computational cycles available, there is an approach called space-time [Cameron90, Hubbard93, Hubbard95]. Some space-time techniques require that the object's motion be known a priori, such as would be provided with dead reckoning or with objects moving in a slow, controlled fashion. Space-time techniques use motion prediction to precompute when a collision might occur and do not check for collisions again until right before that time occurs. Space-time techniques can be used to check if a collision has occurred between the last time step and the current time step. The technique operates exactly according to the intuition provided in the preceding paragraph: It checks the swept volumes of the two objects for possible contacts. The swept volume is generated by taking the object from its last position to its current position. For objects of arbitrarily complex shape, space-time approaches are very expensive. For spheres, cubes, or simple bounding volumes, space-time may be tractable to some scale for use in a net-VE.

An alternate and more efficient solution for detecting collisions between time steps is the scheduling scheme [Lin93, Lin/Canny92, Lin/Manocha95], which utilizes the bounds on acceleration and velocity of the objects and the current interobject separation distances to predict the times to collision for each pair of objects in the virtual environment. Researchers in dynamic simulation often backtrack using bisection methods to locate the exact time and location of collisions [Baraff+98]. All of these methods require additional computation, which is not available on low-end computing platforms.

Collisions that happen for dead reckoned objects but not for the actual objects are also possible in a net-VE. This is the case where the ownship has updated its position in space and has updated the ghosts, the dead reckoned objects. The ownship may determine that it has collided with a dead reckoned object and issue a packet to the network indicating the results of that collision. However, the object collided with is at a slightly different actual location, depending on the error tolerance in the dead reckoning algorithm. That object instead may determine that no collision occurred or it may determine a different level of damage. Needless to say, that object is also operating with incomplete information about the virtual world, since it, too, is dead reckoning remote objects. Indeed, the net-VE designer must establish a mechanism for establishing an agreement on which object reached the "right" (or mutually acceptable) conclusion, while fully well knowing that both may, in fact, have reached entirely the wrong conclusions because of incomplete information. Again, the choice of the net-VE programmer might be not to worry about the problem.

If we want to make sure that both objects see the collision and that both objects make similar determinations of damage, then the simplest approach is to architect the net-VE to recognize arriving packets from other objects that indicate mutual collision and determine the fates of the objects. The easiest decision may be to make the object that missed the collision see the collision and have the same fate. Of course, we then may have a situation where the object that should have collided (but missed the determination) has shot someone or performed some action between the time of the missed collision and the time that it learns that the collision occurred. At some point we have to decide that we cannot roll back time and that we are out of cycles to correct the past. As should be readily apparent, real-time distributed collision agreement is a difficult problem, and few good solutions exist. It is an area of active research.

Computational Resource Management

Figure 6-4 introduced the notion of multiple subsystems for our virtual environment's software. When we began examining the subsystems of that figure, we found that the subsystems were implemented as multiple threads. The notion from that figure is that if we build our virtual world on a multiprocessor machine that has a processor for each thread, then each thread can run in parallel, and we do not need to do much in the way of computational resource management. The usual case, though, is that we have more threads than processors, so what do we do?

In the early days of VR, people tended to ignore this problem and hoped the virtual environment would run well. This is not a bad strategy if the threads are comprised of system calls, such as serial line reads, where the thread will block until the hardware on the other end of the line returns data. In most reasonable operating systems, a blocked thread yields the processor to other waiting threads. Therefore, the input subsystem is probably fine without computational resource management, at least until we have higher speed buses for our input devices rather than slow serial ports. The net read subsystem is also fine if written so that the thread blocks until data is at the network interface. Again, waiting for hardware usually makes our system of multiple threads work well.

The display subsystem is comprised of multiple threads, each thread having significant computation to perform, especially the app and cull threads. Threads with a large amount of computation to perform can lock other threads from executing. Hence, the app and cull threads require computational resource management of some kind. The draw thread of the display subsystem tends to work against graphics hardware that occasionally blocks the thread. On most high-end graphics workstations, some of the computational resource management for the app, cull, and draw threads is provided as part of the scene graph processing software that comes with the graphics hardware. However, support for computational resource management for complex culling is not provided and is something we may have to take care of.

The net write subsystem, in its simplest form, does not require much computational resource management, as we are writing to a network interface, and our thread will tend to block on the write and free the processor. As we move to more scalable systems and begin computing area of interest management (Chapter 7), this subsystem and its threads will require significant computational resource management.

The *modeling subsystem* is also a problem. Computational modeling threads tend not to yield their processors until they are done. If we have successfully parallelized our computational modeling to the point where we have more threads than processors, we may then need to manage those threads' processor usage.

One way to perform computational resource management is to set an alarm that triggers on each executing thread after a set amount of time has passed. A separate thread, a *thread scheduler*, then needs to look at the alarm and determine which thread should next be run. The thread scheduler could decide to continue with the thread that was interrupted by the alarm or wake up another thread that has higher priority. Determining which thread has higher priority is VE application dependent and system design dependent. A good design for this scheduler can make the difference between a VE that performs poorly and one that works well.

CONCLUSION

The system design of virtual environments is an art requiring the balance of computational requirements against performance requirements against the actual available hardware. This chapter has provided a high-level view of how VEs should be constructed in a multithreaded fashion. However, the actual construction of a net-VE system has many application dependent details, and we cannot provide one single, comprehensive guide.

In discussing the important subsystems of a net-VE, we have focused our attention on graphics rendering and computational modeling. In the next chapter, we revisit the distribution of messages among participating net-VE hosts. Reducing the number of messages that must be sent and received aims not only to reduce the bandwidth requirements of the net-VE but also to improve the computational performance of the net read and net write subsystems.

REFERENCES AND FURTHER READING

Example Systems

[Barrus+96] *Barrus, J. W., R. C. Waters, and D. B. Anderson. Locales and beacons: Supporting large multi-user virtual environments. *IEEE Computer Graphics and Applications* 16(6):50–57, November 1996.

[Benford+94] *Benford, S., J. Bowers, L. Fahlen, and C. Greenhalgh. Managing mutual awareness in collaborative virtual environments. In *Proceedings of VRST 1994*, 223–236. River Edge, NJ: World Scientific Publishing, 1994.

[Greenhalgh+97] *Greenhalgh, C., and S. Benford. Boundaries, awareness and interaction in collaborative virtual environments. In *Proceedings of the Sixth Workshops on Enabling Technologies: Infrastructure for Collaborative Enterprises* (WETICE 97), 193–198. Cambridge, MA, June 1997.

[Macedonia95] *Macedonia, M. R. A network software architecture for large scale virtual environments. Ph.D dissertation, Naval Postgraduate School, Monterey, CA. June 1995.

[Macedonia+94] *Macedonia, M. R., M. J. Zyda, D. R. Pratt, P. T. Barham, and S. Zeswitz. NPSNET: A network software architecture for large scale virtual environments. *PRESENCE: Teleoperators and Virtual Environments* 3(4): 265–287, Fall 1994.

[Macedonia+95] *Macedonia, M. R., D. P. Brutzman, M. J. Zyda, D. R. Pratt, P. T. Barham, J. Falby, and J. Locke. NPSNET: A multi-player 3D virtual environment over the Internet. In *Proceedings of the 1995 Symposium on Interactive 3D Graphics*. ACM SIGGRAPH, Monterey, CA, April 1995.

[NPSNET] *NPSNET Web site: *http://www.npsnet.nps.navy.mil/npsnet*

[Robertson/Card/Mackinlay89] *Robertson, G., S. K. Card, and J. Mackinlay. The cognitive coprocessor architecture for interactive user interfaces. In *Proceedings of the ACM SIGGRAPH Symposium on User Interface Software and Technology*, 10–18. ACM SIGGRAPH, Williamsburg, VA, November 1989.

Note: An asterisk * indicates a selection recommended as further reading. Works with no asterisk are references cited in the chapter.

[Rohlf+94] *Rohlf, J., and J. Helman. IRIS performer: A high-performance multiprocessing toolkit for real-time 3D. In *SIGGRAPH 1994 Conference Proceedings*, 381–394. ACM SIGGRAPH, Orlando, FL, August 1994.

[Snowdon/West94] *Snowdon, D., and A. West. AVIARY: Design issues for future large-scale virtual environments. *PRESENCE: Teleoperators and Virtual Environments* 3(4):288–308, Fall 1994.

[Waters+97] *Waters, R. C., D. B. Anderson, J. W. Barrus, et al. Diamond park and spline: A social virtual reality system with 3D animation, spoken interaction, and runtime modifiability. *PRESENCE: Teleoperators and Virtual Environments* 6(4):461–480, August 1997.

[Wloka95] Wloka, M. Lag in multiprocessor VR. *PRESENCE: Teleoperators and Virtual Environments* 4(1):50–63, Winter 1995.

Polygon Culling

[Airey+90] Airey, J. M., J. H. Rohlf, and F. P. Brooks, Jr. Towards image realism with interactive update rates in complex virtual building environments. *Computer Graphics* 24(2):41–50, March 1990. (Special Issue on the 1990 ACM SIGGRAPH Symposium on Interactive 3D Graphics.)

[Bishop+98] *Bishop, L., et al. Designing a PC game engine. *IEEE Computer Graphics and Applications*, 56–63, January–February 1998.

[Brooks86] Brooks, F. P., Jr. Walkthrough: A dynamics graphics system for simulating virtual buildings. In *Proceedings of the 1986 Workshop on Interactive 3D Graphics* (S. Pizer and F. Crow, eds.), 9–21. University of North Carolina at Chapel Hill, October 1986.

[Clark76] Clark, J. Hierarchical geometric models for visible surface algorithms. *Communications of the ACM* 19(10):547–554, October 1976.

[Fuchs+83] *Fuchs, H., G. Anram, and E. Grant. Near real-time shaded display of rigid objects. In *Proceedings of SIGGRAPH 1983*, 65–72, Summer 1983.

[Fuchs+80] *Fuchs, H., Z. Kedem, and B. Naylor. On visible surface generation by a priori tree structures. In *Proceedings of SIGGRAPH 1980*, 124–133, Summer 1980.

[Funkhouser+96] Funkhouser, T., S. Teller, C. Sequin, and D. Khorramabadi. The UC Berkeley system for interactive visualization of large architectural models. *PRESENCE: Teleoperators and Virtual Environments* 5(1):13–44, Winter 1996.

[Funkhouser/Sequin93] *Funkhouser, T. A., and C. H. Sequin. Adaptive display algorithm for interactive frame rates during visualization of complex virtual environments. In *Proceedings of SIGGRAPH 1993*, 247–254, August 1993.

[Funkhouser+92] *Funkhouser, T. A., C. H. Sequin, and S. J. Teller. Management of large amounts of data in interactive building walkthroughs. In *Proceedings of the 1992 Symposium on Interactive 3D Graphics*, 11–20, March 1992.

[Greene95] Greene, N. Hierarchical rendering of complex environments. Ph.D thesis. University of California, Santa Cruz, CA, 1995.

[Mine/Weber96] Mine, M., and H. Weber. Large models for virtual environments: A review of work by the architectural walkthrough project at UNC. *PRESENCE: Teleoperators and Virtual Environments* 5(1):136–145, Winter 1996.

[Naylor95] *Naylor, B. Interactive playing with large synthetic environments. In *Proceedings of the 1995 Symposium on Interactive 3D Graphics*, 107–108, March 1995.

[Teller/Sequin91] *Teller, S., and C. Sequin. Visibility preprocessing for interactive walkthroughs. In *Proceedings of SIGGRAPH 1991*, 61–69. Published as *Computer Graphics* 25(4).

[Zhang+97] Zhang, H., D. Manocha, T. Hudson, and K. Hoff. Visibility culling using hierarchical occlusion maps. In *Proceedings of SIGGRAPH 1997*, 77–88, Summer 1997.

Levels of Detail

[Cohen+96] Cohen, J., A. Varshney, D. Manocha, G. Turk, H. Weber, P. Agarwal, F. Brooks, and W. Wright. Simplification envelopes. In *Proceedings of SIGGRAPH 1996*, 119–128, Summer 1996.

[DeHaemer/Zyda91] DeHaemer, M. J., and M. J. Zyda. Simplification of objects rendered by polygonal approximations. *Computers & Graphics* 15(2): 175–184, 1991.

[Hoppe96a] Hoppe, H. View-dependent refinement of progressive meshes. In *Proceedings of SIGGRAPH 1996*, 189–198, Summer 1996.

[Hoppe96b] Hoppe, H. Progressive meshes. In *Proceedings of SIGGRAPH 1996*, 99–108, Summer 1996.

[Turk92] Turk, G. Re-tiling polygonal surfaces. In *Proceedings of SIGGRAPH 1992*, 55–64, July 1992.

Collision Detection

[Baraff/Witkin98] Baraff, D., and A. Witkin. SIGGRAPH course notes on physically-based modeling. ACM SIGGRAPH Course Notes (CD-ROM), Orlando, FL, July 1998.

[Cameron90] Cameron, S. Collision detection by four-dimensional interaction testing. *IEEE Transactions on Robotics and Automation* 6(3):290–302, June 1990.

[Cameron97] Cameron, S. Enhancing gjk: Computing minimum and penetration distance between convex polyhedra. In *Proceedings of the International Conference on Robotics and Automation*, 1997.

[Cohen+95] Cohen, J., M. Lin, D. Manocha, and M. Ponamgi. I-collide: An interactive and exact collision detection system for large-scale environments. In *Proceedings of the ACM Symposium on Interactive 3D Graphics*, 189–196, 1995.

[Dobkin+90] Dobkin, D. P., and D. G. Kirkpatrick. Determining the separation of preprocessed polyhedra—A unified approach. In *Proceedings of the 17th International Colloquium on Automata Language Programming*, vol. 443 of *Lecture Notes in Computer Science*, 400–413. New York: Springer-Verlag, 1990.

[Garcia-Alonso+94] Garcia-Alonso, A., N. Serrano, and J. Flaquer. Solving the collision detection problem. *IEEE Computer Graphics and Applications* 14:36–43, May 1994.

[Gilbert+88] Gilbert, E. G., D. W. Johnson, and S. S. Keerthi. A fast procedure for computing the distance between objects in three-dimensional space. *IEEE Journal on Robotics and Automation* RA-4:193–203, 1988.

[Gottschalk+96] Gottschalk, S., M. Lin, and D. Manocha. Obb-tree: A hierarchical structure for rapid interference detection. In *Proceedings of SIGGRAPH 1996*, 171–180, 1996.

[Hubbard93] Hubbard, P. M. Interactive collision detection. In *Proceedings of the IEEE Symposium on Research Frontiers in Virtual Reality*, 24–31, October 1993.

[Hubbard95] Hubbard, P. M. Collision detection for interactive graphics applications. *IEEE Transactions on Visualization and Computer Graphics* 1(3): 218–230, September 1995.

[Hubbard96] Hubbard, P. M. Approximating polyhedra with spheres for time-critical collision detection. *ACM Transactions on Graphics* 15(3):179–210, July 1996.

[Hudson+97] Hudson, T., M. Lin, J. Cohen, S. Gottschalk, and D. Manocha. V-collide: Accelerated collision detection for VRML. In *Proceedings of the VRML '97 Conference*, 119–125, 1997.

[Lin] UNC collision detection software on the Web: *http://www.cs.unc.edu/~geom/collision_code.html*

[Lin93] Lin, M. C. Efficient collision detection for robotics and animation. Ph.D dissertation, University of California at Berkeley, 1993.

[Lin/Canny92] Lin, M. C., and J. F. Canny. Efficient collision detection for animation. In *Proceedings of the Third Eurographics Workshop on Animation and Simulation*, Cambridge, England, September 1992.

[Lin/Gottschalk98] Lin, M., and S. Gottschalk. Collision detection between geometric models: A survey. In *Proceedings of the IMA Conference on Mathematics of Surfaces, 37–56,* 1998.

[Lin+98] Lin, M., D. Manocha, J. Cohen, and S. Gottschalk. Collision detection: Algorithms and applications. In *Proceedings of the 1998 Conference on Algorithms for Robotics Motion and Manipulation* (Jean-Paul Laumond, M. Overmars, and A.K. Peters, eds.), 129–142, 1998.

[Lin/Manocha95] Lin, M. C., and D. Manocha. Fast interference detection between geometric models. *The Visual Computer* 11(10):542–561, 1995.

[Pratt93] Pratt, D. R. A characterization of virtual world and artificial reality systems. Ph.D dissertation, Naval Postgraduate School, Monterey, CA, June 1993.

[Preparata/Shamos85] Preparata, F. P., and M. I. Shamos. *Computational Geometry.* New York: Springer-Verlag, 1985.

[Zyda+93] Zyda, M. J., W. D. Osborne, J. G. Monahan, and D. R. Pratt. NPSNET: Real-time collision detection and response. *Journal of Visualization and Computer Animation* 4(1):13–24, January–March 1993. (Special Issue on simulation and motion control.)

Systems and Parallel Programming

[Birman/Marzullo92] *Birman, K., and K. Marzullo. The ISIS distributed programming toolkit and the META distributed operating system: A brief overview. *Mission Critical Operating Systems* (A. Agrawala, K. Gordon, and P. Hwang, eds.), 32–35. Amsterdam: IOS Press, 1992.

[El-Rewini+98] *El-Rewini, H., and T. G. Lewis. *Distributed and Parallel Computing.* Greenwich, CT: Manning Press, 1998.

[Schneider97] *Schneider, F. B. *On Concurrent Programming.* New York: Springer-Verlag, 1997.

Chapter 7

Resource Management for Scalability and Performance

So far, we have been concerned with the fundamental aspects of building net-VEs, including accessing the network, generating interactive graphics, sharing state, and managing the interactions among the various net-VE system components. Using these tools, one can develop net-VEs for LANs and even for the Internet. These net-VEs can support the full range of desired interactions among users. Indeed, the majority of net-VEs in use today are built using these techniques.

However, these basic net-VEs can support only a limited number of users, usually on the order of a few dozen. Moreover, they demand fast networks connecting the participating machines and run on machines having considerable processing capacity. These constraints are entirely reasonable for systems intended for small group interactions within a single organization, but, as we will see in Chapter 8, they are inappropriate for systems that will be deployed over the Internet, where hundreds or even thousands of users will participate in the net-VE simultaneously. For example, networked game players perpetually seek to interact with larger communities of players to form complex and realistic experiences. Even some non-Internet net-VEs demand these numbers of participants. For instance, military war gaming probably represents the most prevalent example of a large-scale net-VE. The military has envisioned systems supporting over 100,000 simultaneous entities [ARPA94], enough to simulate an entire military campaign. To support systems of this size, the net-VE designer must use a variety of new techniques for managing resources such as network bandwidth and processor capacity.

Even when sufficient resources are available for the net-VE, resource management still can be an important issue. Improved resource management can generally improve the interactive performance of the net-VE. For example, reduced processor load means that user actions can be processed more quickly at the local machine. Excess processor capacity then can be used to generate higher-quality graphics for the user. Moreover, reduced network load can lower the transmission latencies caused by network congestion and can therefore ensure that shared state information and updates are exchanged more quickly. By demanding fewer resources, net-VE software can coexist with other applications on the participants' machines and network, instead of demanding a dedicated environment. Indeed, multiple independent net-VEs may need to execute simultaneously over a single network. In general, therefore, the net-VE designer should always strive to avoid wasting available resources.

Resource management for net-VEs is an active area of research. Each net-VE uses a different combination of techniques, and a single commonly accepted suite of techniques has not yet emerged. This chapter provides an overview of the broad range of techniques used to improve the size and performance of net-VEs by reducing network bandwidth and processor resources. In presenting these techniques, we try to place them into a common conceptual framework by which they, as well as techniques created in the future, may be compared and evaluated. The chapter begins by explaining the close relationship between the system resources and the information requirements of a net-VE. It then discusses the four broad categories of resource management: communication protocol optimization, data flow restriction, leveraging of limited user perception, and system architecture modifications.

AN INFORMATION-CENTRIC VIEW OF RESOURCES

Aside from scene rendering and graphics processing, which were discussed in Chapter 6, network bandwidth and information processing are the two most significant bottlenecks in a net-VE. We therefore seek to minimize the demands on these resources to achieve improved scalability and performance. Before trying to manage these resources, however, it is worthwhile to review why net-VE systems place such heavy demands on them.

Network bandwidth provides the cornerstone of a net-VE. As we have seen, the network is used to exchange information so that participants maintain a consistent view of the virtual environment's state and so that participants can engage in real-time conversation. Network bandwidth requirements increase with the number of users in the net-VE. This growth occurs for three reasons.

1. Each of the additional participants must receive the initial net-VE state, as well as updates that the other participants are already receiving. Unless the new users are on the same broadcast LANs as the existing users, additional network resources are required to deliver that information.

2. Each additional participant potentially introduces new updates to the existing shared state of the net-VE and new interactions with existing users. Network bandwidth is required to disseminate these additional updates.

3. Each new user introduces additional shared state to the net-VE. At a minimum, each user has a position, orientation, and graphical representation. Moreover, each user may also bring other objects into the environment, with each of these objects also having its own set of shared state. More network bandwidth is required to share this new state information and updates to it.

In general, new users increase the amount of shared data and the level of interaction in the environment. Therefore, more network bandwidth is required to maintain the data and disseminate the interactions.

The host's processor is required to support the full set of tasks in a net-VE. It needs to maintain a full or partial copy of the virtual environment's current state, apply and disseminate updates initiated by the local user, receive and apply updates initiated by other users, and render the current state of the environment. Put another way, the processor is responsible for graphics generation, user input handling, network packet generation, network packet reception, and virtual environment update processing. As more users enter the net-VE, additional processor cycles are required at each of the existing users' hosts.

1. Each new user introduces more elements that the processor must render for display to the local user. For example, existing users must render the new users as well as the objects that those new users bring to the net-VE.

2. Because each new user introduces new shared state to the net-VE, the processor must cache this additional state, receive updates to this new state, and apply those updates to the cache.

3. Because each new user introduces additional updates to existing shared state and new interactions with existing users, the processor must be prepared to receive and handle the increased volume of updates to that information and support increased interactions with the local user.

In general, by increasing the amount of shared data and levels of interaction in the environment, each new user places an additional burden on the host processors already participating in the net-VE.

The bandwidth and processor implications of net-VE participation parallel each other closely. Ultimately, larger net-VEs contain more user interactions and shared state. These interactions and state updates must be exchanged over the network. This exchange consumes network bandwidth, and those packets must be generated, sent, received, and processed, and rendered by host processors.

This relationship between the networking and the processing in net-VEs represents the foundation for improving the scalability and performance of net-VEs. We refer to this relationship as the *Networked Virtual Environment Information Principle:*

> The resource utilization of a Net-VE is directly related to the amount of information that must be sent and received by each host and how quickly that information must be delivered by the network.

Put another way, the most scalable net-VE is one in which no networking is required (effectively presenting each user with a single-user virtual environment). For each piece of information—a state update, a chat message, an announcement, and so forth—that two hosts must exchange, the system incurs resource penalties in both bandwidth and computation. To achieve scalability and performance, therefore, the net-VE designer should strive to reduce the overall resource penalty incurred within a net-VE.

We may describe the Information Principle more concretely using the following equation:

$$\text{Resources} \approx M \times H \times B \times T \times P$$

where

M = number of messages transmitted in the net-VE
H = average number of destination hosts for each message
B = average amount of network bandwidth required for a message to each destination
T = timeliness with which the network must deliver packets to each destination (that is, large values of T imply that packets must be delivered with minimal delay, while small values of T imply that packets may be delivered with longer delays)
P = number of processor cycles required to receive and process each message

The net-VE designer can reduce the resource utilization by lowering any of the five variables in the Information Principle equation. However, as with any engineered system, the designer cannot improve one aspect of the system without impacting another aspect of the system.

Each reduction of a resource variable typically requires either a compensating increase in another variable or a compensating degradation in the quality of the net-VE experience (for example, its responsiveness to user actions, or the accuracy and realism of the rendered view of the environment). The choice of which Information Principle variables to reduce and, accordingly, which variables to penalize, depends on the purpose of the net-VE application and on what resources represent the most significant system bottlenecks.

We have already seen one example of applying the Information Principle equation. In Chapter 5, dead reckoning reduced the frequency of transmitted state updates. The approach effectively reduced the value of M (fewer messages sent per second) and compensated by increasing P (to compute and maintain the predicted position) and potentially degraded the realism the net-VE experience (because of the likely inaccuracy of the predicted position). We will now turn our attention to a variety of other techniques for adjusting the resource balance within a net-VE system. Table 7-1 summarizes these techniques and their impact on the Information Principle equation variables.

TABLE 7-1   Approaches to Resource Management

Approach	Impact on Information Principle equation	Description
Packet compression	Reduce B Increase P	Reduce size of packets by employing lossy or lossless techniques
Packet aggregation	Reduce M, B Increase P, T	Merge multiple updates into a single packet using timeout- or quorum-based techniques
Multicasting	Reduce H Increase M	Transmit updates to a subset of participating entities employing a group for each source entity or for each net-VE region
Area-of-interest filtering	Reduce H Increase M, P, T	Define explicit information filters and process at a subscription manager
Projection aggregations	Reduce H, B Increase M, P, T	Predefine fine-grain multicast groups for particular subscription filters
Reduced level-of-detail	Reduce H, B Increase M, P	Provide low-fidelity data channels for distant viewers
Temporal contour	Reduce T Increase P	Render remote entities using delays corresponding to perceived network latency
Server clusters	Reduce P (per host) Increase T	Employ servers that communicate peer-to-peer Create server hierarchies
Peer-server communication	Reduce T, B, M Increase T, B, M	Select between peer-to-peer and client-server communication based on network characteristics

OPTIMIZING THE COMMUNICATIONS PROTOCOL

Up to this point, whenever we needed to transmit data in the net-VE, we simply allocated a buffer for that packet, wrote the data into that buffer, and transmitted a packet containing the buffer contents. Although this transmission approach is simple, it is not always the most optimal. As we have seen, every network packet incurs a processing penalty at the sender and receiver. Moreover, every network packet must include TCP/IP, UDP/IP, or multicast header information that describes who sent the data, who should receive the data, and other transmission information.

We can improve resource usage, therefore, by applying simple optimizations that reduce the size of each network packet and that reduce the number of network packets that are actually transmitted. These optimizations fall under the categories of packet compression and aggregation. Broadly speaking, they seek to reduce the M (number of transmitted messages) and B (bandwidth per message) variables in the Information Principle equation while increasing P (processor requirements per packet) or affecting the presentation quality.

Packet Compression

Packet compression seeks to reduce the size of the packets transmitted within a net-VE. The sender is responsible for shrinking data for transmission, while the receiver is responsible for restoring the actual data. Table 7-2 summarizes the range of available compression options for net-VEs.

Compression may be either lossless or lossy. *Lossless compression* simply shrinks the data by changing its encoding format in the transmitted packet, but it does not affect what information is transmitted. For example, run-length encoding (RLE) replaces a sequence of zeroes with a token denoting a run of zeroes, followed by a count of the number of zeroes in that run; the destination host can easily reconstruct the original information content as long as it recognizes the token indicating the run of zeroes.

On the other hand, *lossy compression* may eliminate some of the transmitted information from the packet as part of the compression process. This type of data reduction makes particular sense if the information is relatively insignificant, is likely to be inaccurate, or consumes packet space that does not correspond to its value. For example, if an object is located at position (10.000000001, 13.999999999), a lossy compression scheme might round the data to (10,14) and transmit the position in 2 bytes instead of 8.

Packet compression can be either internal or external. *Internal compression* is what we normally think about when thinking of data com-

TABLE 7-2   Four Categories of Compression Techniques

Compression technique	Lossless compression	Lossy compression
Internal compression	Encode the packet contents in a more efficient format and eliminate redundancy within the packet	Filter information that is irrelevant or reduce the detail of the transmitted information
External compression	Avoid retransmitting information that is identical to that sent in previous packets	Avoid retransmitting information that is similar to that sent in previous packets

pression. This type of compression manipulates a packet based solely on its own content, without regard to what data has been transmitted in previous packets. Most forms of internal compression operate by detecting redundancy within the data being transmitted. For example, instead of sending the same byte sequence multiple times, the compression algorithm may provide the byte sequence once, associate that sequence with an ID number, and simply specify that ID number instead of including that byte sequence a second time in the packet.

In contrast, *external compression* manipulates the packet data within the context of what has already been transmitted in previous packets. For example, such a scheme might shrink a packet by representing it as a set of deltas from the most recently transmitted packet. Net-VE data streams tend to include a fair amount of duplicated information, particularly because much of the state in the net-VE does not change between successive packet transmissions. Consequently, external compression can yield greater bandwidth reduction than internal compression. However, external compression also introduces a dependency between different packets in the data stream. Because the compression takes advantage of data contained in previously transmitted packets, successful decompression requires that the receiver has received all of those previous packets. External compression therefore usually requires that packets be transmitted reliably or, at a minimum, that lost packets be recoverable.

The right choice (or combination) of compression algorithms tends to depend on the particular net-VE application in which they are being deployed. The decision depends on the frequency of packet updates, the content of those packets, and the communication architecture and protocols being used for packet distribution. The choice of optimizations is therefore typically derived by analyzing the traffic generated in prior executions of the net-VE to detect data duplication and other inefficiencies.

Protocol Independent Compression Algorithm

The Protocol Independent Compression Algorithm (PICA) [Van Hook+94] is a lossless, external compression algorithm used in early versions of the U.S. military's Strategic Theater of War (STOW) program. PICA eliminates redundant state information from successive update packets. As shown in Figure 7-1, the source host occasionally transmits numbered "reference" state snapshots for the entity being described, and receivers cache these snapshots. Subsequent update packets designate an associated snapshot number and a list of which

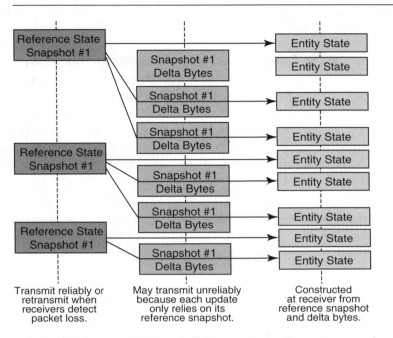

FIGURE 7-1   Using PICA, a host transmits entity state snapshots and byte deltas to those snapshots.

bytes in that snapshot have changed. The receiver uses the snapshot and the update packet to reconstruct the current entity state. Because each state update describes changes from the state snapshot, instead of simply from the previous packet, only the state snapshots need to be transmitted reliably. PICA can even be used over an unreliable communication protocol such as UDP/IP or multicast. Because each update identifies the number of the corresponding reference state, the receiver can detect when a state snapshot was not received and can request retransmission from the source. The receivers can therefore effectively implement a lightweight reliability protocol for state snapshots over the unreliable communications protocol.

The sending application delivers the complete state of an entity to the PICA compression module. The compression module is responsible for constructing the update packet by selecting the differences between the current state snapshot and the current entity state. When the number of byte differences exceeds a threshold, the PICA compression module transmits a new reference state snapshot containing a new sequence number and the entity's full state.

Localized Compression Using Application Gateways

Normally, compression and decompression would occur on the source and destination hosts. However, compression really only needs to be localized to areas of the network having limited bandwidth availability. By eliminating compression where bandwidth is ample, the system frees client hosts from wasting computational cycles for manipulating the data needlessly. In the STOW exercises, for example, WAN bandwidth was at a premium, so compression and decompression were performed only when the packet was leaving and entering the high-bandwidth LANs, as shown in Figure 7-2. In STOW, hosts transmit packets in their uncompressed form over the LAN, and they are intercepted by an *application gateway* (AG) application that compresses them before they enter the WAN [Calvin+95]. Similarly, packets arriving from the WAN reach an AG at the destination LAN where they are locally broadcast in their decompressed form.

Application gateways can provide other types of localized compression services for the net-VE. For example, in military simulations,

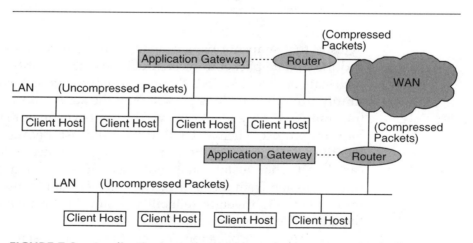

FIGURE 7-2   Application gateways reduce the processing burden on net-VE hosts by compressing and decompressing packets as they enter and leave areas of high bandwidth availability.

up to half of the network traffic has been attributed to dead or inactive entities that need to periodically broadcast their current (unchanging) state in order to announce their continued presence on the battlefield [VanHook93,VanHook94]. (This behavior is intrinsic to the DIS protocol [IEEE95] and makes the net-VE resilient to packet loss or intermittent breaks in network connectivity.)

To optimize this behavior, the STOW system used AGs to provide a *quiescent entity service* (QES) [Calvin+95] which eliminates these repeated update transmissions from the low-bandwidth WANs. The AG server detects when an entity has become inactive, or a host explicitly informs the server that a particular entity is no longer active. The AGs periodically exchange lists of dead or inactive entity IDs. While an entity is inactive, its local AG filters its updates from being transmitted over the WAN. Similarly, each AG is responsible for locally generating periodic state updates on behalf of inactive entities located on remote LANs and depositing those update packets onto the local LAN.

Packet Aggregation

Packet compression sought to reduce the average *size* of each packet by eliminating repetition both within an individual packet and between successive packets. *Packet aggregation*, on the other hand, seeks to reduce the *number* of packets that are actually transmitted by merging information from multiple packets into a single packet.

This packet merging saves network bandwidth by reducing the number of packet headers that are sent over the network. For example, every UDP/IP packet and every TCP/IP packet contains a protocol header of 28 and 40 bytes, respectively. If two packets are merged, therefore, then one of the headers is eliminated. Depending on the net-VE application protocols and the amount of data contained within each packet, aggregation can eliminate as much as 50% of the bandwidth requirements in a net-VE.

In some cases, aggregation can be implemented by simply capturing state information from all of the entities that reside on the local machine and merging that information into a single packet. Typically, this basic approach is appropriate when packets are transmitted at a regular frequency, as is done with frequent state regeneration schemes (see Chapter 5). In these schemes, each host transmits all of its entity updates at the same time, and the aggregation step simply collects those updates together into a single packet transmission. Consequently, aggregation does not adversely affect the quality of the net-VE experience in this case, because it does not artificially delay the transmission of entity updates.

However, updates for multiple entities generally are not generated simultaneously. For example, if a dead reckoning or prediction algorithm is used to reduce the frequency of update transmissions, then each entity generates update packets independently. In this case, for packet aggregation to occur, the source host must wait until it has enough packets to merge before it can actually send an aggregated packet over the network. The aggregation process therefore may need to artificially delay the transmission of update packets, meaning that receivers will rely on stale information for longer than they otherwise would have.

Aggregation Tradeoffs and Strategies

Packet aggregation imposes a tradeoff. By waiting longer to transmit an aggregated packet, aggregation offers greater potential for bandwidth savings (more packets might get merged) but reduces the value of the data (by delaying it). The transmission policy employed by the aggregation software defines how this tradeoff is managed [Singhal96].

With a *timeout-based transmission policy*, the packet aggregator collects individual packets and transmits them after waiting for some fixed timeout period:

```
create an empty packet
loop until an entity has generated an update
add that entity update to the packet
initialize the timeout
loop collecting entity updates and adding them to the packet

on timeout
    send packet
    restart procedure
```

This policy guarantees an upper bound on how much delay is introduced on an individual update packet and, therefore, the impact of aggregation on the quality of the net-VE.

On the other hand, the bandwidth and packet rate reduction provided by this policy varies depending on how often individual entities generate packets. At the extreme, it is possible that during the timeout period, no other entity generates any updates, so no aggregation (or bandwidth savings) occurs at all even though the transmitted packet still pays the aggregation delay penalty.

With a *quorum-based transmission policy*, the packet aggregator merges individual updates until the aggregated packet contains a certain number (the quorum) of updates:

```
create an empty packet
while the number of entity updates in the packet is less than the quorum
    wait for an entity update to be generated
    add the entity update to the packet
send packet
restart procedure
```

The quorum-based policy guarantees a particular bandwidth and packet rate reduction. The level of bandwidth reduction is determined by the quorum, which designates how many updates are merged into each aggregated packet. However, the quorum policy imposes no limitation on how much delay may be introduced to a particular entity update. Indeed, a single update can be delayed indefinitely while the aggregator waits for enough packets to merge into the transmission.

These two aggregation strategies force the net-VE designer to make an explicit decision about whether to prioritize the net-VE data timeliness (impose a timeout) or the net-VE bandwidth reduction (impose a quorum). Timeout-based transmission bounds the delay placed on updates at the expense of a higher update rate. Moreover, the transmission behavior is independent of the number or types of entities that are generating updates. This independence is desirable because it frees the net-VE designer from the difficult task of selecting appropriate quorum values in environments where each host may manage a different type or number of entities and where the type or number of entities at each host may dynamically change during the net-VE execution. On the other hand, though its delay characteristics are less predictable, the quorum-based approach can manage to transmit considerably fewer packets than timeout-based transmission.

It is possible to merge these two aggregation strategies to achieve a middle-ground solution. For example, one can designate a transmission timeout and preempt the timeout once a quorum of entity updates has been aggregated:

```
create an empty packet
loop until an entity has generated an update
```

```
add that entity update to the packet
initialize the timeout
while the number of entity updates in the packet is less than the quorum
   wait for an entity update to be generated
   add the entity update to the packet
cancel timeout
send packet
restart procedure

on timeout
   send packet
   restart procedure
```

This hybrid transmission approach offers the advantage of adapting to the dynamic entity update rates. At a slow update rate, the timeout prevails and bounds the amount of delay on the updates. At a rapid update rate, the quorum prevails and achieves the target level of update aggregation. As a further positive side effect, when the net-VE is changing rapidly and entities are generating updates at a fast rate, the hybrid strategy accordingly increases the rate of packet transmission, allowing remote hosts to react more quickly to these changes.

Aggregation Servers

So far, we have considered aggregation strategies that a single host may use to merge update packets from the multiple entities that it manages locally. However, these strategies face inherent limitations. Aggregation is only possible on those hosts that manage multiple entities, but in many simulations, each host only manages a single entity. Moreover, the tradeoff between network bandwidth and data timeliness is largely determined by which entity updates are available to be aggregated. In general, with a larger pool of available entity updates, larger aggregation packets can be generated more quickly, hence providing an improvement along both dimensions (timeliness and bandwidth) of the aggregation tradeoff. With a larger pool of entity updates available, one may furthermore be able to separate the updates into *projection aggregations*, each representing a set of entities having a common characteristic such as virtual world location or entity type. Projection aggregations are discussed in more detail later in this chapter.

These limitations can be addressed by introducing *aggregation servers* into the net-VE system. Instead of (or in addition to) disseminating entity updates directly to other participants over the network, hosts transmit those updates to one or more aggregation servers. These servers collect updates from multiple source hosts and, using one of the aggregation strategies that we have discussed, disseminate aggregated update packets. The aggregated updates may therefore contain entity data from multiple source hosts.

A single net-VE may have multiple aggregation servers. For example, each aggregation server might be responsible for managing updates generated from a different LAN. Alternatively, each aggregation server might handle updates for a different entity type. One server might handle fast-moving airplanes while another server handles slow-moving bicycles, or one might handle the red team while another handles the blue team. Finally, each aggregation server might handle updates for a different region of the virtual world. In short, the net-VE designer has considerable flexibility in defining the precise configuration of aggregation servers.

The use of multiple aggregation servers offers several advantages. Clearly, it reduces the need for a single high-power machine by distributing the workload across multiple processors. It improves the fault-tolerance characteristics of the net-VE should one of the servers fail. The use of multiple servers also can improve the overall performance of the aggregation process. For example, placing an aggregation server on each LAN ensures that updates do not need to travel far from their source hosts before entering an aggregation queue. Moreover, if a single entity type is assigned to a server, then the aggregation packets for that entity type tend to be generated at a more predictable frequency and a more predictable size because similar entities tend to generate updates at a common rate.

Finally, a sophisticated net-VE configuration may include servers that construct aggregations based on different entity characteristics, such as location, type, or LAN. An entity must therefore transmit its updates to multiple aggregation servers. When combined with the flow restriction techniques described in the next section, the availability of many aggregation types can prove to be quite powerful. For example, recipients have more flexibility to subscribe to aggregations representing only those entities that are of local interest.

CONTROLLING THE VISIBILITY OF DATA

The protocol optimizations that we have discussed so far have sought to reduce the network bandwidth requirements of the net-VE by reducing the average number of bits required to describe a particular entity. The second class of resource optimizations aims to reduce bandwidth by reducing the average number of hosts that receive each message. Broadly speaking they seek to reduce the H (number of hosts) and B (bandwidth per message) variables in the Information Principle equation while slightly increasing M (number of transmitted messages).

The underlying assumption behind data flow restriction is that the net-VE contains a tremendous amount of information, yet an individual user only needs to know a small portion of the total available information. Therefore, instead of broadcasting each packet to every participating host, the net-VE designer should strive to send information only to those hosts that really need it. By limiting the dissemination of data, the aggregate bandwidth requirements of the net-VE can often be reduced.

Data flow optimizations can be expressed generally using the *aura-nimbus* information model [Greenhalgh/Benford97], as illustrated in Figure 7-3. Entity data should only be made available to those entities that would be capable of perceiving that information; this sphere of influence constitutes the source entity's *aura* and may restrict destination entities based on virtual world location, entity type, sensor capabilities, or any other set of characteristics. Similarly, each entity is only interested in receiving information from a particular set of entities in the virtual world, as again defined by virtual world location, entity type, or other characteristics; this sphere of interest constitutes the destination entity's *nimbus*. In an ideal world, each piece of information would be processed individually and delivered only to entities whose nimbi intersect with the source entity's aura.

Unfortunately, the aura-nimbus approach, which was used in the MASSIVE-1 system [Greenhalgh/Benford95], does not scale effectively to large numbers of entities. The system requires considerable processing resources. Moreover, because each packet is associated with a custom set of destination entities, the system cannot easily take advantage of network data dissemination efficiencies such as multicasting. Therefore, most of the techniques that this section discusses attempt to approximate the pure aura-nimbus model in a scalable manner.

Data flow management can be divided into three broad categories: area-of-interest filters, multicasting, and subscription-based aggregation. Area-of-interest filters are explicit data filters provided by each host, allowing the net-VE to perform fine-grained data management to

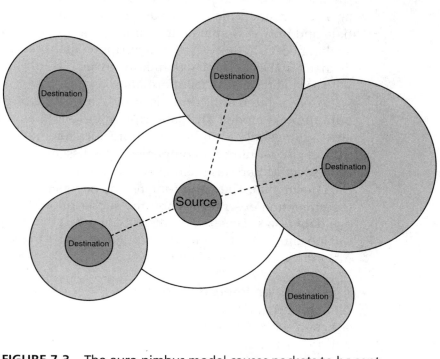

FIGURE 7-3 The aura-nimbus model causes packets to be sent between a source entity whose aura intersects with the nimbus of a destination entity.

deliver only the information that the host needs. Multicast involves taking advantage of subscription-based network routing protocols to restrict the flow of data. Subscription-based aggregation represents a hybrid between these two approaches, grouping the available data into fine-grain "channels" to which destination hosts may subscribe.

Area-of-Interest Filtering Subscriptions

Under an *area-of-interest filtering* scheme, hosts transmit information to a set of *subscription managers,* alternatively referred to as "area-of-interest managers" or "filtering servers." These subscription managers also receive subscription descriptions from each of the participating hosts in the net-VE. For each piece of transmitted data, the subscription managers determine which of the subscription requests are satisfied by that data and only disseminate the information to the corresponding subscribing hosts. In this way, the subscription managers can be thought of as matchmakers, who try to link the available information with hosts who are interested in that information.

Area-of-interest filtering is simply a restricted form of the pure aura-nimbus model. The subscription descriptions really specify the subscribing entity's nimbus. In a pure aura-nimbus system, each piece of data also would be accompanied by a dissemination description, an aura specification designating which entities are permitted to receive the information. The area-of-interest managers would process both the dissemination descriptions and the subscription descriptions to manage data flows. The area-of-interest approach that we consider in this section eliminates the aura descriptions in order to reduce the processing and bandwidth load on the system.

A Subscription Interest Language

A subscription description can be arbitrarily complex. It usually consists of a sequence of filters or assertions based on the values of fields within each packet. These assertions may furthermore be joined together via conjunction ("and") or disjunction ("or") operators. More sophisticated filter languages may support programmable functions, where the subscribing client can invoke arbitrary Boolean function modules from within the interest subscription. For example, these function modules might be packaged as Java class files that are uploaded for execution at the subscription manager.

To illustrate the use of subscription filtering languages, we consider the following Lisp-like syntax, which is a popular way of specifying a subscription filter:

```
(OR  (EQ TYPE "Tank")
     (AND (EQ TYPE "Truck")
          (GT LOCATION-X 50)
          (LTE LOCATION-X 75)
          (GT LOCATION-Y 83)
          (LTE LOCATION-Y 94)
          (EQ PACKET-CLASS INFRARED)))
```

The EQ, GT, and LTE operators in this expression correspond to the standard binary "equals," "greater than," and "less than or equal" operators. Similarly, OR and AND denote the standard conjunctive operators.

The expression terms reference the values of various packet fields, namely TYPE, LOCATION-X, LOCATION-Y, and PACKET-CLASS. By asserting this expression, a host indicates that it is interested in all packets generated by tanks, as well as any infrared packets generated by trucks located within the region bounded by (50,83) (not-inclusive) and (75,94) (inclusive).

The filter grammar may be described more formally using the following Backus-Naur grammar:

```
Subscription ::= Directive
Directive    ::= Negation | Conjunction | Disjunction | Expression
Negation     ::= "(NOT" Directive ")"
Conjunction  ::= "(AND" Directive Directive+ ")"
Disjunction  ::= "(OR" Directive Directive+ ")"
Expression   ::= "(" Operator Packet-Field-ID Constant ")"
Operator     ::= "EQ" | "GEQ" | "GT" | "LEQ" | "LT"
```

Upon receiving an interest subscription in this language, the subscription manager can compile it at runtime for efficient execution. To support this compilation, the subscription manager defines the following base class:

```
class Expr {
    // Constructor takes a list of Expr objects
    Expr(Expr[]);
    // Returns the i-th element of the Expr list
    Expr getExpr(int i);
    // Evaluate the expression for the given packet
    int eval(packet);
}
```

This class is extended, or subclassed, for each type of expression supported by the filtering language. Some examples of such extensions are shown in Listing 7-1. Clearly, additional classes would be provided in similar style for other packet fields, for other logical operators such as "equals" and "not equals," and for other conjunctive operators such as "or" and "not."

LISTING 7-1   Sample Expression Classes for a Filtering Language

```
class EqualsExpr extends Expr {
    int eval(packet) {
        return (getExpr(0).eval(packet) == getExpr(1).eval(packet));
    }
}
class AndExpr extends Expr {
    int eval(packet) {
        Expr expr;
        int i = 0;
```

```
             // Return false if any of the expressions is false
        while ((expr = getExpr(i++)) != null) {
            if (! expr.eval(packet))
                return false;
        }
        return true;
    }
}
class ConstantExpr extends Expr {
        // Stores an int value for expression
    ConstantExpr(int value) { /*... */ }
    int eval(packet) {
        return /* ... */ ;    // Returns constant value
    }
}
class PacketLocationXExpr extends Expr {
    int eval(packet) {
            // X location is in slot zero
        return (packet.getLocation())[0];
    }
}
```

An interest subscription can be compiled using a simple parser. The basic pseudocode is shown in Listing 7-2. This parser simply reads the operator keyword for each expression and instantiates an appropriate Expr subclass to represent that expression. The parser invokes itself recursively to process the subexpressions that make up the arguments for each expression. Finally, the parser outputs the single top-level Expr object that represents the entire filter subscription.

LISTING 7-2   Pseudocode for Compiling an Interest Expression at Runtime

```
/* We assume that InterestExpression provides methods for
 * accessing the components of an expression.  For example,
 * given an InterestExpression "ie" representing:
 *    (OR (EQ X 3) (GT Y 8) (LT Z 9))
 * then
 * ie.getOperator() returns the string "OR"
 * ie.getArgCount() returns 3
 * ie.getArg(0) returns an InterestExpression holding "(EQ X 3)"
 * ie.getArg(1) returns an InterestExpression holding "(GT Y 8)"
 * ie.getArg(2) returns an InterestExpression holding "(LT Z 9)"
 */
Expr parse(InterestExpression ie) {
    String op = ie.getOperator();
    if (op is an integer)
        return new ConstantExpr(op.toInt());
    if (ie equals "LOCATION-X")
```

```
            return new PacketLocationXExpr();
            /* Handle other packet fields similarly */
        if (op equals "EQ") {
                /* Recursively parse the two equality arguments */
            Expr [] exprList = new Expr[2];
            exprList[0] = parse(ie.getArg(0));
            exprList[1] = parse(ie.getArg(1));
            return new EqualsExpr(exprList);
        }

            /* Handle GT, LT, etc. similarly */
        if (op equals "AND") {
                /* Recursively parse the conjunction arguments */
            int count = ie.getArgCount();
            Expr [] exprList = new Expr[count];
            for (int i = 0; i < count; i++)
                exprList[i] = parse(ie.getArg(i));
            return new AndExpr(exprList);
        }

            /* Handle OR and NOT similarly */
    }
```

Once an interest subscription has been compiled in this manner, it can be evaluated at runtime by simply invoking the `eval()` method on the packet, as follows:

```
if (expr.eval(packet))
    /* Transmit packet to interested client */
```

The type of top-level `Expr` object returned by the parser determines which `eval()` function is actually invoked by the above code.

That `eval()` function encodes the operation represented by the interest subscription and can therefore efficiently determine whether the given packet satisfies the subscribing client's data request. If the expression accepts the packet (for example, the `expr()` function returns true), then the packet should be transmitted to the client that registered this interest subscription.

We may extend our filtering subscription language so that source hosts can include priority values with each filter expression. For example, information originating from distant regions or from regions that are partially occluded is generally of less importance than information originating from nearby regions. These priority values can be used by the subscription manager to more closely manage its own system resources. For example, when network bandwidth or computational resources are at a premium, the subscription manager may choose not to evaluate the low-priority filter expressions [Capps/Teller97]. As a result, the high-priority filters ensure that the most important information is delivered to each client, but as system resources are exceeded, the less important information may be blocked because the corresponding low-priority filter is not executed.

JPSD: A Sample Filtering Subscription-Based System

The Joint Precision Strike Demonstration (JPSD) [Powell+96] is a military net-VE built to train army tactical commanders. Most of the entities in the system are artificially constructed entities that do not have any human controller. The system has been demonstrated with up to 6,000 participating entities modeled on 80 hosts.

Rather than introducing distinguished subscription manager hosts, JPSD places the subscription management responsibility directly at each source host in the system. A host manages the subscriptions for all of its local entities. The host then sends packets directly to interested clients using peer-to-peer unicast protocols.

The interest subscriptions are described as logical predicates similar in form to the subscription interest language described above. The interest language operators include equality and "within range" (essentially a merged greater-than and less-than operator). In addition, the interest subscription language includes facilities for invoking external function modules. However, the implementation avoids the complexity of dynamically migrating client code to the subscription managers. Instead, the function modules are provided in a library that resides at each subscription manager host. This use of function modules effectively allows the subscription language to be extended statically without having to change the parser. To extend the subscription language, the net-VE designer adds new function modules to the filtering language library at each host.

Evaluating the Role of Filtering Subscriptions

Because each host can specify its own subscription request and because the subscription descriptions may be arbitrarily complex, an area-of-interest subscription can ensure that a host does not receive extraneous information that it will subsequently discard. Each host receives a customized flow of information. This model is appropriate under five circumstances.

1. Participating hosts have limited processor capacity and cannot afford the cost of receiving and processing unnecessary packets.

2. Participating hosts are connected over extremely low-bandwidth links, so network utilization must be minimized at all costs.

3. Multicast and/or broadcast protocols are not available, so point-to-point transmission is the only available method for exchanging information.

4. Client subscription patterns change rapidly so that the host cannot tolerate the delay introduced as the network adjusts the multicast group routing to accommodate its entry into or departure from the multicast group.

5. The net-VE designer cannot determine any a priori categorizations of net-VE data, and the group-per-entity approach is too resource-expensive.

The biggest cost of area-of-interest filtering is the increased network bandwidth required when a significant number of hosts are interested in the same piece of information. Because each receiver effectively receives a customized data stream, data generally must be unicast from the subscription managers to each recipient. As a result, a piece of data may travel multiple times over the same network link on its way from the filtering server to the interested hosts. Network multicasting directly serves to eliminate this duplication, but it cannot be used with area-of-interest filtering.

Area-of-interest filters provide what can be called *intrinsic filtering* because the filter must inspect the application content within each packet to determine whether it should be delivered to a particular destination host [Morse96]. The set of fields that must be inspected is determined by the area-of-interest filter provided to the subscription manager. By being aware of the packet contents, intrinsic filtering can dynamically partition data based on fine-grained entity interests. An alternative approach, *extrinsic filtering*, does not consider application-level information but instead filters packets based on network properties such as the packet's destination address. Extrinsic filtering can be implemented more efficiently than intrinsic filtering and may even be performed within the network itself. On the other hand, the level of filtering cannot be as sophisticated as that provided by intrinsic filtering. Instead, the net-VE designer must statically partition the data based on assumptions about the subscription patterns of the participating entities. These subscriptions are the topic for the next subsection.

Multicasting

Multicasting is a network protocol technique whereby the application transmits each packet to a *multicast group* by supplying a special *multicast address* as its destination (see chapter 3 for more details on multicasting and how programs may use it). The packet is only delivered to those hosts who have subscribed to the multicast group. To receive a multicast packet, therefore, a host must first subscribe to (join) the corresponding multicast group. Similarly, to stop receiving those packets, the host must unsubscribe from (leave) the multicast group. A host may be subscribed to multiple multicast groups simultaneously. Any host may transmit data to any multicast group, regardless of whether it is currently subscribed to that group.

Compared to broadcast protocols, multicasting is relatively efficient, as shown in Figure 3-3. From each data source, the multicast group is represented as a shortest-path tree through the network with the source host at the root and the destination hosts at the leaves. The branches of the tree are network links, and the internal tree nodes are routers and gateways in the network. When a packet is transmitted, a single copy of the packet travels along each network link in the multicast tree. Whenever the packet encounters an internal node in the multicast tree, the packet is copied so that it may travel along the descendant branches.

As a result of this distribution method, the packet only travels to parts of the network that have interested subscribers. If no remote hosts are currently interested in the packet, then it travels no farther than the source host's local LAN. In general, if only a few hosts are members of the multicast group, the packet is likely to travel only over a small fraction of the network links that a broadcast packet otherwise would traverse to reach all participants in the net-VE.

The key challenge for implementing multicast-based solutions is determining how to partition the available data among a set of multicast groups. Successful multicasting demands that each multicast group deliver a set of related information. In other words, subscribers to a multicast group should be interested in receiving most, if not all, of the information that is transmitted to that group. If a multicast group delivers many types of completely unrelated information, then it will attract subscribers who are only interested in a subset of the transmitted information. As a result, much of the group's transmissions will be disseminated to network locations where they are not required. In the worst case, each client might be interested in a small subset of information from every multicast group and consequently must subscribe to every available multicast address. In this case, the whole multicast system would degenerate into a broadcast system.

Group-per-Entity Allocation

One approach to the multicast group mapping problem is to assign a different multicast address to each entity in the net-VE [Abrams/Watsen/Zyda98]. Like the area-of-interest filtering scheme, this approach allows each host to receive information about all hosts that lie within its nimbus. Each net-VE host executes its subscription filter locally, based on available information about what entities exist in the net-VE. It then subscribes to the multicast groups for entities that are of local interest. However, unlike the area-of-interest approach, information subscriptions can only be made on a per-entity basis, rather than on a per-packet basis. Because information is transmitted on a fixed multicast group per entity, entities cannot specify their aura and have no control over which hosts will receive that information.

This multicast allocation approach was employed in the Stanford PARADISE system [Singhal/Cheriton96]. Each entity subscribed to information for entities located nearby in the virtual environment. Entities could also control their directional information interests. For example, a vehicle could subscribe to nearby entities that are behind it and subscribe to both nearby and distant entities located in front.

This multicast allocation technique can be extended to assign multiple multicast group addresses to each entity. The entity can then transmit specific types of information to each of these multicast groups. For example, an entity's position updates may flow on one group while its infrared data may be transmitted in another group. In this way, heat sensors can choose to receive only the infrared information without being burdened with the physical position data. By introducing more multicast groups into the system, a net-VE provides information at a finer granularity, allowing a host's nimbus to be more closely approximated by multicast group subscriptions.

To deploy the group-per-entity technique effectively, the net-VE must provide a way for hosts to learn about the entities that are located nearby in the virtual world and the multicast addresses used by those entities. To provide these capabilities, the net-VE typically provides some sort of entity directory service that tracks the current state of participating entities. Each entity periodically transmits state information over one or more designated directory multicast addresses. The directory servers collect these periodic state announcements and provide the information to any entity that requests an updated list of entities in its nimbus.

Such an entity location service is provided by the Diamond Park net-VE developed at Mitsubishi Electric Research Laboratories (MERL) [Barrus+96]. Directory servers, known as *beacon servers*, exist for each region of the virtual environment, as shown in Figure 7-4. Each beacon server has a designated multicast address for receiving information about entities in the associated region. The beacon servers also share a well-known beacon multicast group used by clients to query for and locate the appropriate beacon server for a particular virtual world region.

This allocation of one multicast group per entity is potentially costly in large net-VEs. It consumes a large number of multicast addresses. Because the pool of multicast addresses is shared among all Internet multicast applications and is only weakly regulated, a large net-VE is likely to collide with one or more other applications using those multicast addresses. Many multicast groups also create an overhead on net-

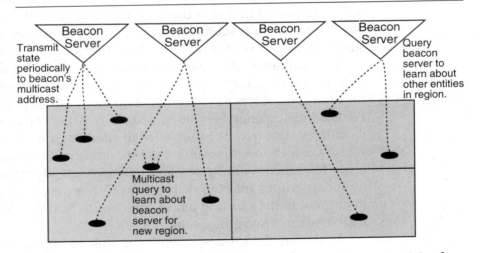

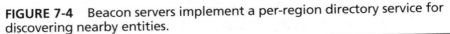

FIGURE 7-4 Beacon servers implement a per-region directory service for discovering nearby entities.

work routers, which must process the corresponding large number of group membership join and leave requests. It introduces network traffic for group discovery, as hosts need to learn the multicast addresses for each of the entities in which they are interested. Finally, most network cards today can only support a limited number (in the dozens) of simultaneous multicast address subscriptions. When a host exceeds this limit, the card enters "promiscuous mode" and receives all multicast packets sent on the local LAN. Promiscuous mode reduces system performance because it forces packet processing to be performed within the software protocol stack.

To address these limitations, the net-VE designer can impose an upper bound on the number of multicast addresses that are used by the net-VE. Once all of the available addresses have been assigned to entities, they are then recycled for use by other entities [Milner95]. It is possible that multiple entities may share a single address; however, that single address can still be thought of as representing multiple logical multicast groups. Entities can be dynamically reassigned to multicast groups that become available as other entities depart the net-VE. To change its multicast address assignment, the entity simply needs to update the directory service and transmit a reliable notification to its current subscribers about the new multicast address.

It is worth noting that group-per-entity multicasting has a number of properties that make it amenable to optimizations as the Internet evolves [Holbrook/Cheriton98]. Each multicast group only has a single sender, and that sender's identity does not change. Consequently, the network routers only need to maintain a single multicast distribution tree for each multicast group. Consequently, the amount of router state information can be reduced and multicast packet processing within the routers can be enhanced. These and other optimizations to the multicast routing protocols represent an active area of research.

Group-per-Region Allocation

Instead of assigning a multicast address to each entity, net-VE designers may partition the virtual world into regions and assign each region to one or more multicast groups. Each entity simply transmits its data to groups corresponding to regions that cover its current location. Similarly, each entity subscribes to groups corresponding to the regions in which it has interest, generally corresponding to the regions that are immediately adjacent to the entity.

The group-per-region design permits entities to have limited control over their aura by permitting information dissemination to be restricted to particular regions of the net-VE. However, subscribers have even less control over their nimbi, because they can only filter information according to the sender's location. The group-per-region approach effectively manages communication overhead by limiting aura and nimbus specifications to fall within a small number of spatial categories.

Unlike the group-per-entity approach in which each entity transmits over the same multicast group throughout its lifetime, the group-per-region approach requires each entity to change its target group(s) as it travels throughout the virtual world. The transmitter must track the bounds of its current region and, upon entering a new region, learn the multicast addresses associated with that region. The region boundaries and the mappings from region to group addresses are often defined statically and installed as part of the net-VE software on each host. However, more sophisticated systems collect this information in a central directory service, similar to the beacon servers described above.

Traditionally, the virtual environment is partitioned into rectangular grid regions. Experimental versions of the Modular Semi-Automated Forces (ModSAF) system statically assigned multicast addresses to each grid region and achieved good performance using 5-kilometer grids [Russo+95, Smith+95, Rak/VanHook96]. The Close-Combat Tactical Trainer (CCTT) uses a similar approach, assigning a multicast address to each 5-kilometer grid [Mastaglio/Callahan95]. The system goes a step further, however, by allowing the application to designate interest in a grid region as well as a particular packet type such as motion, detonation, etc. The interest specification is implemented as a multicast group subscription based on the grid region, with client-side software filtering incoming packets based on their type.

Grid-based region assignments have the disadvantage of having many points at which multiple grids meet. As an entity approaches one of these corners, it must subscribe to groups corresponding to all of the regions that meet at that corner, as shown in Figure 7-5. To alleviate this difficulty, the NPSNET system divides the virtual environment into hexagonal regions, in which only three regions intersect at any given point, instead of four [Macedonia+95]. In a hexagonal system, entities within each region cooperate to implement a dynamic directory service. The entity that has been active within the region for the longest time

This is History City, an application built on top of NetEffect. To date, 5,000 copies of History City have been distributed to children in Singapore and the system has been operational since 1997. Further information on History City is available at *http://www.historycity.org.sg* The picture here shows one of the 21 History City communities and avatars of several children exploring the community. *Source:* Image courtesy of Dr. Gurminder Singh, Director, Learning Lab, Kent Ridge Digital Labs, 21 Heng Mui Keng Terrace, Singapore 119613. Fax: +65 774-4998; Tel: +65 874-3651; Email: gsingh@krdl.org.sg; *http://www.krdl.org.sg/RND/learning*

Narrative Immersive Constructionist and Collaborative Environment (NICE) is a collaborative learning environment to teach young children the concept of how to plan and grow a virtual garden. The broader research goal of this project is to develop techniques for collaborative interaction and learning. *Source:* Image courtesy of Jason Leigh, Andrew E. Johnson, Maria Roussos, Christina Vasilakis, Thomas G. Moher, Craig Barnes. Electronic Visualization Laboratory and the Interactive Computing Environments Laboratory, University of Illinois at Chicago, 1996; *http://www.evl.uic.edu/cavern*

This image presents the Community Place Browser used to navigate within virtual worlds. Here the avatars represent other players. The right window is the multiuser window where the player can send and/or receive text and trigger some behaviors (waving, and so forth). *Source:* Image courtesy of Hubert Le Van Gong and the Sony Corporation.

The U.S. Army's Close Combat Tactical Trainer (CCTT) is one of the larger-scale net-VEs. CCTT is the centerpiece of the Combined Arms Tactical Trainer (CATT) program. CCTT will train armor, cavalry, and mechanized infantry platoons through battalion task force on their doctrinal mission training plan collective tasks. The CCTT system consists of the following components: networked simulator manned modules, semiautomated forces, operation center workstations, after action review systems, and computer networks and protocols. CCTT provides a robust VE that can be used for other simulators designed to be CCTT interoperable. *Source:* U.S. Army Simulation, Training and Instrumentation Command (STRICOM), Donnie Martello and Mike Macedonia; *http://www.stricom.army.mil*

Virtual environments can accommodate individual soldiers as well as vehicles. Simulated entities can take into account physical and natural structures such as buildings and trees. *Source:* Image courtesy of Warren Katz and Fred Wersan of MÄK Technologies; *http://www.mak.com*

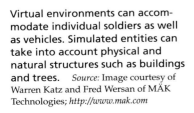

The CyberCafe lobby, where the user selects an avatar and attaches behavior and personality before entering the VRML-based virtual environment. *Source:* Courtesy of David Lection, IBM Corporation.

This is a Schmoozer avatar about to cross locale boundaries. The Schmoozer authoring environment includes "Port" objects, which are the small gold diamonds with green upper faces just above door's threshold. Beacon objects attached to these Ports are used to make the connection, and the origins of two diamond Port objects are overlayed to designate the spatial relationship between the two locales—the white brick hallway the avatar is in at present and the large room directly ahead. *Source:* Image courtesy of Bill Lambert, Mitsubishi Electric ITA, and David Anderson, Mitsubishi Electric Research Laboratories; *http://www.meitca.com/opencom* and *http://www. meitca.com/opencom/schmoozer*

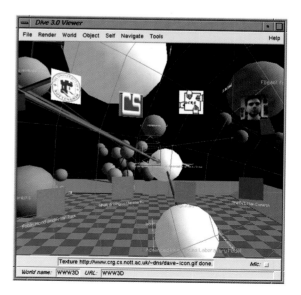

WWW3D, a 3D collaborative Web browser, constructed using the DIVE 3.0 system. *Source:* Courtesy Dave Snowdon, Nottingham University, UK. "A 3D Collaborative Virtual Environment for Web Browsing," Dave Snowdon, Steve Benford, Chris Greenhalgh, Rob Ingram, Chris Brown, Dave Lloyd, Lennart Fahlén and Mårten Stenius, presented at *Virtual Reality Universe '97*, April 2–5 (Westin Santa Clara Hotel, California, USA).

The Fraunhofer collaborative virtual environment (CVE). Participants are avatars with live video textures. Various other types of data are used in the environment including shared models, application sharing, and spatialized conferencing audio. The avatars are equipped with telepointers for rudimentary data interaction and referencing within the environment. *Source:* This work is a joint collaboration between the Fraunhofer Center for Research in Computer Graphics and the Institute for Graphics, Darmstadt, within the Transatlantic Research and Development Environment program. Image courtesy of Bob Barton and Lars Karle, Fraunhofer CRCG, Providence, Rhode Island; *http://www.crcg.edu*

This is the Sarcos I-port input device, the NPSNET-IV networked virtual environment, and the University of Pennsylvania Jack ML human. *Source:* Image courtesy of Michael Zyda, Naval Postgraduate School; *http://www.npsnet.nps.navy.mil*

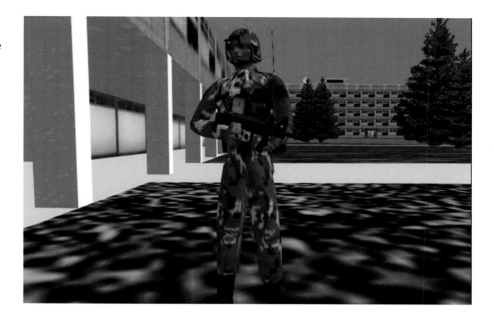

The NPSNET-IV networked virtual environment and the Boston Dynamics BDI-Guy human.
Source: Image courtesy of Michael Zyda, Naval Postgraduate School; *http://npsnet.nps.navy.mil*

The Sarcos Treadport input device, the NPSNET-IV networked virtual environment, and the University of Pennsylvania Jack ML human. The Treadport is a hospital treadmill, with a robot arm to recenter the human in the rear-projected virtual environment.   *Source:* This demonstration took place at the AUSA '95 Conference, Washington, DC. Image courtesy of Michael Zyda, Naval Postgraduate School; *http://www.npsnet.nps.navy.mil*

The Virtual Space Devices Omni Directional Treadmill, the NPSNET-IV networked virtual environment, and the Boston Dynamics BDI-Guy human.   *Source:* Image courtesy of Michael Zyda, Naval Postgraduate School; *http://www.npsnet.nps.navy.mil*

A virtual environment for exploration of business information.   *Source:* The image appeared in Thomas A. Funkhouser, Ingrid Carlbom, Gary Elko, Gopal Pingali, Mohan Sondhi, and Jim West, "A Beam Tracing Approach to Acoustic Modeling for Interactive Virtual Environments." *Computer Graphics* (SIGGRAPH '98), 21–32, Orlando, July 1998. The work was sponsored by Bell Laboratories, Lucent Technologies.

A view from the seventh floor of Soda Hall, as seen in the Berkeley Interactive Walkthrough Program. *Source:* Image courtesy of Richard Bukowski and Carlo Sequin, Computer Science Department, University of California at Berkeley.

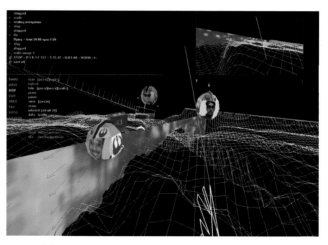

Five collaborators at four sites (using 3 ImmersaDesks and 2 desktop workstations) tour a virtual Chesapeake Bay. CAVE5D 2.0 displays the bay's bathymetry, measured time-dependent turbidity, and flow-velocity data. The Virtual Director framework provides navigation in space and time, virtual camera control, and communication between participants. *Source:* Courtesy of Glen Wheless, Cathy Lascara (CCPO, Old Dominion University); Virtual Director: Donna Cox, Robert Patterson, Stuart Levy (NCSA, UIUC), Marcus Thiebaux (EVL, UIC). Participating during Supercomputing 1998: Russell Burgett (ODU), Satheesh Subramanian (EVL), Umesh Thakkar (NCSA), and several of the others mentioned here.

The Virtual Tennis system of the University of Geneva and Ecole Polytechnic Féderal du Lausanne. *Source:* Image courtesy of Nadia Magnenat-Thalmann, University of Geneva, and Daniel Thalmann, EPFL; *http://miralabwww.unige.ch/*

Hacienda screen capture from Rainbow Six game.
Source: Courtesy of Red Storm Entertainment, Morrisville, NC; *http://www.redstorm.com*

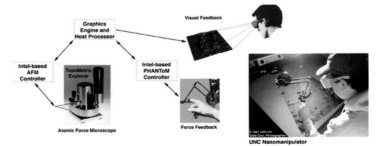

This is the UNC nanoManipulator (nM) system. The networked components here are the graphics, haptics, and microscope systems.
Source: The nM project is a collaboration between the UNC departments of Computer Science, Physics and Astronomy, and Chemistry; the School of Library Science; and the School of Education. The project is developing an improved, natural interface to scanning probe microscopes, including Scanning Tunneling Microscopes and Atomic Force Microscopes. The nM couples the microscope to a VR interface to provide a telepresence system that operates over a scale difference of about a million to one. Courtesy of Russell Taylor, UNC at Chapel Hill.

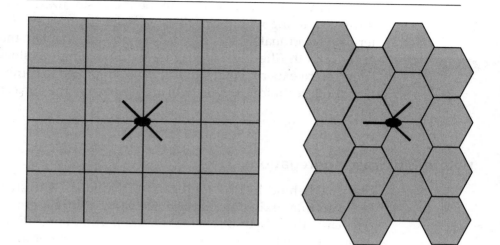

FIGURE 7-5 In a rectilinear grid (*left*), an entity may need to transmit to up to four multicast groups; a hexagonal grid (*right*) requires a maximum of three simultaneous group transmissions.

plays the role of group leader. As an entity enters the region, it multicasts a *join packet*, and it sends a *leave packet* upon leaving the group. That leader maintains a list of all of the entities currently in the region and provides that list to any host that transmits a join packet in the region.

Though easy to implement, a regular tessellation of the virtual environment may cause a region boundary to fall in an inconvenient location. For example, if a region boundary falls in the middle of a hallway, then all entities traveling along that hallway must subscribe to the multicast groups for both adjacent regions. Ideally, therefore, the regions should be constructed around the actual structure of the virtual environment. In the Diamond Park system [Barrus+96], each region, called a locale, can have an arbitrary geometric structure and an independent coordinate system. The locales are then "stitched" together to form the complete virtual environment. The boundary of each locale is associated with a translation, rotation, and scaling matrix that provide a transformation between the local coordinates of that locale and the local coordinates of the adjacent locale.

Ideally, a net-VE would combine the customized subscriptions of ̇rinsic filtering with the multicast efficiency provided by extrinsic fil- ̇ing. Unfortunately, it is generally impossible to retain the full advantages of both filtering approaches within a single system. However, some recent experimental systems have attempted to combine elements from both techniques. This hybrid approach is the subject of the next subsection.

Hybrid Multicast Aggregation

The goal behind hybrid aggregation techniques is to strike a balance between fine-grain data partitioning and multicast grouping. On the one hand, these hybrid schemes aim to partition net-VE data into fine-grain multicast groups, thereby allowing each client to tune its set of subscriptions based on local interests; fine-grain multicast grouping allows each client to receive a form of intrinsic filtering that approximates its nimbus. At the same time, hybrid schemes ensure that the partitioning is not so fine-grained that data transmission degenerates into simple unicast; in other words, the multicast groups must still be broad enough to include multiple source entities and multiple potential recipients, thereby guaranteeing some level of extrinsic filtering within the network.

The three-tiered interest management system [Abrams+98] provides one example of a hybrid technique providing fine-grain multicast groups. The system provides three levels of data filtering.

1. A group-per-region scheme segments data based on location within the virtual environment. The regions are themselves organized into a spatial hierarchy (such as a quadtree or octree), and each region in the hierarchy is associated with its own multicast address. As each entity moves through the virtual environment, it transmits updates at a particular depth of the hierarchy; the hierarchy depth is chosen based on the entity's size and speed of motion. To subscribe to all information within a region, a host subscribes to all levels of the hierarchy that intersect the desired region.

2. A group-per-entity scheme allows receivers to select individual entities at a fine-grain level of detail.

3. Area-of-interest filter subscriptions are supported by library routines on each subscriber's host. Although the interface to this filtering library is portable, its implementation depends on the particular protocols and services available in the net-VE. At its simplest, the filtering library operates locally by inspecting inbound packets and discarding them before they are processed by the net-VE application.

The three-tiered interest management framework effectively partitions the nimbus filter into a portion that is processed by extrinsic filtering within the network and a portion that is processed by intrinsic filtering at the destination host. The hierarchical region groups are of particular interest because, besides *explicitly* segmenting information according to location within the virtual environment, they also *implicitly* segment information based on entity size and speed.

The concept of fine-grain multicast groups can be generalized to explicitly represent multiple parameter values [Singhal96]. For example, suppose that each entity in a net-VE has a type and a location. Each multicast group therefore may be associated with a set of entity types and entity locations, as shown in Figure 7-6. One multicast group might include tanks located between (10,25) and (35,40) while another group includes cars located between (85,70) and (110,85) in the net-VE. In this way, the entity type attribute therefore is effectively "projected" onto the entity location attribute.

These multiattribute multicast groups are referred to as *projections*, and data transmitted to each projection typically satisfies multiple attribute constraints. A projection is formally described using the following restricted interest language:

```
(AND expr₁ expr₂ expr₃ ... exprₙ)
```

where each expression may be one of the following three types:

```
(GTE Packet-Variableᵢ Value)
(LT Packet-Variableᵢ Value)
(EQ Packet-Variableᵢ Value)
```

In other words, each projection restricts the values of one or more variables in the entity's packets. Each attribute value must either fall into a particular range or equal a particular value.

To send a packet, a host simply determines which projection's requirements are satisfied by the packet and transmits the packet to the

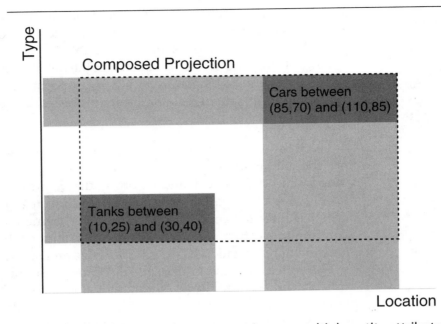

Type

Composed Projection

Cars between
(85,70) and (110,85)

Tanks between
(10,25) and (30,40)

Location

FIGURE 7-6   Projections impose constraints on multiple entity attributes.

corresponding multicast address, much as was done for the three-tiered spatial hierarchy groups. The restricted interest language described above also lends itself to efficient processing at the transmitting host because each projection specification can be processed using a simple table-driven interpreter. In many systems, the set of projection filters and associated multicast group assignments can be specified statically, meaning that the projection analysis can be compiled directly into the net-VE application.

A client host subscribes to the set of projections whose information corresponds to data of local interest. This subscription is performed by comparing each projection's interest filter with the client's intrinsic filter (nimbus). If the two filters have a nonempty intersection, then the client subscribes to the projection's multicast address. As the client's interests change, it dynamically adjusts the set of outstanding projection subscriptions.

For additional bandwidth reduction, projections can be combined with aggregation. Instead of transmitting data directly to the projection's multicast group, source hosts can send data to an appropriate *projection aggregation server*. Each server is responsible for managing one or more projections. These servers are responsible for collecting data for each projection and transmitting aggregated packets that contain multiple individual updates. The resulting *projection aggregations* consume less network bandwidth than standard projections. They provide an efficient way to subscribe to information from a large set of entities. Projection aggregations are therefore perfect for supporting the needs of pan-view displays, radar, and other system monitoring entities.

To further support subscriptions to large numbers of entities, projection aggregations may also be defined to group information from multiple projections [Singhal/Cheriton96]. For example, consider the projections given previously (in Figure 7-6): one including tanks located between (10,25) and (35,40) and a second including cars located between (85,70) and (110,85) in the net-VE. A projection aggregation may be defined that contains all vehicles located between (10,25) and (110,85) in the net-VE.

We can extend the projection filter language to support efficient projection composition. Using a new operator, one may define a high-level projection by simply merging the interest specifications of the component projections:

```
(INCLUDE group_1 group_2 group_3 . . . group_k)
```

This assertion, which is used instead of an AND expression, simply causes the packet to be transmitted to the associated projection group if it was also sent to one of the listed projection groups.

Visibility filtering is a topic of active research. As we have seen, there is a rich range of options, many of which can be tuned to the particular net-VE data characteristics and execution environment. We now turn our attention to the third broad class of resource reduction techniques, leveraging knowledge about human perception.

TAKING ADVANTAGE OF PERCEPTUAL LIMITATIONS

Up to this point, we have considered techniques that reduce network bandwidth by either sending fewer bits in each packet or by reducing the number of hosts that receive each message. However, if a host is interested in receiving information about a particular entity in the net-VE, neither of these techniques reduces the actual number of entity updates that the host receives from the source or relaxes the demand on the network to deliver the data in a timely manner. The third class of optimizations addresses both of these concerns by tuning the data flows and data processing to match more closely the fidelity requirements of the users at the receiving hosts.

This class of optimizations essentially reduces H (the number of hosts that receive each message), B (the average size of each message), and T (delivery timeliness requirements) in the Information Principle equation. To achieve these results, the techniques introduce a higher value of M (number of transmitted messages) by requiring each host to transmit more packets. This balance may at first seem paradoxical: By transmitting more packets, the net-VE, in fact, reduces its overall resource requirements. This situation arises because the additional packet counts are more than offset by the significant reductions in both the average number of destinations and the average size of each packet.

This class of optimization techniques exploits knowledge that the net-VE participant, be it a human user or a computer-controlled sensor, has inherent perceptual limitations. By recognizing these perceptual limitations, the net-VE system can reduce the amount and timeliness of information that must be presented to that participant.

For example, humans have limited visual capabilities. If an object is far away, humans cannot discern intricate appearance or location details. Moreover, human perception is relatively forgiving about small inaccuracies in a rendered scene. Small inaccuracies do not necessarily disrupt the overall sense of realism underlying the net-VE experience. In many situations, the net-VE can take advantage of this knowledge of the human user to reduce how much information must be delivered to each receiver.

In this section, we consider two ways in which human perceptual limitations are exploited to reduce net-VE resource requirements. First, information about entities in the virtual environment can be provided at multiple levels of detail and at different update rates. Only the users who are located near the entity in the virtual environment need to receive the high-detail (more data within each update and higher frequency of updates) information, while others can be adequately serviced with less detail (less data within each update and lower frequency of updates). Second, hosts can take advantage of perceptual limitations to mask the timeliness characteristics of information that they are receiving about remote entities. If particular information does not directly concern the local user, then the user need not see up-to-date representations. By presenting the user with a slightly out-of-date representation of distant entities, the net-VE reduces the real-time delivery requirements of the network without noticeably affecting the realism of the user's net-VE experience.

Exploiting Level-of-Detail Perception

Up to this point, we have treated all of the data transmitted by a net-VE entity in a uniform manner. In other words, when a user wishes to learn about the entity, that user receives all of the update packets generated by that entity, whether it be through a dedicated multicast address, through a region-based multicast address, or via an aggregation service. However, a single data stream is inappropriate for servicing all net-VE participants.

On the one hand, nearby viewers expect to see the entity rendered with full graphical detail and with accurate structure, position, and orientation. In some cases, these users may require update rates approaching their local frame rate to achieve accurate graphical display. They may require even higher rates if they are performing collision detection, collision resolution, or physical force modeling.

On the other hand, distant viewers can tolerate rendering the entity with less graphical detail and with less accurate information about its current structure, position, and orientation. Many inaccuracies cannot even be detected on a finite-resolution graphical display; for example, if an entity is rendered at a distance, then small position errors will not actually cause the entity to be rendered at a different pixel location. Moreover, because the distant entity is unlikely to be the focus of attention, small errors are not generally of critical importance. Thus, transmitting high-resolution to these distant viewers imposes unnecessary bandwidth burdens on the network and processing burdens on the receiving hosts.

A Multiple-Channel Architecture

To meet the needs of these different viewer constituencies, each entity can transmit multiple independent data *channels*, each providing information at a different level of detail and with a different frequency. For example, a low-resolution channel might provide updates once every

20 seconds and contain only the entity's position. A high-resolution channel, on the other hand, might provide updates every 3 seconds and include the entity's position, orientation, and dynamic structure. Viewers only subscribe to the channel providing the required level of detail.

Although the source host transmits more packets overall, the overall network bandwidth requirements of the net-VE are actually reduced. The multiple channels allow distant viewers to shift their data subscriptions away from high-frequency, high-bandwidth information and toward low-frequency, low-bandwidth information. Moreover, in general, relatively few viewers actually demand the high-resolution data at any one time. Therefore, although the source host actually transmits more packets, each receiver, on average, receives fewer and smaller packets. The overall network resource demands are reduced by substituting expensive channels with cheaper channels for most receivers.

The entity's data channels may be implemented in a variety of ways, corresponding to the network software architecture in use by the net-VE. For example, in client-server systems, the server is responsible for dispatching data from the individual channels to the attached clients according to their information needs. Each transmission to the server must identify which channel should be associated with the update packet. However, the receiving client can be largely oblivious to the existence of multiple channels, because the server dynamically determines which channel information is needed by that client.

In systems that assign a multicast address for each region of the virtual environment, channels are introduced by simply designating multiple addresses for each region. For example, one address provides all of the entities' high-resolution channels, while another provides all of the entities' low-resolution channels. Assuming that the regions are not too large, most users will not need to subscribe to multiple addresses simultaneously for the same region of the virtual environment; it is rare for a viewer to demand high-resolution from one entity while requiring low-resolution from a neighboring entity.[1]

---

[1] Our previous discussion of projection aggregations would seem to contradict the view that a receiver would treat all entities within a particular geographic region equivalently. Strictly speaking, it is rare for a viewer to demand high-resolution from one entity while only requiring low-resolution from a neighboring entity, *as long as the entities are of the same type*. If a net-VE designer wishes to segment entities within a region by type, then he or she would allocate a multicast address for each entity type and level-of-detail combination within each region.

In systems that assign each entity to an independent multicast address, channels may be introduced by simply allocating multiple addresses to each entity; subscribers can therefore subscribe to the appropriate multicast address for the entity's channel that satisfies the local information needs. The different multicast addresses are registered in the entity directory service, where subscribers can locate them. The directory must provide sufficient information with each address to allow viewers to autonomously select among the available channels based on needed graphical detail and display accuracy, available network bandwidth, and processor availability. For example, a directory entry should indicate the expected packet frequency and packet size, a list of information provided within each update packet, and the average expected remote modeling errors that viewers will experience by relying on the channel.

Finally, because each channel corresponds to a different level of data frequency, a system may also introduce different levels of reliability to each channel [Kessler/Hodges96]. For example, for channels that generate low-frequency updates, a lost packet can have a significant impact on receivers because they will rely on stale information for an extended period of time. Consequently, these channels may require the use of a reliable multicast scheme allowing receivers to quickly detect packet loss without waiting for the next update to be transmitted. For frequently updated channels, however, such reliability mechanisms are not needed because lost packets will be quickly replaced by subsequent updates. Therefore, the entity directory must also indicate which transmission protocol is used for each channel.

Selecting the Channels to Provide

Source hosts face a tradeoff in deciding how many channels to provide for an entity. By offering more channels, the source increases the chances that each remote host can select a channel that closely matches its particular rendering accuracy and computational requirements. However, each supported channel also imposes a cost, both in terms of computation at the source host and in terms of bandwidth on the host's local network (because that link must carry traffic for all of the channels, even if no receivers are interested in receiving those packets). Moreover, if each channel has a small number of subscribers, then multicasting offers fewer efficiencies because there are fewer opportunities to eliminate transmission redundancies over each network link.

Experimentation has shown that to satisfy this tradeoff between supporting a large variety of viewer needs while controlling computation and bandwidth near the source, the source typically only needs to provide three channels for each entity [Singhal96]. The channels provide order-of-magnitude differences in structural and positional accuracy and also provide order-of-magnitude differences in packet rate. The three channels—which we refer to as the rigid-body channel, approximate-body channel, and full-body channel—support far-range, mid-range, and near-range viewers, respectively.

Rigid-Body Channel

The *rigid-body channel* demands the least network bandwidth and processor computation. The source host transmits enough information to allow remote hosts to represent the entity as a rigid body, hence ignoring most changes to the entity's structure. Consequently, this channel is used when the entity is distant from the local viewer; structural changes would be imperceptible or uninteresting. When a viewer can see hundreds or thousands of entities in the net-VE, the host must subscribe to rigid-body channels for most visible entities, to avoid consuming excessive bandwidth and computational resources. The channel provides three types of updates.

1. *Position:* The current location of the entity in the virtual environment
2. *Orientation:* The current rotation of the entity in the virtual environment
3. *Structure:* A significant structural event has occurred to the entity. A structure update announces the new geometry to use for rendering the entity. Receivers do not learn about minor changes to entity structure.

A particular packet transmission may include any one or multiple update types. The position and orientation updates are transmitted relatively infrequently to ensure that the packet rate is kept low.

Approximate-Body Channel

The *approximate-body channel* provides more frequent position and orientation information to remote hosts. In addition, it enables remote hosts to render a rough approximation of the entity's dynamic structure (including the location of appendages or other articulated parts). Because it provides some information about the entity's structure, this channel consumes more bandwidth than a rigid-body channel, and receivers must dedicate more computational resources to handle the higher update rate and process the additional entity attributes. Remote hosts subscribe to the approximate-body channel for nonrigid entities that are close enough so that the local viewer can notice structural changes, but are far enough away so that the viewer can tolerate some structural inaccuracy.

The type of structural information provided in an approximate-body channel is entity-specific. The updates correspond to a simple physical model chosen to correspond to the dominant changes that occur to the entity's structure. The common structural approximations include the following.

1. *Radial length:* This model is appropriate for entities whose dominant structural change involves motion toward and away from a center point. For example, an inflatable balloon or a blowfish may be modeled in this way. As shown in Figure 7-7(a), update packets include the entity's current average radius. Remote hosts use this information to expand or shrink the image of the entity on their display.

2. *Articulation vector:* When the entity has well-defined appendages, the update packet can simply designate a vector to describe the current direction of the appendage, as shown in Figure 7-7(b). This approach is appropriate, for example, when modeling the rotating turret of a tank or the arms and legs of a human. It should be noted, however, that the approximation only describes the appendages' attachment points and not all of the entity's movable joints. The viewer therefore sees the appendage rotated into the correct direction but still does not see a fully accurate rendering of either the entity's or appendage's structure.

3. *Local coordinate system points:* The structural approximation may describe the current location of a subset of the entity's significant vertices relative to the entity's local coordinate system. As shown in Figure 7-7(c), this approach is appropriate when the entity is composed of multiple components which may move independently of each other or when the entity's structure is completely ill defined. It is appropriate, for example, when describing wiggling Jello. The receiving host simply

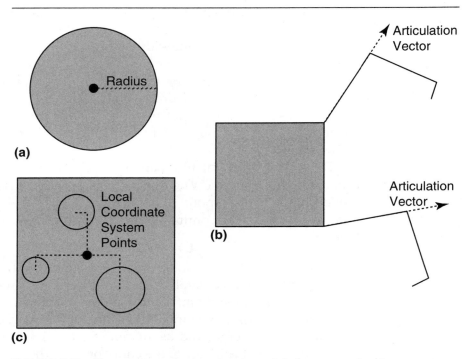

FIGURE 7-7 Three common structural models for approximate body channels: (a) radial length, (b) articulation vector, and (c) local coordinate system points

perturbs the entity's structure by moving vertices according to information contained in the packet and by interpolating the entity's structure between those vertices.

Full-Body Channel

A *full-body channel* provides the highest level of detail about the entity's dynamic position, orientation, and structure. To provide this level of information, these channels impose higher bandwidth and computational requirements than either the rigid-body or approximate-body channels. Consequently, a viewer can only subscribe to a limited number of full-body channels at any one time; in particular, a viewer needs this information when the entity is located nearby in the virtual world or when the viewer is interacting with the entity. The frequent updates transmitted along this channel include the entity's current position and orientation. The entity's structure is described by providing the location of every movable vertex. Upon receiving the update, the viewing host can construct a new geometric model for the entity and render the current structure.

The three-channel system can be augmented with receiver-initiated feedback to enable greater flexibility. Normally, the update frequencies or dead reckoning error thresholds, if prediction is being used to remotely model entity position and orientation, are fixed in advance for each channel. However, source hosts can also support *dynamic rethresholding* based upon feedback provided by active subscribers to each channel. Each remote host subscribes to the channel most closely matching the locally desired bandwidth and accuracy. The subscriber then periodically (for example, once per minute) notifies the source of its ideal bandwidth utilization and modeling error. Based on the set of recently received requests, the source then chooses an appropriate error threshold, either by satisfying the average of the requests, by satisfying the highest fidelity requirement, or by satisfying the lowest bandwidth requirement.

Summary of Multiple Channels

In summary, by providing multiple channels, a source host simultaneously supports the low-fidelity, medium-fidelity, and high-fidelity requirements of its entity viewers. Multiple channels improve scalability by allowing each viewer to independently determine its rendering accuracy requirements for each entity, as well as how much bandwidth and computation to allocate. In the worst case, when compared to the traditional single-channel approach, multiple channels introduce some additional overhead, particularly more computation at the source host, additional traffic on the network links closest to the source, and potentially some additional bandwidth at destination networks if multiple hosts subscribe to different channels. However, in the common case, multiple channels reduce the aggregate traffic and computation throughout the net-VE by shifting most subscriptions toward the lower frequency, lower data volume updates.

Exploiting Temporal Perception

The use of multiple-fidelity channels provides receivers with less frequent updates about an entity's location and behavior. Hosts use those received updates to dead reckon the entity's current position. Consequently, the user sees what should be an up-to-date representation of the entity, though that representation is largely inaccurate because it is based on stale or incomplete information. In other words, the rendered location approximates the entity's current location, though the entity might never actually have been located at the rendered location. As we have seen, this approach improves net-VE scalability by reducing the amount of detailed information that must be transmitted over the network.

An alternative approach to exploiting perceptual limitations is to render the entity in an accurate, albeit slightly out-of-date, location; the entity was actually at the rendered location, though it was there at some time in the past. As long as the local user is not interacting directly with the rendered entity, these small temporal inaccuracies can be safely hidden inside the rendered net-VE. This approach, which is essentially a formalization of the frequent state regeneration techniques discussed in Chapter 5, has a number of advantages.

1. Because packet recipients can explicitly hide the effects of network latency, the net-VE can be safely deployed over wide area networks having greater latency.
2. These techniques can further enhance the use of packet aggregation techniques that artificially delay the transmission of data to reduce network bandwidth requirements, as described earlier in this chapter.
3. These techniques can enhance the use of dead reckoning and other prediction techniques by significantly reducing the required prediction time interval and consequently limiting the potential prediction error. When temporal techniques are used, prediction is used primarily to hide the effects of short-term network latency bursts rather than to provide an accurate model of the entity's current position.

Active and Passive Entities

This manipulation of temporal perception mirrors how information is conveyed in the real world [Ryan/Sharkey97]. For example, when looking at stars in space, we perceive them as they looked in the past, because the accuracy of our perception is limited by the speed of light. "Information" from each star has its own time delay according to the source's physical distance from the Earth; planets in our solar system, for example, have a latency of several minutes, while distant stars can have a latency of several million years. The temporal perception model for net-VEs applies the same principle by rendering the net-VE scene according to the network latency encountered by information arriving from the remote entity.

Temporal perception techniques distinguish between active and passive entities. An *active entity* is one that takes actions (and therefore generates update notifications) on its own. Active entities include all human participants, as well as computer-controlled entities. Because receivers generally cannot predict the behavior of an active entity with complete accuracy, these entities are rendered using state updates that they transmit, adjusted for the network latency required to deliver these events to the remote viewer. A *passive entity*, on the other hand, only reacts to events from its environment and does not generate its own actions. Passive entities include all inanimate objects in the net-VE, such as rocks, balls, and books. Because active entities interact with passive entities, the net-VE must render each passive entity according to the network latency (that is, in the same time frame) of its nearest active entity. In this way, users perceive that the passive entity reacts instantaneously to actions taken by its adjacent active entity.

A Simple Example

As an example of manipulating temporal perception with active and passive entities, consider a networked version of the old *Pong* arcade game [Buckwalter77]. In this two-player game, which is essentially a two-dimensional version of Ping-Pong, each player controls a paddle that can only move vertically. As shown in Figure 7-8, a ball bounces back and forth between the players, and a player loses by allowing the ball to move past his or her paddle.

This distributed application consists of two active entities, namely the users' paddles [Harvey97]. Because the paddles are controlled by human users, their movement is mostly unpredictable. In particular, a remote computer cannot predict whether a player will actually hit the ball. The ball, on the other hand, is a passive entity because once it is hit by a player's paddle, its motion is determined and predictable. For example, once the ball is hit, it travels along a straight path or bounces deterministically against the walls of the playing region until it reaches the other player's paddle.

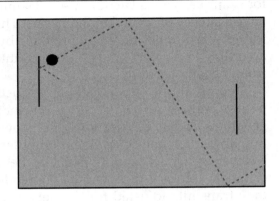

FIGURE 7-8   The game of *Pong*. The dashed line shows the expected trajectory of the ball as it moves from left (Player 1) to right (Player 2).

Now, let us consider how the game is rendered on Player 2's display. The network introduces a delay of d seconds on all information about Player 1's movements. In particular, Player 2's machine cannot determine whether the ball was hit by Player 1's paddle until d seconds after the event occurred. Consequently, to avoid seeing inaccurate information, Player 2 must see Player 1's location as it was d seconds in the past [Harvey97], as shown in Figure 7-9(a) with Player 1 on the left and Player 2 on the right. Obviously, if Player 1's past actions are being rendered, then the ball must also be rendered as it was d seconds in the past in order to give the appearance that Player 1 is actually interacting with the ball; if Player 1's paddle and the ball were to be rendered in different time frames, then the ball would not appear to touch Player 1's paddle, even though it is hit by the paddle.

Once the ball has been hit by Player 1, it begins to travel toward Player 2. Because the local user may now potentially interact with the ball, Player 2's display must begin to render the ball's location at the current time because otherwise, Player 2 would attempt to move his or her paddle according to the ball's previous location (d seconds in the past). As the ball moves across the playing field toward Player 2, therefore, it effectively travels at an artificially faster rate. As shown in Figure 7-9(b, c), the displayed time frame for the ball accelerates from d seconds in the past toward the current time. By the time the ball reaches

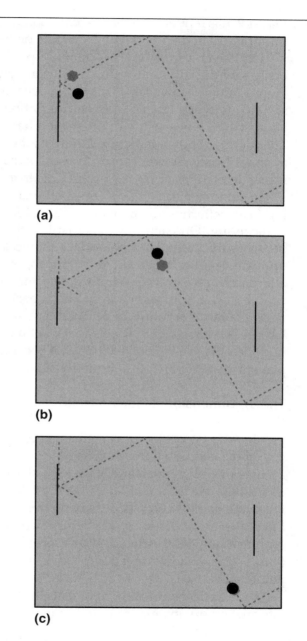

(a)

(b)

(c)

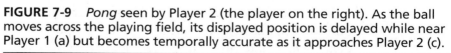

FIGURE 7-9 *Pong* seen by Player 2 (the player on the right). As the ball moves across the playing field, its displayed position is delayed while near Player 1 (a) but becomes temporally accurate as it approaches Player 2 (c).

Player 2, it is rendered in the current time, which is the same as the time frame associated with Player 2's paddle on his display.

On Player 1's display, the opposite process occurs. Player 1 previously saw the ball rendered at its current actual location, as shown in Figure 7-10(a). However, as the ball moves toward Player 2, there is a d second network latency for learning about the ball's true position because of the possibility of interaction between Player 2 and the ball. Therefore, as shown in Figure 7-10(b, c), the ball must effectively travel at an artificially slower rate on Player 1's display, as its displayed time frame decelerates from the current time to d seconds in the past.

In summary, each player sees a different representation of the playing field, reflecting the network latencies for information that the host is receiving. On each player's display, the ball accelerates as it approaches the local player's paddle and decelerates as it approaches the opposing player's paddle. In doing so, the ball's rendered position alternates between the current time reference (for the local player to enable meaningful interaction) and a past time reference (for the remote player to account for network latency). As long as the network latency is not too big, the ball's variable time frame should be relatively unnoticeable to each player, though it becomes quite obvious if the two players' displays are placed side-by-side.

The 3½-Dimensional Playing Field

We may represent each player's perception of the *Pong* game from the previous section as a four-dimensional coordinate system, (x,y,z,t). The x, y, and z coordinates correspond to the spatial position of each point in the game playing area relative to the local player's current position. (Naturally, in this particular game, the z value of all points is 0 because the game is played on a flat playing field.) For example, the center of the player's paddle is always positioned at $(0,0,0)$, with $(1,0,0)$ representing a point to the right, $(-1,0,0)$ corresponding to a point to the left, $(0,1,0)$ corresponding to a point above, and $(0,-1,0)$ corresponding to a point below.

The fourth coordinate, t, represents the time associated with rendered information originating from that spatial location. For example, because the player's paddle is rendered at the current time, its position has $t = 0$. Indeed, the entire vertical path of the player's paddle has $t = 0$. On the other hand, because the opposing player's paddle is rendered with a delay of d, it (and indeed all points along its vertical path) has $t = -d$.

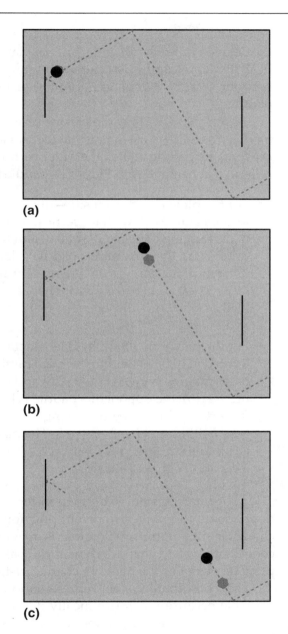

(a)

(b)

(c)

FIGURE 7-10 *Pong* seen by Player 1 (the player on the left). As the ball moves across the playing field, its displayed position is temporally accurate while near Player 1 (a) but becomes delayed as it approaches Player 2 (c).

As the ball moves across the playing field, it accelerates and decelerates smoothly between the present time ($t = 0$) of the local player and the delayed time ($t = -d$) of the remote player. Each point on the playing field therefore can be associated with an appropriate t value, ranging between 0 and $-d$, depending on the distance from the local player's paddle.

Assuming that a linear interpolation is used, the *Pong* playing field is modeled as follows, assuming that the playing field has horizontal width w (from one paddle to the other) and vertical height h. Player 1's paddle is located at height h_1 and Player 2's paddle is located at height h_2.

- For the player on the left side—that is, Player 1—the paddle is located at $(0,0,0,0)$ with its vertical motion region having coordinates ranging between $(0,-h_1,0,0)$ and $(0,h-h_1,0,0)$. As shown in Figure 7-11(a), the opponent's paddle is located at $(w,h_2-h_1,0,-d)$ with its vertical motion region having coordinates ranging between $(w,-h_1,0,-d)$ and $(w,h-h_1,0,-d)$. The playing field may be characterized as $(x,y,0,t)$ with x between 0 and w, y between $-h_1$ and $h-h_1$, and t equal to $-xd/w$.

- For the player on the right side—that is, Player 2—the paddle is located at $(0,0,0,0)$ with its vertical motion region having coordinates ranging between $(0,-h_2,0,0)$ and $(0,h-h_2,0,0)$. As shown in Figure 7-11(b), the opponent's paddle is located at $(-w,h_1-h_2,0,-d)$ with its vertical motion region having coordinates ranging between $(-w,-h_2,0,-d)$ and $(-w,h-h_2,0,-d)$. The playing field may be characterized as $(x,y,0,t)$ with x between $-w$ and 0, y between $-h_2$ and $h-h_2$, and t equal to $-(w+x)d/w$.

The coordinate system is defined independently for each player and depends on the player's current position and on the network delay characteristics of information that is arriving at that player's host. The coordinate system changes dynamically as the player moves about the playing area or as the network characteristics change.

This coordinate system representation of the *Pong* playing area is valuable because it algorithmically defines how any passive object in the playing area should be rendered. For example, if the *Pong* game is extended to include multiple balls (and other flying objects), the local coordinate system for each player determines the appropriate time for

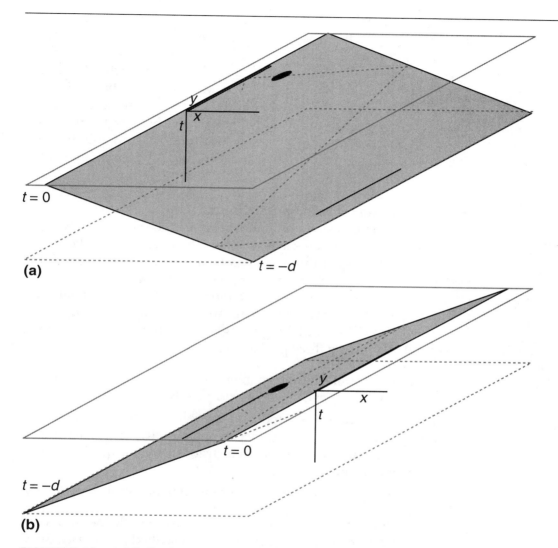

(a)

(b)

FIGURE 7-11   A 3½-dimensional coordinate system for the *Pong* game, as perceived by (a) Player 1 and (b) by Player 2. Network latency (*t*) represents the additional dimension (depicted vertically). Each player is locally rendered at the origin with *t* = 0, and each player is remotely rendered with *t* = –*d*.

rendering each object. The coordinate system ensures that two interacting objects (that is, two objects that are located at the same location) are rendered at the same time reference point. Consequently, each user perceives all object collisions correctly, including all interactions between those objects and the opposing player. Moreover, all objects that approach the local user are rendered in the user's current time frame, so the user can interact naturally with them. Finally, because the time field is smooth and continuous, objects appear to move smoothly through the playing field even though they are traveling between different time reference frames.

Generalizing the Local Temporal Contour

Our *Pong* example has two limitations. First, each player is only capable of moving along a single axis. In a net-VE, users expect to be able to move freely through a three-dimensional environment. Second, the system only supports two active objects. A large-scale net-VE would contain many more active users. The four-dimensional coordinate system defined in the previous section can be generalized to support a richer set of net-VEs. In making this generalization, the system must preserve the following three properties.

1. The local user must be able to interact (collide, acquire, relinquish) naturally with passive objects in the vicinity.
2. The local user must see remote interactions (between passive objects and between passive objects and an active object) naturally. These interactions include object collisions, object acquisition, and object relinquishment.
3. The local user must perceive smooth motion of remote objects.

The generalization, as described in [Sharkey+98], defines a smooth four-dimensional contour for each user. As described previously, the x, y, and z coordinates for the region are determined relative to the local user's current position, with the local user positioned at (0,0,0). Each active object in the net-VE is assigned a t value corresponding to the network latency experienced by the local host for updates originating from that object; the local user has a t value of 0. The four-dimensional coordinates assigned to each active object, including the local user, constitute a set of anchor points, as shown in Figure 7-12. A differentiable

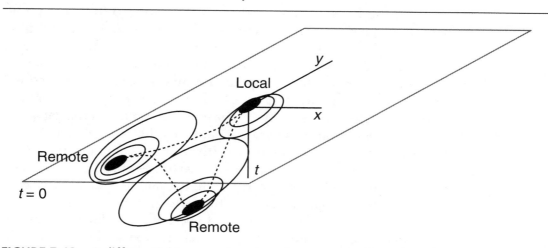

FIGURE 7-12   A differential temporal contour is constructed based on the network latency for updates originating from remote entities.

contour is then interpolated over the anchor points to define a suitable t value for each spatial point in the net-VE.

To define the contour for every point P, we denote the local user as user L and number the remote active entities from 1 to n. Each active entity i has a locally perceived network delay of d_i and is located at position P_i relative to the local user L. We use r_i to denote the distance between point P and point P_i. The t value at any point P is then computed as:

$$t(P) = \Phi_L \times \sum_{i=1}^{n} \left(d_i e^{\frac{-r_i^2}{2v_i}} \right)$$

The value v_i denotes a variance value which affects how flat the contour is around P_i. Larger values of v_i yield a contour whose t values vary smoothly from one anchor point to the next. However, if two adjacent anchor points are far apart, all passive entities located between them will always be rendered in the past (with a nonzero t value).

Smaller values of v_i, on the other hand, yield a contour that has an affinity to $t = 0$, so the contour around a particular anchor point is more steep. Passive entities that are distant from any active entity are rendered in the present time (with a t value close to 0). Function Φ_L denotes an adaptation function that equals 0 at the local user's position $P_L(0,0,0)$ and graduates to 1 for any position beyond a particular radius. It is used to force the t value to be exactly 0 at the local user's position.

This contour equation computes a composite of the active entities' network latencies by weighting each one by the corresponding entity's distance from that active entity. As one moves closer to a particular active entity, the contour approaches that entity's individual latency. As one moves into empty regions of the net-VE that are distant from any particular active entity, the contour approaches 0 (if v_i is small) or a weighted average of the adjacent entity latencies (if v_i is large). Moreover, the contour function also adjusts itself smoothly as each entity moves.

The contour function only needs to be computed for each passive entity that is rendered on the user's display. To use the contour, the local machine simply adjusts the equation parameters on each frame according to updates received from the remote active entities and the results of dead reckoning algorithms. It then applies the equation to determine the appropriate latencies to apply to each of the passive entities. These computed latencies determine the rendered position for each passive entity.

Extensions and Limitations to the Temporal Contour

The temporal space filter provides an effective technique for hiding the effects of network latencies in net-VE systems. The basic technique can be extended in a number of ways to improve its performance.

First, the contour equation does not respond well to net-VE environments that experience highly dynamic network latencies. For example, as a remote entity's latency varies across successive packets, it can cause the temporal contour to shift quite dramatically, possibly causing passive entities to unnaturally jump forward or backward in time. To reduce the impact of these effects in bursty networks, we can use a smoothed weighted average of recent latency values instead of relying on the most recent latency value. The smoothed average dampens the impact of a sudden latency change.

When a new latency estimate d_i^{new} is received, the new value of d_i is computed as follows:

$$d_i = \alpha d_i^{new} + (1 - \alpha)d_i^{old}$$

where α is a dampening factor between 0 and 1 which determines how much a new latency sample impacts the current value used in the contour computation. A reasonable value for α is ⅛, which also enables an efficient binary implementation.

An alternative approach for managing the latency estimate involves keeping a record of the recent latency estimates and fitting a best-fit line through those samples [Roberts/Sharkey97]. If the slope of this line is near 0, then the network latency is stable and the samples may safely be averaged to produce a usable latency estimate. Otherwise, the network is presumed to be exhibiting erratic behavior, and the latency estimate is increased to a maximum level until the network behavior stabilizes.

A related problem arises when an update from an active entity is delayed by considerably more than the current estimate built into the temporal contour. The local host has no information that it can use to update the entity's rendered position while waiting to receive a new update and, consequently, update the temporal contour to reflect the increased network latency. To address this problem, we can introduce into the system dead reckoning and other event prediction techniques. Whenever an update is delayed, the dead reckoning algorithm generates an estimated position prediction for the affected entities until the delayed update arrives. When used in this way, dead reckoning is no longer used to predict the entity's current position. Instead, it is used to predict the entity's *past* position according to the expectations of the current temporal contour. When updates are arriving at a steady rate, dead reckoning therefore has limited value because the rendered entity position matches the in-the-past position provided by the entity update. Because dead reckoning is only used to account for variations in the network latency, rather than the entire network latency, the prediction period is usually relatively short, and the prediction accuracy is also considerably better.

The computational requirements on the contour filter increase linearly with the number of active entities in the net-VE. However, the impact of a particular active entity on the temporal contour also decreases rapidly as one moves away from it. Therefore, to save computational costs in the presence of many active entities, it makes sense to compute the contour using only the nearest active entities. For each passive entity, the host determines the k closest active entities and computes the contour based only on those entities' latencies. It is important to employ the k closest entities instead of, for example, all active entities located within a radius r, to ensure the ability to compute the contour in regions that are located far from any active entity.

A final extension to the temporal contour involves forcibly flattening it within a radial vicinity of each active entity. By forcing the contour's values to equal that entity's network latency at all points within a certain radius, the system can ensure that all interactions with that active entity within the flattened radius occur with proper realism. For example, a remote user can reach out to catch a ball that is flying by. As long as the ball lies within the flattened contour radius, it is rendered at the same time frame as the user, and the interaction can be seen naturally. Without this flattening, the user's hand (rendered in the same time frame as the rest of the body) may not actually be rendered as touching the ball (which is rendered at a slightly different time frame from the user's body). The alternative, of course, would be to render different parts of the user's body in different time frames, but this approach is both computationally expensive and visually unappealing.

Despite their advantages, temporal contour filters also have a few limitations that make them unsuitable for many net-VE environments. The contour equation requires considerable computation, particularly in the presence of many active entities. Even with the optimization of bounding the number of active entities, as described above, the computational complexity is still significant. Though the temporal contour may serve to reduce the computational requirements of the dead reckoning algorithm, it does pose a net increase to the computational costs at each host.

To be effective, the temporal contour as defined above assumes that active entities do not move near each other. As two active entities approach each other, the perceived latency (t) values for locations between them increases, possibly approaching the sum of those entities' individual latencies. Clearly, this is not ideal, and neither of the available solutions is particularly desirable. One could decrease the value of v_i, thereby reducing the impact that a particular active entity has on its immediately surrounding contour. However, as shown in Figure 7-13(a), this approach reduces the flatness of the overall contour. It yields a rather complex, unnatural temporal field throughout the net-VE, and it also does not eliminate the problem when the two entities are colocated.

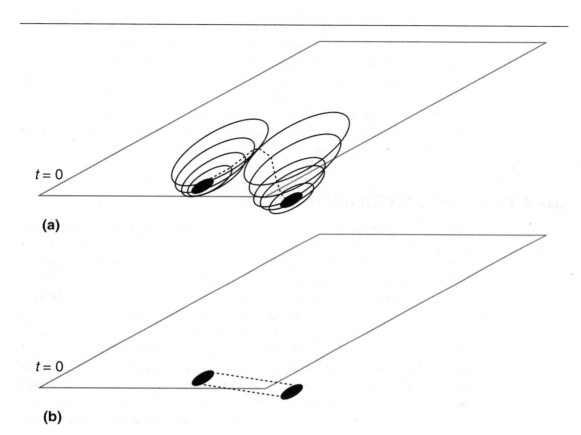

FIGURE 7-13 Behavior of temporal contour as active entities approach each other: (a) decreasing the value of v_i reduces the flatness of the contour, and (b) a weighted average contour complicates the processing of interactions originating at the higher-latency entity.

Alternatively, one could modify the contour formula itself to eliminate impact of the latency summation. For example, one could divide the computed t value by the sum of the individual exponential terms

$$\sum_{i=1}^{n} \left(e^{\frac{-r_i^2}{2v_i}} \right)$$

to yield a perfect weighted average of the active entities' latency elements. However, besides increasing the computational costs, this approach causes two colocated entities to be placed at a time frame equal to the average of their individual latencies. As shown in Figure 7-13(b), information about interactions between the two entities is likely to arrive late to the rendering host, particularly if the update originates from the entity exhibiting a longer latency.

The final approach to improving scalability and performance in net-VEs involves changing the underlying network architecture. Two recent innovations in this area are discussed in the next section.

ENHANCING THE SYSTEM ARCHITECTURE

All of the optimizations considered so far have reduced resource consumption by altering the content and information transmitted to the network, the set of host destinations for each packet, and how the net-VE is represented on participant hosts. The final class of optimizations involves changing the network software architecture of the net-VE system to enable more efficient information dissemination. By optimizing information delivery, these techniques can save network bandwidth (B), reduce the number of hosts that receive each packet (H), and reduce the timeliness requirements on packet delivery (T) in the Information Principle equation. To offset these advantages, these techniques demand additional computational resources (P) among the net-VE hosts and supporting infrastructure to determine the optimal message routing and delivery.

We discussed net-VE network software architectures in chapter 4. In particular, net-VEs were divided into two basic structures, client-server and peer-to-peer, and up to this point, our discussion of net-VE techniques has relied almost exclusively on these two architectures. Rather than defining radically new architectures, recent research has explored ways of augmenting or combining these basic structures to support greater scalability or performance.

In this section, we consider two ways in which net-VE network architectures can be changed to provide more efficient packet delivery in large-scale systems. First, as discussed in Chapter 4, the basic client-server architecture may include a federation, or cluster, of servers that communicate in a peer-to-peer manner. Alternatively, these servers may themselves behave as clients in a hierarchical client-server relationship. Second, the client-server and peer-to-peer structures may be merged into a so-called peer-server architecture, in which packets travel to some destinations in a peer-to-peer manner and to other destinations via a server.

Server Clusters

In a traditional client-server environment, a central server acts as a communication hub for packets exchanged by the participating hosts in the net-VE. All packets are sent to that server, which, in turn, forwards them to the appropriate destination hosts. A server may act as a simple broadcast reflector, in which case all packets are forwarded to all participating clients. Alternatively, the server may act as a filtering reflector, in which case packets are forwarded only to those participating clients who need to receive the information. Finally, the server may serve a packet aggregation role, combining information from multiple inbound packets into a single packet transmission to destination clients.

The basic client-server approach encounters scalability problems because all traffic must pass through the central server. As the number of net-VE participants increases, this server must scale to handle more traffic. This server rapidly becomes the bottleneck component that impedes further growth in the number of net-VE participants.

Partitioning Clients across Multiple Servers

As we saw in Chapter 4, this server bottleneck can be eliminated by introducing multiple servers into the net-VE system. Each client sends and receives all updates via one of the servers, as shown in Figure 7-14. The servers themselves communicate using peer-to-peer protocols [Funkhouser95]. When a client sends an update message to its server, that server forwards the update to its clients who would be interested in that information. Moreover, the server forwards the update to other servers having clients interested in the information. The other servers, in turn, forward the update to their interested clients.

To support the required server-to-server communications, the servers periodically exchange control messages containing composite information about the information interests of their respective clients. Using these control messages, the servers can avoid broadcasting all data to each other, instead limiting information flow to those peer servers having clients that might be interested in that information.

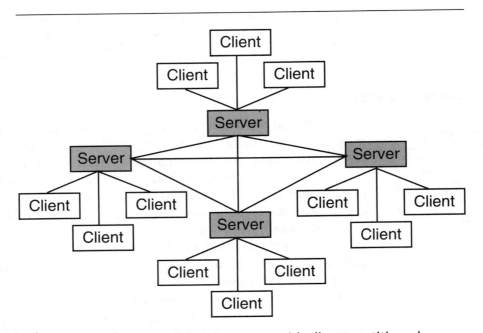

FIGURE 7-14   Client-server configuration with clients partitioned among multiple servers.

These control messages may include, for example, a list of entity locations or a summary of net-VE grid regions occupied by those entities [Farcet/Torguet98]. They may also include information about the entities' functional interests (for example, types of information in which they are interested) [Capps/Teller97], such as the projection aggregation requests and filtering subscriptions discussed previously.

Having multiple servers reduces the workload on each server because the clients are divided among them. The introduction of multiple servers does incur some cost, however. First, because updates need to be exchanged through multiple servers, they encounter a greater latency than through a single-server system. Second, the aggregate amount of processing and bandwidth required by the servers is greater than the resources required in a single-server system. For example, in a multiple-server system, each server must generate and distribute composite information about its clients; moreover, each server must also ensure that updates are forwarded to servers whose clients might have an interest in the data. However, because the number of servers is usually far fewer than the number of clients, these additional processing overheads are more than offset by the flexibility gained by dividing up the server workload onto multiple machines. Because the servers can often be connected by high-speed LANs, the additional network traffic usually does not affect the overall net-VE performance adversely.

This approach to server partitioning also can be applied in wide area network environments having a limited supply of multicast groups. In such environments, one cannot deploy hundreds or thousands of content-specific multicast groups over the WAN. However, one can establish *bilevel multicast groups* [Calvin+95,Van Hook+96], where the content-specific multicast groups are established on all of the LANs. Each LAN also has an application gateway (AG) that subscribes to all multicast groups. A sender transmits a packet to the appropriate content-specific LAN multicast group G, and it is received by the local AG. The AG then forwards the packet over the WAN by multicasting it to the set of remote AGs whose LANs have local subscribers to multicast group G. The recipient AGs each forward the packet to group G on their respective LANs. Using this approach, which is structurally identical to the server cluster described above, the number of multicast groups on the WAN only needs to scale according to the number of participating LANs instead of according to the number of content-specific groups on those LANs.

Partitioning the Net-VE across Multiple Servers

Instead of partitioning the clients among multiple servers, one can also partition the net-VE itself among those servers [Funkhouser96], as shown in Figure 7-15(a). With this technique, each server is responsible for clients located within a particular region of the net-VE, and each client communicates with different servers as it moves through the environment. The servers play the same role as in other client-server systems—that is, receiving updates from the clients and forwarding updates to clients who are interested in that information.

Partitioning the net-VE can eliminate almost 95% of the information exchange among the servers. The servers' areas of responsibility closely align to the locality behavior of the information within the net-VE. However, this technique also requires more advanced configura-

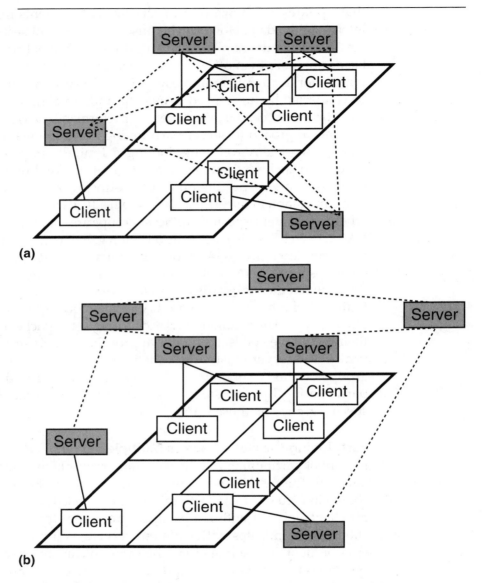

FIGURE 7-15   Partitioned net-VE among multiple servers: (a) one server per region, and (b) servers organized into a hierarchy.

tion work by the net-VE designer to enable proper information exchange among the servers. Servers need to exchange information, for example, whenever one region of the net-VE is visible to another region. To enable this exchange, the net-VE designer statically defines a table whose rows and columns correspond to various regions of the net-VE; each server may manage multiple regions represented in the table. Element (i,j) of the table equals 1 if region i is visible to region j, and the element equals 0 otherwise. When a server receives a packet from an entity, it checks the table to determine which regions can potentially see that update. It then forwards the update to the servers that manage the region.

Astute readers will notice that partitioning the net-VE across multiple servers seems quite similar to the use of aggregation servers to collect and merge a set of related updates for forwarding to an interested client. Indeed, aggregation servers are a particular instance of the more general net-VE server partitioning technique. Aggregation servers are primarily responsible for collecting updates having a well-defined characteristic and rebroadcasting them to a set of clients. Generally, however, servers may provide a variety of additional services, including filtering of irrelevant updates on a per-client basis (effectively creating customized aggregations for each connected client), information summarization, logging and recovery, and so forth.

Server Hierarchies

We may carry the parallel between server partitioning and aggregation servers one step further. Having introduced aggregation servers, we also discussed the use of aggregation server hierarchies, with higher-level servers taking responsibility for creating aggregations of information over larger regions of the net-VE. The same technique can be applied to partitioned server environments to reduce the overhead of peer-to-peer communication among the servers in a large cluster.

Using this technique, the servers themselves act as clients in a client-server relationship with higher-level servers, as shown in Figure 7-15(b). Each higher-level server is responsible for coordinating information on behalf of the net-VE regions represented by its client servers. The higher-level servers can, in turn, also be clients to even higher-level servers. The servers therefore form a rooted hierarchy for exchanging messages.

Upon receiving a packet, each server applies the algorithm shown in Listing 7-3. When a packet arrives from the upstream server, the server simply determines which of its downstream clients should receive the information and queues the update for delivery to the appropriate set of destinations. On the other hand, when a packet arrives from a downstream client, the server determines which of its other downstream clients should receive the information and queues the update for delivery to the appropriate set of destinations. It then determines whether clients in any other regions might be interested in the information. If the information is of interest to other regions, then it forwards the information to its upstream server.

LISTING 7-3   Algorithm for Packet Processing at a Server
             Hierarchy Node

```
/* This algorithm executes in a server node within a hierarchy.
 * It has a plurality of connectd downstream clients C₁...Cₙ,
 * which may be either net-VE user clients or other servers
 * in the cluster.  It may also be connected to an upstream
 * server S.
 */
if packet originates from S
   loop Cᵢ from C₁ to Cₙ
         /* Forward the packet to interested downstream clients */
      if packet might be of interest to user Cᵢ or to its
            downstream users
         queue packet for delivery to Cᵢ
      end if
   end loop
end if
else    /* packet originates from Cₖ */
   loop Cᵢ from C₁ to Cₙ
         /* Forward the packet to interested downstream clients */
      if Cᵢ != Cₖ    /* Avoid forwarding back to the source */
         if packet might be of interest to user Cᵢ or to its
               downstream users
            queue packet for delivery to Cᵢ
         end if
      end if
   end loop
   if packet might be of interest to regions not represented by
         this node
      queue packet for delivery to S
   end if
end else
```

The biggest efficiency derived from net-VE partitioning comes from reducing the interserver communication by taking advantage of information locality among clients of a particular server. The same principle applies when servers are arranged in a hierarchy. In particular, if no information locality exists among the server partitions, then the server cluster degenerates into a server-to-server broadcast system; all packets are funneled through the root server, and that server clearly becomes the system bottleneck. In deploying a server hierarchy, therefore, the net-VE designer must ensure that at each level of the hierarchy the servers' regions of responsibility correspond to natural regions of information locality in the environment.

Peer-Server Systems

Traditional peer-to-peer and client-server systems each have their own advantages and disadvantages. Peer-to-peer systems have the advantage of minimizing the latency for packet delivery by sending packets via the shortest path from source to destination, but they potentially consume considerable bandwidth because they afford minimal opportunity to perform data merging and other multisource optimizations. Client-server systems, on the other hand, can provide effective data aggregation and filtering services, but they introduce additional latency because packets must travel to the destination via an indirect path through the server.

The hybrid *peer-server* technique [Singhal+97] attempts to merge the best characteristics of these two network software architectures. Over short-haul, high-bandwidth links, it seeks to preserve the use of peer-to-peer communication, but over long-haul, low-bandwidth links, it seeks to preserve the efficiency of client-server communication.

Each entity in the net-VE is associated with its own multicast group over which it transmits updates. Destination hosts that are well connected to the entity's host subscribe directly to the multicast group and receive updates via peer-to-peer communication. However, if the latency is significant or the bandwidth is insufficient, then the destination attaches to a *forwarding server*. The forwarding server subscribes to the multicast groups for entities of interest to the destination host, performs appropriate aggregation and filtering functions, and forwards the updates to the destination host.

The system is managed by a monitoring directory server that collects information about the environment and dynamically determines which hosts should receive transmissions from each entity in the environment. Whenever the directory server determines that a new host H_{dest} should receive updates from a source entity located at host H_{src}, it instructs H_{src} and H_{dest} to perform a latency and bandwidth test by exchanging a burst of UDP packets. If the latency is below a threshold and the bandwidth is sufficient, then H_{dest} is instructed to subscribe to the multicast group corresponding to the source entity. Otherwise, H_{dest} is instructed to add the subscription to its forwarding server subscription list. Finally, while a subscription is in force, bandwidth and latency tests are repeated periodically to account for changes to the network topology and delivery characteristics.

The bandwidth and latency tests implicitly include a *reachability test* that determines whether H_{src} can actually communicate with H_{dest} via multicast. This test enables the system to account for network firewalls that block connectionless data traffic or network routers that do not support multicasting. The reachability test ensures that the net-VE can operate over complex network environments, such as those encountered over the Internet. Moreover, the test can be extended to investigate the availability of alternative peer-to-peer connectivity protocols such as UDP or TCP when multicasting is unavailable.

The peer-server technique represents an example of an *adaptive net-VE system architecture* that dynamically adjusts to account for network topology, host location, and network dynamics. As we will see further in Chapter 8, net-VE deployment over the Internet and over other complex, dynamic, and heterogeneous network environments is a difficult task. A one-size-fits-all approach to system architecture will no longer be sufficient. Considerable work remains to be done in this area, and, indeed, it remains a subject of ongoing research.

CONCLUSION

This chapter has introduced issues of net-VEs that: have large numbers of users, execute on machines with limited processor capacity, and run over networks having variable latency and limited bandwidth. These constraints require the net-VE designer to ensure that limited system resources are not used to generate, transport, and process extraneous information. Resource optimization techniques can broadly be divided into four areas: optimizing the communication protocol via compression and aggregation, controlling the visibility of data through multicasting and filtering, exploiting human perceptual limitations through reducing the level of detail and creating temporal inaccuracies, and changing the net-VE network software architecture by merging traditional peer-to-peer and client-server techniques.

Unfortunately, the set of available optimizations is diverse, and it is impossible to provide a formula for which resource management techniques should be used in a particular net-VE. The net-VE designer must iteratively deploy the target system, evaluate the bottlenecks, and selectively introduce optimizations according to the consistency and performance requirements of the application. A real net-VE system uses multiple techniques simultaneously, and to date, each deployed system employs a unique combination of features.

Resource management is an active area of research for several reasons. Net-VE users are seeing the value of having multiple simultaneous participants in the system, and they are demanding real-time collaboration or competition among ever-increasing numbers of participants. Increasing graphic processor speeds are driving users to expect net-VEs to provide higher quality visualization experiences, but wide area network bandwidth is not increasing at the same pace. Network latency is not improving much and may actually be deteriorating as more links become congested. As net-VE resources become more constrained, resource management techniques will gain heightened importance.

One of the driving forces behind the need for resource management is the emergence of the Internet. As long as net-VEs were confined to high-cost private networks such as the Defense Simulation Internet sponsored by the Department of Defense, it was possible to simply invest in greater network capacity. However, the Internet represents a limited shared resource that cannot be upgraded unilaterally. Because of its universal accessibility, the Internet is also encouraging rapid growth in the expected number of participants within net-VEs. After all, the Internet provides a virtually unlimited supply of potential participants, and given sufficiently compelling content, net-VE sizes are staged to explode.

Because of its heterogeneity, the Internet represents a difficult environment for deploying net-VEs. Network firewalls, routers having different capabilities, intermittent connectivity, and unpredictable latency are just a sampling of the problems that the Internet brings to the fore. Finally, the Internet is driven by standards, and successful deployment of net-VEs over the Internet calls for standardized protocols, APIs, and content. This drive toward standardization over the Internet is the subject of the next chapter.

REFERENCES

[Abrams+98] Abrams, H., K. Watsen, and M. Zyda. Three tiered interest management for large-scale virtual environments. In *Proceedings of Virtual Reality Systems and Technology* (VRST) *1998*. ACM, Taipei, Taiwan, November 1998.

[ARPA94] Advanced Research Projects Agency. STOW 97 program plan. May 1994.

[Barrus+96] Barrus, J. W., R. C. Waters, and D. B. Anderson. Locales and beacons: Efficient and precise support for large multi-user virtual environments. In *Proceedings of the 1996 Virtual Reality Annual International Symposium* (VRAIS), 204–213. IEEE Neural Networks Council. Santa Clara, CA, March 1996.

[Buckwalter77] Buckwalter, L. *Video Games.* New York: Grosset & Dunlap, 1977.

[Calvin+95] Calvin, J. O., D. C. Miller, J. Seeger, et al. Application control techniques system architecture. Technical Report RITN-1001-00, MIT Lincoln Laboratories, Lexington, MA, February 1995.

[Capps/Teller97] Capps, M., and S. Teller. Communication visibility in shared virtual worlds. In *Proceedings of the Sixth IEEE Workshop on Enabling Technologies: Infrastructure for Collaborative Enterprises* (WETICE), 187–192. IEEE Computer Society, Cambridge, MA, June 1997.

[Farcet/Torguet98] Farcet, N., and P. Torguet. Space-scale structure for information rejection in large-scale distributed virtual environments. In *Proceedings of the 1998 IEEE Viirtual Reality Annual International Symposium* (VRAIS), 276–283. IEEE Neural Networks Council, Atlanta, GA, March 1998.

[Funkhouser95] Funkhouser, T. A. RING: A client-server system for multi-user virtual environments. In *Proceedings of the 1995 Symposium on Interactive 3D Graphics*, 85–92. ACM SIGGRAPH, March 1995.

[Funkhouser96] Funkhouser, T. A. Network topologies for scalable multi-user virtual environments. In *Proceedings of the 1996 IEEE Virtual Reality Annual International Symposium* (VRAIS), 222–228. IEEE Neural Networks Council, San Jose, CA, April 1996.

[Greenhalgh/Benford95] Greenhalgh, C., and S. Benford. Virtual reality tele-conferencing: Implementation and experience. In *Proceedings of the Third European Conference on Computer Supported Cooperative Work* (ECSCW'95). Stockholm, September 1995.

[Greenhalgh/Benford97] Greenhalgh, C., and S. Benford. Boundaries, awareness, and interaction in collaborative virtual environments. In *Proceedings of the Sixth IEEE Workshop on Enabling Technologies: Infrastructure for Collaborative Enterprises* (WETICE), 193–198. IEEE Computer Society, Cambridge, MA. June 1997.

[Harvey97] Harvey, W. The future of Internet games. *Modeling and Simulation: Linking Entertainment and Defense*, 140–143. Computer Science and Telecommunications Board, National Research Council. Washington, DC: National Academy Press, 1997.

[Holbrook/Cheriton98] Holbrook, H. W., and D. R. Cheriton. EXPRESS multicast. January 1998.

[IEEE95] Institute for Electrical and Electronics Engineers. *IEEE Standard for Distributed Interactive Simulation—Application Protocols*. IEEE Standard 1278.1-1995. Piscataway, NJ: IEEE Standards Press, September 1995.

[Kessler/Hodges96] Kessler, G. D., and L. F. Hodges. A network communication protocol for distributed virtual environment systems. In *Proceedings of the 1996 IEEE Virtual Reality Annual International Symposium* (VRAIS), 214–221. IEEE Neural Networks Council, San Jose, CA, April 1996.

[Macedonia+95] Macedonia, M., M. Zyda, D. Pratt, and P. Barham. Exploiting reality with multicast groups: A network architecture for large-scale virtual environments. In *Proceedings of the 1995 Virtual Reality Annual International Symposium* (VRAIS). IEEE Neural Networks Council, Research Triangle Park, NC, March 1995.

[Mastaglio/Callahan95] Mastaglio, T. W., and R. Callahan. A large-scale complex virtual environment for team training. *IEEE Computer* 28(7):49–56, July 1995.

[Milner95] Milner, S. STOW real-time communications architecture: Requirements, approach, and rationale. Presentation to STOW Technical Evaluation Team, May 1995.

[Morse96] Morse, K. L. Interest management in large-scale distributed simulation. 1996.

[Powell+96] Powell, E. T., L. Mellon, J. F. Watson, and G. H. Tarbox. Joint precision strike demonstration (JPSD) simulations architecture. In *Proceedings of the 14th Workshop on Standards for the Interoperability of Distributed Simulations*, 807–810. Orlando, FL, March 1996. (Published as Technical Report

IST–CF–96–03, Institute for Simulation and Training, University of Central Florida, Orlando, FL.)

[Rak/VanHook96] Rak, S. J., and D. J. Van Hook. Evaluation of grid-based relevance filtering for multicast group assignment. In *Proceedings of the Fourteenth Workshop on Standards for the Interoperability of Defense Simulations*, II:739–747. Orlando, FL, March 1996. (Published as Technical Report IST–CF–96–03, Institute for Simulation and Training, University of Central Florida, Orlando, FL.)

[Roberts/Sharkey97] Roberts, D. L., and P. M. Sharkey. Maximising concurrency and scalability in a consistent, causal, distributed virtual reality system, whilst minimizing the effect of network delays. In *Proceedings of the Sixth IEEE Workshop on Enabling Technologies: Infrastructure for Collaborative Enterprises* (WETICE), 161–166. IEEE Computer Society, Cambridge, MA, June 1997.

[Russo+95] Russo, K. L., L. C. Shuette, J. E. Smith, and M. E. McGuire. Effectiveness of various new bandwidth reduction techniques in ModSAF. In *Proceedings of the 13th Workshop on Standards for the Interoperability of Distributed Simulations*, 587–591. Orlando, September 1995.

[Ryan/Sharkey97] Ryan, M. D., and P. M. Sharkey. Causal volumes in distributed virtual reality. In *Proceedings of the 1997 IEEE International Conference on Systems, Man and Cybernetics*, 1067–1072. Orlando, October 1997.

[Sharkey+98] Sharkey, P. M., M. D. Ryan, and D. J. Roberts. A local perception filter for distributed virtual environments. In *Proceedings of the 1998 IEEE Virtual Reality Annual International Symposium* (VRAIS), 242–249. IEEE Neural Networks Council, Atlanta, GA, March 1998.

[Singhal96] Singhal, S. K. *Effective remote modeling in large-scale distributed simulation and visualization environments.* Ph.D dissertation. Department of Computer Science, Stanford University, Stanford, CA, August 1996.

[Singhal/Cheriton96] Singhal, S. K., and D. R. Cheriton. Using projection aggregations to support scalability in distributed simulation. In *Proceedings of the 16th International Conference on Distributed Computing Systems* (ICDCS), 196–206. IEEE Computer Society, Hong Kong, May 1996.

[Singhal+97] Singhal, S. K., B. Q. Nguyen, R. Redpath, M. Fraenkel, and J. Nguyen. InVerse: Designing an interactive universe architecture for scalability and extensibility. In *Proceedings of the Sixth IEEE International Symposium on High-Performance Distributed Computing* (HPDC). IEEE Computer Society, Portland, OR, August 1997.

[Smith+95] Smith, J. E., K. L. Russo, and L. C. Shuette. Prototype multicast IP implementation in ModSAF. In *Proceedings of the 12th Workshop on Standards for the Interoperability of Distributed Simulations*, 175–178. Orlando, FL, March 1995. (Published as Technical Report IST–CF–95–01, Institute for Simulation and Training, University of Central Florida, Orlando.)

[VanHook93] Van Hook, D. J. Simulation tools for developing and evaluating networks and algorithms in support of STOW 94, 19–20. Presented at Scalability Peer Review, San Diego, CA, August 1993.

[VanHook94] Van Hook, D. J. Personal communication, September 1994.

[VanHook+94] Van Hook, D. J., J. O. Calvin, and D. C. Miller. A protocol independent compression algorithm (PICA). Advanced Distributed Simulation Memorandum 20PM-ADS-005, MIT Lincoln Laboratories, Lexington, MA, April 1994.

[VanHook+96] Van Hook, D. J., D. P. Cebula, S. J. Rak, C. J. Chiang, P. N. DiCaprio, and J. O. Calvin. Performance of STOW RITN application control techinques. In *Proceedings of the 14th Workshop on Standards for the Interoperability of Distributed Simulations*. Orlando, March 1996.

Chapter 8

Internet Networked Virtual Environments

This chapter discusses virtual environments on the Internet, including VRML-based worlds, the virtual reality transfer protocol, and Internet gaming. This chapter also addresses the evolving technologies and standards that enable networked virtual environments to enter the mainstream and be deployed over the Internet. It provides an overview of some of the difficulties in developing virtual environments and games on the Internet. It also provides an overview of the performance issues specifically associated with the Internet.

VRML-BASED VIRTUAL ENVIRONMENTS

To place a net-VE on the Internet presupposes that the environment and its supporting software can be downloaded to a Web browser running on any machine and that users can subsequently see and interact with the net-VE. Assuming that we have sufficient computational power and sufficient graphics power, Web-based net-VEs first require a standardized encoding for supporting the display of those worlds and their objects. The Virtual Reality Modeling Language (VRML) is one such encoding [VRML]. VRML has unfortunately been developed before most Web users have access to sufficient graphics and computational power to assure its universal success, but it represents the most promising technology for constructing Web-based virtual environments.

To anyone who has grown tired of encoding graphics objects as a series of C function calls, the idea behind VRML is quite simple and natural: If we wish to place 3D VEs on the Web, we need a standard, machine-independent way of encoding that 3D information into a file downloadable across the Web. VRML originates from one such file format, the Silicon Graphics Inventor toolkit [Wernecke94]. A VRML file contains a hierarchical scene graph for describing the 3D geometry, as well as texturing, lighting, and pseudospatial sound effects for objects described by the file. In addition, VRML scene elements can exchange user events, timer events, and other messages. A scripting interface (through a special scene graph node called a ScriptNode) allows an external programming environment to communicate with and manipulate the VRML scene graph. In this way, Java and JavaScript code can add and delete scene graph nodes, generate events, and receive event notifications.

VRML files, once retrieved over the Web, are handled by a VRML browser that renders the VRML scene graph and supports user navigation through the virtual environment. Numerous free VRML browser plug-ins exist today for both Netscape Navigator and Microsoft Explorer. By far, the most popular VRML plug-in is the SGI Cosmo3D browser. The Intervista WorldView and Sony Community Place browsers are also popular.

VRML-based worlds have always been regarded as the poor stepchild of the virtual environment community. Performer-based VEs written in C to execute on high-end SGI machines have always generated more compelling environments with better rendering performance than those written in VRML. For this reason, it has been difficult to justify development in VRML—it has not offered good support for the full programming of a VE with significant physical modeling. This attitude is starting to change as people develop their physics models in Java, with Java providing hooks into the VRML scene [Brutzman98]. Despite these limitations, VRML-based VEs have been developed and deployed.

Some Existing Networked VRML Worlds

Due to the hardware limitations of most machines connected to the Internet and the lack of investment in a VRML technology, relatively few organizations have experimented with networked VRML-based worlds. The few systems that have been developed usually support only a small number of players, under 16 in most cases. To understand how such net-VEs are being constructed, this subsection examines some of these efforts and their architectures.

To enable Web-based net-VE interoperability, the following three architectural questions are key [DIS-Java-VRML].

1. What types of information need to be transferred between Web-based net-VEs?
2. What protocol should be used to transfer that information over the Internet?
3. What is the network software architecture (NSA) for Internet-based net-VE software?

The types of information that need to be transferred between networked VEs are easily specifiable.

1. State changes and entity interactions (exchanged using peer-to-peer protocols)
2. Heavy-weight objects (retrieved using HTTP client-server requests)
3. Network pointers and references (represented as URLs)
4. Real-time media streams (transmitted as multicast audio/video)

A design that allows the transfer of any of these types of information over the Web is a rather large effort (see the virtual reality transfer protocol section below).

DIS-Java-VRML

The DIS-Java-VRML project of the Naval Postgraduate School is an archetype for VRML-based net-VEs. As a first step into understanding the design of Web-based net-VEs, the project concentrated its efforts on transferring state change and entity interaction information for VRML-

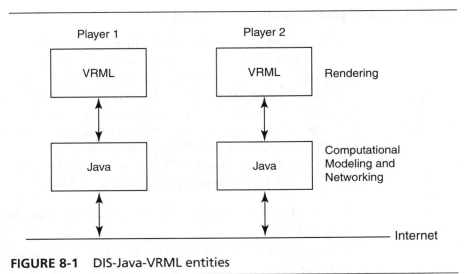

FIGURE 8-1   DIS-Java-VRML entities

based net-VEs. Rather than invent a wholly new protocol design, the project developed a Java class library and an architecture for exchanging DIS packets over the Internet. With the protocol already an IEEE standard, the remaining task was to develop the network software architecture.

At a high level, the DIS-Java-VRML architecture looks like that shown in Figure 8-1. In that figure, we see that rendering is handled by VRML and that Java provides the modeling computation and networking required. Figure 8-2 shows the DIS-Java-VRML architecture in more detail. The behavior stream buffer thread reads entity state PDUs (ESPDUs) from the network and places them into a memory buffer.[1] This thread is implemented in Java as a static class. The entity dispatcher thread reads the ESPDUs from memory and demultiplexes those PDUs to the corresponding ESPDU transform by writing again

---

[1]In traditional net-VEs, as discussed in Chapter 6, this memory buffer would exist in shared memory so that it could be shared by multiple threads. Because a Java virtual machine provides a single address space for all threads, there is no need to use an operating system shared memory buffer; instead, a reference to the memory buffer is simply placed in a global (static) variable, accessible to all threads.

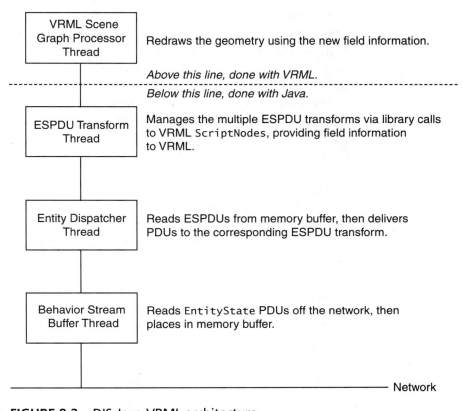

FIGURE 8-2   DIS-Java-VRML architecture

into memory queues. The entity dispatcher thread is also implemented as a static Java class.

The ESPDU transform thread performs the transformations mandated by the ESPDUs via library calls to VRML ScriptNodes in the scene graph. Those ScriptNode calls provide field information to the VRML scene, information that causes the VRML geometry to be drawn in different positions and orientations. The final thread is the scene graph processor. The scene graph processor redraws the display as fast as the VRML browser is capable, usually not very fast if graphics hardware acceleration is not available.

There are some important qualifications to this architecture. It can be implemented in two different ways. The method that usually produces working systems is to perform both the Java interpretation and VRML processing inside the VRML browser. To enable this, the VRML browser providers have had to write a ScriptNode support class library that is utilized by the ESPDU transform thread.

The other way to implement this architecture is to execute the net-VE program as a regular Java system application or browser applet, with VRML processing handled by a VRML browser. Because the VRML browser and Java interpreter are written by two different organizations, this requires that some sort of political agreement be accomplished by the different software authoring organizations in order for the ScriptNode class library to get implemented and be made available to the Java virtual machine.

Despite all of this, the DIS-Java-VRML working group has had some success. Performance measures indicate that 300 PDUs per second can be processed within the Java part of the architecture. With VRML plugged in and a rich graphics scene, the VRML browser scene graph processing rapidly becomes the performance bottleneck, with unaccelerated PCs reporting 1 frame per second or less, completely unacceptable performance for an interactive net-VE. If we assume the availability of sufficient graphics cycles at a later date, 300 PDUs per second corresponds to 9 to 37 players in our DIS-Java-VRML–based net-VEs. DIS-Java-VRML worlds run in Web browsers and have the potential to be downloaded over the Internet.

LivingWorlds

LivingWorlds is a working group of the VRML/Web3D Consortium [VRML-LivingWorlds, VRML]. The goal of that working group is to define a set of VRML 2.0 conventions for interoperable virtual environments. LivingWorlds is not a complete net-VE architecture but rather provides a set of standards for using VRML, a set of standards that have been utilized by a number of VE efforts [blaxxun, Community-Place, OpenCommunity, Singhal+97].

The LivingWorlds standard defines how to support "multiplayer virtual presence," the interaction of people with people and people with objects in the VRML-defined scene. It also defines how multiplayer worlds can be made interoperable, even though those worlds are dynamically assembled from components (user avatars, shared models, virtual rooms, and so forth) built by different developers whose only commonality is their use of VRML and the LivingWorlds APIs. For example, the LivingWorlds project aims to support an Internet in which each Web user has a personal VRML avatar which includes geometry and scripted behaviors and is associated with other personal information. A user may bring that avatar into any LivingWorlds-compliant net-VE and automatically access and interact with the full virtual environment. Similarly, the user may take an object from one LivingWorlds net-VE and transport it into another (independently developed) net-VE.

The LivingWorlds draft defines a library of VRML scene nodes representing shared objects, avatars, and shared events. Through the standard Java interface to VRML, a LivingWorlds net-VE application can learn of actions taken by the local user in the VRML browser and transmit network messages describing those actions. Similarly, the Java code receives packets over the network and makes corresponding modifications to the VRML scene graph.

The LivingWorlds draft specification defines the following five interfaces.

1. Coordination of the position and state of shared objects (including avatars)
2. Information exchange between objects in a scene
3. Personal and system security for VRML applications
4. A library of utilities and workarounds for VRML 2.0 limitations
5. Runtime identification and integration of the interaction capabilities implemented by VRML scripts

The LivingWorlds working group believes these interfaces can support a first generation of shared VRML worlds. Though successful worlds have been constructed that claim to adhere to the LivingWorlds specification, these worlds are barely interoperable at this time. Moreover, some of these worlds are not usable in a Web browser as they are not fully written in Java and VRML.

blaxxun Interactive

blaxxun Interactive has an entire product line based on the work of the LivingWorlds working group [blaxxun]. Their Community Platform is a client-server architecture that supports VRML-based, interactive net-VEs. The planned customer base is anyone wishing to deploy a 3D Web-based VE, particularly for product promotion.

The blaxxun CCpro (Community Client pro) system fully supports shared virtual environments, including all activities that modify the environment [blaxxun]. Activities supported include the following:

- Object activation and movement
- Object assembly
- Object behavioral modeling
- Object usage
- 3D information visualization

blaxxun CSobjects is the name of the distributed object manager (server). CSobjects distributes entity state information to all relevant users (CCpro clients) and provides persistence for those state changes. Objects placed in the blaxxun VE stay until the objects are again changed by a user of the world.

The blaxxun VE requires its own VRML browser. Changes to the VRML world are accomplished via Java applets utilizing the VRML External Authoring Interface (EAI) [VRML-EAI]. Java applets can interact with VRML by [blaxxun]:

- Accessing the functionality of the browser interface (that is, to create new geometry)
- Sending events to nodes inside the scene (that is, to change positions or colors of objects)
- Reading the most recent event values sent from nodes inside the scene (that is, to find the last position of an object)
- Receiving notifications when events are sent from nodes inside the scene (that is, when an object is being clicked)

Some of the resulting VRML net-VEs are particularly impressive [Colony-City].

Sony's Community Place

Sony's Community Place is another Java- and VRML-based set of software that supports the construction of net-VEs based on the Living-

Worlds draft specification. Community Place (CP) is the name of the browser that supports the Java-VRML software [CommunityPlace, Lea+97]. The Community Place browser supports the usual (non-networked) VRML world navigation and additionally supports worlds with embedded musical and video clips and interaction with behaviorally animated objects. Textual chat is also supported via a pop-up window.

Multiuser worlds are supported through the client-server paradigm. The multiuser worlds operate across the Internet by connecting to a server called a Bureau. In such worlds, movement of an avatar is communicated through the server to other players connected to the same Bureau (world). Behaviorally animated objects have interactions whose results are communicated across the Internet for other players to see.

The goal of the Community Place project was to develop an architecture to support users connected via low-bandwidth modem to the Bureau server [Lea+97]. The server holds a copy of the initial VRML scene, which is downloaded at start time by the CP browser. The server provides information about the other players in the scene, including their location and state. Additionally, the server updates the VRML display with 3D objects that are not in the originally downloaded base world.

Java code drives VRML ScriptNodes, which fill data fields in the VRML scene graph to change the display. The Java code can add new entities and objects into the scene as well as move already known objects around the scene. The CP browser communicates to the server via a protocol called the Virtual Society Client Protocol (VSCP), which runs over TCP/IP [Lea+97], hence guaranteeing delivery of state change information. The packets are designed for extensibility, with application-specific messages as well as standard geometry state change messages.

The server tracks the positions of all players and informs players of relevant state changes via the aura-based area of interest management scheme pioneered in MASSIVE and DIVE (see Chapter 7). The server also forwards messages that are specific to particular players. This directed messaging is sufficient to support chat and other person-to-person interactions. The Community Place server architecture is quite scalable. Assuming mayhem (high packet rates), the system can support between 400 and 630 connections and/or players with high-end servers (Sony NEWS, SGI, and Sun machines) [Lea+97]. Assuming more realistic packet flows (lower packet rates), the system can support up to 1,000 connections and/or players utilizing a high-performance Sun server. These performance numbers are based on network traffic and server capability only. Again, the VRML nature of the system limits the visual performance of a CP browser except on the highest price setups.

Open Community

Open Community is an Internet-capable, VRML-based virtual environment architecture developed by Mitsubishi Electric Research Lab (MERL) located in Cambridge, Massachusetts [OpenCommunity]. Open Community's implementation is based on the Spline (Scalable Platform for Large Interactive Networked Environments) system developed by MERL [Waters+97]. Open Community itself is a software library that provides services for network communications, real-time audio transport, transport of large objects such as VRML models, and area of interest management.

The architecture for Open Community is shown in Figure 8-3 (derived from [OpenCommunity]). The user application makes calls to the Open Community library. The Open Community library writes data into a shared memory space called the World Model. Open Community spawns processes that read that shared memory to perform other operations. For example, Open Community spawns a visual renderer that draws its display by reading the state of the world from the shared memory. The visual renderer (spVisual process) is a C process that communicates with a VRML scene graph processor. Connection to the network is via an Interactive Sharing Transfer Protocol (ISTP) process [OpenCommunity, Waters/Anderson/Schwenke97].

The most notable part of the architecture is that its world model uses locales to manage areas of interest and beacons to support entity discovery [Barrus+96a, Barrus+96b, Barrus+96c]. Each application process only has information about the relevant area of interest in its shared memory. Open Community does not require a central server but can be configured with one depending on the application.

Open Community, with its area of interest management and multicasting, should be able to support large numbers of players, again assuming available high-speed graphics hardware for the VRML scene

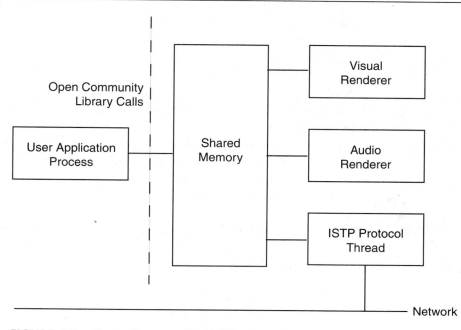

FIGURE 8-3   Open Community architecture

Source: From [OpenCommunity]. Used with permission.

graph rendering, available multicast-capable network, and sufficient cycles to process the multiple processes that make up an Open Community session. On the other hand, the development of large parts of Open Community in the C programming language on particular operating systems reduces its ability to operate on heterogeneous platforms. An effort is underway at MERL to port Open Community to Java to eliminate this issue. When that fully Java and VRML world is constructed, Open Community may then be downloadable via Web browsers across the Internet.

VNet

VNet is another client-server Java- and VRML-based net-VE [VNet]. Avatars can be selected from the VNet server or developed individually. Those avatars can be displayed in a shared world, a world where users can also communicate via textual chat. VNet has simple area of interest management based on spatial location, with chat text provided to all screens whose avatars are located within 30 meters in the VE.

VNet defines an application layer protocol, VRML Interchange Protocol (VIP), for sending VRML field change information across the Internet. That protocol allows multiuser participation in the VRML-defined world. The VNet protocol runs across TCP/IP for reliable state change transmission and uses a binary encoding for efficient transmission across the expected modem-based communications medium. The VIP packet structure is hard-coded, like DIS, but it is designed for application-specific extension, with the ability to send any valid VRML field.

VNet was one of the first networked VRML-based worlds. The following list, taken from the developer's Web site, indicates the plan for VNet's future development [VNet]:

Phase I. Shared movement and chat, custom avatars. These functions are supported in VNet 1.0.

Phase II. Shared building, object ownership, a client-user interface for adding new objects, server-side database for saving object state.

Phase III. Shared behaviors of objects and avatars, although this can be developed within the current VIP protocol.

Phase IV. Server-side Java objects and behaviors. The VNet developer additionally indicates the need to improve bandwidth utilization, perhaps through the implementation of dead reckoning and the utilization of UDP to speed up the overall network architecture performance.

virtual reality transfer protocol

The virtual reality transfer protocol (vrtp) project is an attempt to develop an application layer protocol to support Internet-based net-VEs in a standard fashion [Brutzman+95, Brutzman+97, Zyda+97]. Such standardization allows interoperability and composability of networked virtual environments, allowing us to build very large VEs that are more comprehensive and interactive than those currently attempted.

The main idea behind vrtp is to support the transfer of all types of net-VE information using a unified framework [Brutzman+97]; several examples are discussed next.

- *Entity state processing:* Lightweight messages composed of state, event, and control information as used in DIS entity state PDUs or other behavior reports. These messages are communicated using unicast or multicast. Complete message semantics are included in a single packet encapsulation without fragmentation. Lightweight interactions are received completely or not at all.

- *Heavyweight objects:* Large data objects requiring reliable connection-oriented transmission. These are typically delivered as an HTTP response to a network pointer request.

- *Network pointers:* Lightweight network resource references (that is, a global address space) that can be multicast to receiving groups. These pointers can be cached so that repeated queries can be answered by other group members instead of servers. Unlike lightweight interactions, pointers do not contain a complete object, instead containing only a reference to an object.

- *Real-time streams:* Live video, audio, DIS behaviors, sequential graphics images, or other continuous stream traffic that requires real-time delivery, sequencing, and synchronization. These are typically implemented using multicast channels.

The vrtp framework consists of a collection of protocol modules and an application-layer protocol to provide the necessary connectivity to a net-VE client. As shown by the implementation architecture of Figure 8-4, vrtp provides a protocol module for each of the four types of data to be communicated to the net-VE client. The vrtp application-layer protocol is used to wrap together these four dissimilar protocol modules.

INTERNET GAMING

Games on the Internet provide an interactive experience that is rapidly usurping network television. Internet-capable games tend to be networked versions of single-user games mediated by either a charged or free server. The main thing all such games share in common is the ability

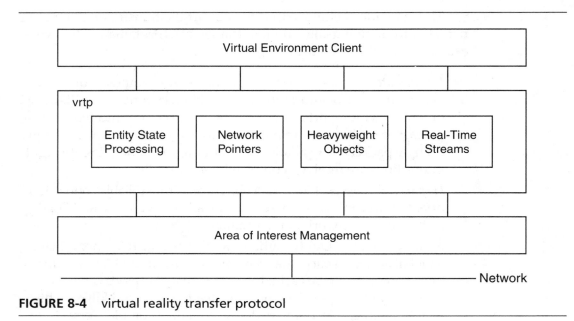

FIGURE 8-4   virtual reality transfer protocol

to pair oneself up with a distant opponent in combat, with a chat window for communication and coordination. Almost all of the games suffer serious lag problems. A recent demonstration of the game *Mechwarrior2: Mercenaries* showed that the essential skill required to play against a networked opponent was to figure out their direction of travel so you could shoot *in front* of them. With lag of some 300 to 400 ms, there was no chance of hitting the opponent by firing directly, even when the game is played over a LAN connected to the Internet by a relatively high-speed T-1 link. Nonetheless, a sustained compelling experience can be had with such games, as players learn to live with the lag.

Overview of Online Gaming Services

There are several commercial enterprises that provide subscription-based network gaming. The largest are Kesmai, HEAT.NET, Internet Gaming Zone, Kali, Mplayer, and Total Entertainment Network [Ryan98]. Not much technical information is available on these services, because most tend to maintain proprietary architectures. They all seem to perform equally, with their most distinguishing characteristic being their advertising style, in *Next Generation Gaming* magazine. Besides network gaming services, individual game companies are also getting into the business of placing free game servers onto the Internet, with those free sites making money from advertising and associated product sales.

Kesmai's GameStorm client software provides a billed monthly service for unlimited access to Kesmai's suite of games (*AirWarrior II*, *Aliens Online*, and *Legends of Kesmai*), as well as access to HEAT.NET and *Engage!* Games Online [Ryan98, GameStorm]. The service provides networked games, automatic software updates, chat, e-mail, and Web page support for its members.

HEAT.NET is a free service provided by SegaSoft [HEAT.NET]. HEAT.NET's bread and butter is action games, where large numbers of players (up to 32) can play online. Game play on HEAT.NET is plagued by lag problems, problems serious enough for complaints about it to be common [Ryan98].

Microsoft's Internet Gaming Zone (IGZ) is the home of card and board games, but it does offer some action games [Ryan98]. The service is free if you own a copy of the networked game to be played, though some special games and zones require fees. There is a low-latency capability called the Dwango-zone, which provides a dedicated dialup server for a subscription fee.

Kali is not itself a gaming service but rather software support for networked gaming provided for a fee [Kali]. The Kali client software provides connectivity from your Internet connection to a Kali server running elsewhere on the Internet. By selling their server software for a relatively low cost, Kali encourages individuals to set up Kali game servers. A single Kali server can support almost any popular action game currently on the market, though the performance for Kali games depends on the game and number of users [Kali]. Some games generate 200 bytes per second per user, with 500 bytes per second per user being typical. Some games consume all available bandwidth no matter what the connection speed.

Mplayer is a gaming service that provides a free basic membership, with a fee-based premium service available [Mplayer]. Mplayer's underlying networked game technology is that of Mpath Interactive, which is discussed in more detail in the next section [Mpath]. As with many of the gaming services, Mplayer users complain about lag and latency with respect to the service [Ryan98].

Total Entertainment Network (TEN), following the lead of others, provides a free gaming service for individually owned games and a premium plan for special games and tournament play [TEN]. Many people consider TEN to be the premier gaming service, with the best-developed interface and best connections to the Internet [Ryan98]. TEN has achieved this best performance on the Internet by negotiating with the ISPs for listing at the top of their router tables and by connecting themselves to the Internet with optical speed (OC-3) connections.

Internet Gaming Software Architectures

As stated earlier, not many of the networked gaming companies provide information on their systems architecture. However, all are client-server-based, so it is not hard to imagine their connectivity and the contents of their packets. Some systems, however, offer a bit more information, and we cover those briefly here.

RTIME

RTIME provides a suite of software called the RTIME Interactive Networking Engine [RTIME]. Their software supports the client-server paradigm over the Internet, as needed by networked game services companies and networked game developers. RTIME's software is tuned to "mitigate the effects of high latency and low bandwidth that affect performance of multiplayer games" [RTIME]. Their support software includes frame-rate decoupling (support for multithreaded game architectures), dynamic motion modeling (dead reckoning and smooth object movement support), a global time base, data filtering (area of interest management), and persistent universe support [RTIME]. RTIME's founders were members of the original SIMNET development effort, and that software architecture experience is clearly evident in the RTIME software. RTIME claims that their engine supports up to 2,000 users and spectators interacting in real-time over the Internet. RTIME's software has been utilized in networked games, simulation, education, training, and just about any other type of multiuser application.

Mpath Interactive

Mpath Interactive developed the support software underlying the Mplayer gaming network [Mpath]. Mpath's software is named POP.X and is focused on providing an architecture for supporting Internet-based online forums, interactive polls, auctions, customer support services, virtual classrooms, talk shows, and multiplayer games. According to Mpath, POP.X provides an off-the-shelf solution to scalability, performance, accessibility, ease-of-use, security, and content management [Mpath]. POP.X has a three-level architecture. It has a user interface module called the WebTop. It has a client proxy module that is capable of being tailored on a per-user basis (think of this as being the net-VE/game client). Finally, it has an application server that provides multiuser logic and area of interest management. The application server is based on the CORBA Object Request Broker architecture, which limits its scalability characteristics but provides a simpler application programming model.

DirectPlay

The DirectPlay software architecture is provided by Microsoft for building Windows-based multiplayer games that are capable of communicating over the Internet, over LAN protocols such as IPX, over serial lines, through direct modem-to-modem connections, or over proprietary protocols such those used by America Online (AOL) [DirectPlay]. DirectPlay provides a network-independent API and support libraries for performing many of the following basic services required by a multiplayer game.

- Implementation of a "lobby server" that can serve as a registry of available games that players may join, and association of each game with properties such as maximum player count
- Ability to locate and connect to a lobby server, retrieve a list of available games, and join a game
- Ability to learn about the identity of other players in the game
- Ability to associate each game player with an application-defined data structure containing application state that should be made available to other players
- Ability to modify the player data structure and propagate those changes to other players

- Ability to send player-to-player, player-to-group, and broadcast messages
- Integration with standard Windows services such as NTLM security and cryptography

The DirectPlay infrastructure has gained popularity because it is free and because its low-level services are well integrated with the Windows operating system. It provides a useful abstraction away from low-level WinSock programming, and the gaming-centered API has proven to be quite popular. The Microsoft lobby server implementation also provides a standard platform for game services, including Microsoft's own Internet Gaming Zone (IGZ), that can therefore host games built by multiple vendors.

DirectPlay supports both peer-to-peer and client-server communication models. The newest version of DirectPlay supports asynchronous messaging with application-provided message priorities and inspectable message queues. Across each asynchronous messaging connection, DirectPlay provides flow control. On top of this asynchronous messaging service, DirectPlay also provides a reliable messaging protocol to serve as an alternative to TCP/IP.

The game is represented within the application by a Session object that describes the maximum number of players, security parameters, and so forth. The lobby server maintains a collection of these Session objects, which a client may retrieve and browse. After joining a session, each user is represented by a Player object. Users may also be associated with Group objects for purposes of message addressing.

Despite its many strengths, the platform also has many limitations. First, games implemented using DirectPlay cannot interoperate with non-Windows game implementations, and lobby servers must run on Windows NT. Second, the DirectPlay implementation is not particularly well suited to large-scale games of more than a few players, and highly interactive games are equally problematic. The DirectPlay system does not provide any of the state management techniques that are required for larger systems or systems that must execute in bandwidth-constrained networks, such as the Internet. Third, DirectPlay works quite poorly through firewalls. To work, the firewall administrator must configure a port to support both inbound and outbound TCP/IP and UDP/IP connections and packets. Finally, though a marked improvement over low-level networking APIs, DirectPlay is still relatively difficult to learn and use. Without a doubt, higher-level APIs would certainly be of some value to support early game prototyping.

Future Internet Gaming Directions

It is striking to observe the similarities among the various attempts to support gaming and other net-VEs over the Internet. They are all primarily client-server systems, and most rely on TCP/IP. Some advanced infrastructures support some level of dead reckoning, area of interest management, and multithreading, but these features are clearly the exception rather than the rule.

It is unlikely that the Internet will be tamed by these straightforward net-VE systems for several reasons. The Internet is extremely heterogeneous in almost all respects. Network bandwidth links range from small numbers of kilobits per second to several gigabits per second. Network latencies are generally quite high (and growing worse), with a broad range from milliseconds to seconds. Some hosts are on the MBone, while others can only do TCP/IP. Different ISPs provide different levels of service, with some discarding or severely delaying UDP traffic and others providing guaranteed levels of service. Finally, the presence of security firewalls renders many existing systems essentially unusable because the only viable connectivity option is through outbound HTTP.

To give an indication of how unforgiving the Internet environment is to simple client-server systems, consider the latency of a simple modem connection [RTIME, TEN]. A roundtrip packet from a modem-connected client to a game server on the Internet takes from 180 to 350 ms. This is much slower than is needed to accurately control and interact with a game world, unless the interactions are predictable. Just passing through a 28.8 modem takes some 40 ms for packet compression and decompression. Therefore, a roundtrip to the ISP requires 80 ms. At the ISP, the questions then become: how many hops (routers) are there to the Internet backbone from the originating player, what is the transit time between backbones (sometimes 100 ms), and how many hops are there along the final backbone to the destination machine? Each router (hop) adds several milliseconds of latency. Transiting between backbones on the Internet is fraught with packet loss, with 20% loss common for some overloaded backbone connections. For this reason, many gaming companies have been forced to create their own backbone network and require users to connect directly to that backbone.

The experimental Interactive Universe (InVerse) system, started at IBM T.J. Watson Research Center in 1996, represents one of the few attempts to systematically revisit the fundamental network architecture assumptions made by traditional net-VEs and consider Internet-based net-VE deployments [Singhal+97]. From the start, InVerse is designed around heterogeneity and dynamic reconfigurability to address network concerns.

The techniques adopted by the InVerse system include the four that follow.

1. *A hybrid peer-server communication system:* When disseminating information, a host transmits data to some hosts directly and to other hosts through a central server. The balance between the peer-to-peer and client-server aspects of information dissemination is established dynamically based on the network bandwidth availability at source and destination hosts and the latency characteristics of the different information distribution paths. As a result, a LAN-based client will typically communicate with other players on the LAN in a peer-to-peer fashion but would communicate with a low-bandwidth modem-based player through a server that can aggregate and compress packets for delivery.

2. *Integration of peer-to-peer unicast, client-server unicast, and multicast communications protocols:* Hosts dynamically perform protocol discovery tests to determine the range of communication options available between them. Using these communication probes, hosts determine whether they can communicate directly by multicast, UDP, TCP/IP, or HTTP or whether they must direct packets through a central server. Thus, the InVerse system can handle communication through fairly complex network infrastructures.

3. *Use of plug-in channels and agents to process all network events:* Rather than being designed as a monolithic system, the InVerse system is implemented in a highly modular fashion, thereby allowing the client software to be incrementally downloaded over the Internet. Each type of packet event processing is packaged into a protocol handler module that can be installed or uninstalled from the InVerse runtime while the net-VE is executing. This design greatly reduces the time required for the initial Web download of InVerse and allows the software to dynamically adapt to the changing needs of the net-VE environment.

4. *Hierarchical servers:* Rather than demanding the use of a single centralized server to manage the entire net-VE, the InVerse system dynamically spawns servers at capable client hosts to manage different parts of the network environment. As a region of the net-VE is no longer populated, server function is then absorbed back to the higher-level servers in the hierarchy. At the highest levels, each game is treated as a separate (nonoverlapping) net-VE region, and a server is spawned on one of the participants' machines to manage the game. This design effectively removes almost all of the computational burden from the top-level lobby server.

InVerse is being used to provide the network infrastructure for a number of commercial Internet-based multiplayer games.

Taken together, these techniques enable a richly dynamic software infrastructure for Internet-based net-VEs. Although we hope that the Internet will grow to accommodate better the needs of net-VEs, progress in delivering the required bandwidth and latency guarantees has been slow. In the meantime, the burden falls upon the net-VE designer to consider ways to mask the Internet limitations as much as possible.

CONCLUSION

In this chapter, we have examined Internet-based virtual environments, including VRML, and looked at Internet-based gaming. Despite the age of the Internet, we are at the early stages in its development as a medium for the delivery of networked virtual environments and entertainment.

The next chapter concludes this book, with an examination of the future, highlighting some of the difficult issues remaining, with respect to networked virtual environments.

REFERENCES

[Barrus+96a] Barrus, J. W., R. C. Waters, and D. B. Anderson. Locales and beacons: Efficient and precise support for large multi-user virtual environments. *IEEE Virtual Reality Annual International Symposium*, 204–213. IEEE Computer Society, Santa Clara, CA. March 1996.

[Barrus+96b] Barrus, J. W., R. C. Waters, and D. B. Anderson. Locales and beacons: Efficient and precise support for large multi-user virtual environments. Technical Report 95-16a, Mitsubishi Electric Research Laboratories, Cambridge, CA, August 1996.

[Barrus+96c] Barrus, J. W., R. C. Waters, and D. B. Anderson. Locales: Supporting large multi-user virtual environments. *IEEE Computer Graphics and Applications* 16(6):50–57, November 1996.

[blaxxun] blaxxun Web site: *http://www.blaxxun.de/products/index.html*

[Brutzman98] Brutzman, D. P. The virtual reality modeling language and Java. *Communications of the ACM* 41(6):57–64, June 1998.

[Brutzman+95] Brutzman, D. P., M. R. Macedonia, and M. J. Zyda. Internetwork infrastructure requirements for virtual environments. *White Papers— The Unpredictable Certainty*, 110–122. Washington, DC: National Academy Press, 1997. (Also published in *Proceedings of the Virtual Reality Modeling Language* (VRML) *Symposium*, San Diego, December 1995.)

[Brutzman+97] Brutzman, D., M. Zyda, K. Watsen, and M. Macedonia. virtual reality transfer protocol (vrtp) design rationale. In *Proceedings of the IEEE Sixth International Workshops on Enabling Technologies: Infrastructure for Collaborative Enterprises* (WETICE '97), Distributed System Aspects of Sharing a Virtual Reality workshop, 179–186. IEEE Computer Society, Cambridge, MA, June 1997.

[ColonyCity] Colony City Web site: *http://www.colonycity.com/index.html*

[CommunityPlace] Web site for retrieving Community Place information in English: *http://vs.spiw.com/vs/browser_manual/index.html* (note that this is not the official Web site).

[DirectPlay] DirectX Web site, including DirectPlay: *http://www.microsoft.com/ directx*

[DIS-Java-VRML] Dis-Java-VRML Web site: *http://www.stl.nps.navy.mil/dis-java-vrml/*

[GameStorm] Kesmai's Game Storm network: *http://www.gamestorm.com*

[HEAT.NET] HEAT.NET Web site: *http://www.heat.net*

[Kali] Kali networked game support software: *http://www.kali.net*

[Lea+97] Lea, R., Y. Honda, K. Matsuda, and S. Matsuda. Community Place: Architecture and performance. In *Proceedings of the 1997 Symposium on the Virtual Reality Modeling Language*, 41–50. ACM SIGGRAPH, Monterey, CA, February 1997.

[Mpath] Mpath Interactive Web site: *http://www.mpath.com/papers/*

[Mplayer] Mplayer gaming Web site: *http://www.mplayer.com*

[OpenCommunity] Open Community Web site: *http://www.meitca.com/ opencom/*

[RTIME] RTIME networked game support software: *http://www.rtimeinc.com*

[Ryan98] Ryan, M. E. Online Gaming Review. *PC Magazine.* March 10, 1998. (Available at *http://search.zdnet.com/pcmag/features/onlinegames/intro.html*)

[Singhal+97] Singhal, S. K., B. Q. Nguyen, R. Redpath, M. Fraenkel, and J. Nguyen. InVerse: Designing an interactive universe architecture for scalability and extensibility. In *Proceedings of the Sixth IEEE International Symposium on High-Performance Distributed Computing.* IEEE Computer Society, Portland, OR, August 1997.

[TEN] Total Entertainment Network game site: *http://www.ten.net*

[VNet] Web sites with information on VNet: *http://ariadne.iz.net/~jeffs/vnet/ FAQ.html* and *http://ariadne.iz.net/~jeffs/vnet/VRML_Interchange_Protocol.html*

[VRML] VRML Web site: *http://www.vrml.org*

[VRML-EAI] VRML EAI Web site: *http://www.vrml.org/WorkingGroups/vrml-eai/*

[VRML-LivingWorlds] VRML Living Worlds Web site: *http://www.vrml.org/ WorkingGroups/living-worlds/*

[Waters+97] Waters, R. C., D. B. Anderson, J. W. Barrus, D. C. Brogan, M. A. Casey, S. G. McKeown, T. Nitta, I. B. Sterns, and W. S. Yerazunis. Diamond Park and spline: A social virtual reality system with 3D animation, spoken interaction, and runtime modifiability. *PRESENCE: Teleoperators and Virtual Environments* 6(4), August 1997.

[Waters/Anderson/Schwenke97] Waters, R. C., D. B. Anderson, and D. L. Schwenke. Design of the interactive sharing transfer protocol. In *Proceedings of the Sixth IEEE Workshops on Enabling Technologies: Infrastructure for Collaborative Enterprises* (WETICE '97). IEEE Computer Society, Cambridge, MA, June 1997.

[Wernecke94] Wernecke, J. *The Inventor Mentor: Programming Object-Oriented 3D Graphics with Open Inventor Release 2.* Reading, MA: Addison-Wesley, 1994.

[Zyda+97] Zyda, M., D. Brutzman, R. Darken, R. McGhee, J. Falby, E. Bachmann, K. Watsen, B. Kavanagh, and R. Storms. NPSNET—Large-scale virtual environment technology testbed. In *Proceedings of the International Conference on Artificial Reality and Tele-Existence*, 18–26. Tokyo, December 1997.

Chapter 9

Perspective and Predictions

The previous chapters have addressed aspects of a net-VE system's design, implementation, and deployment. It should be apparent that a net-VE system must address a complex combination of constraints. While experience has demonstrated how to handle many of these constraints, our knowledge is still far from complete. For example, as we have seen several times, most net-VE design choices must be carefully tuned to the particular application and deployment environment.

This chapter discusses the needs of the net-VE community today. We discuss library support for net-VEs and the need for better support from the Internet. We highlight some net-VE open research issues. We conclude with some observations about the past, present, and future directions for networked virtual environments.

BETTER LIBRARY SUPPORT

Many of the networked virtual environments described in this text have been outstanding successes in their own right. However, in the long run, they have done little more than prove that working together on an immersive application connected via a network was not only feasible but also a "good thing," or that playing a game across a distance was more fun then just playing alone. In general, these systems have not contributed much to the big picture, nor have they addressed the important question of how to make developing net-VEs easier, faster, and cheaper. Most of the systems examined so far are rather monolithic. By monolithic, we mean that the net-VE software is large, ranging around 150,000 lines of code, and hence hard to reuse in building new systems. While many of these systems have proved out small pieces of the net-VE design puzzle, these pieces have not been easy to reuse. The current focus in the net-VE arena is on the development of toolkits that simplify the development of net-VEs and provide a standard framework for net-VE application development.

Toolkits themselves do not make networked virtual environments pervasive, unless the toolkits are widely available and easily understood. In today's climate, this means the toolkits need to be nearly free, with readily available source code somewhat like Linux. Additionally, this means that the learning curve for the toolkit's use must be very short. Toolkits that require weeks of study and expensive development environments for use are not going to achieve universal appeal among net-VE developers. The "not invented here" (NIH) problem pervades the software industry, and net-VE developers are no exception. Unless a toolkit provides clear, immediately perceived value, developers are predisposed to start with new code; by the time the potential value of the toolkit is recognized, it is often too late.

The following subsections examine some of the available toolkits that provide support for networking virtual environments and discuss how they fit into this realm of low-learning curve and freely available source code.

Bamboo

Bamboo[1] is a toolkit for developing dynamically extensible, real-time networked virtual environments [Bamboo, Watsen/Zyda98a, Watsen/Zyda98b]. Bamboo's design focuses on the ability of the system to con-

---

[1]The discussion of Bamboo is a distillation of [Watsen/Zyda98a] with updates.

figure itself dynamically without explicit user interaction, allowing applications to take on new functionality after execution. The Bamboo framework facilitates the discovery of virtual environments on the network at runtime and facilitates their orthogonal decomposition. Bamboo offers a complete, interoperable set of mechanisms needed for a wide variety of real-time, networked applications.

The goal of Bamboo is to enable dynamically scalable virtual environments to be hosted on the Internet. Bamboo accomplishes this by implementing the plug-in metaphor popularized by commercial packages such as Adobe Photoshop and Netscape Navigator. Dynamically loaded modules may be retrieved from memory, from disk, or from the Web via HTTP. Modules can define geometry, textures, sounds, behavior, interface, and so forth. However, assuming its use within large-scale networked environments and the need for explicit linking at runtime, Bamboo extends the original plug-in metaphor by adding specifications of intermodule dependencies and intramodule security.

Bamboo is designed to be cross-platform portable. Though it would be desirable to provide a "compile once and run everywhere" model using the Java programming language, current Java virtual machine (JVM) performance complicates the effective development of real-time, interactive applications such as net-VEs. Instead, Bamboo provides a write once, compile everywhere API in C++ to achieve the real-time, interactive speeds necessary for networked virtual environments.

Bamboo is built on the Adaptive Communication Environment (ACE) toolkit developed at Washington University, St. Louis, and is built around a framework of object-oriented design patterns [Schmidt93]. Bamboo's graphics component is itself pluggable, depending on the desires of the programmer, with Fahrenheit and Java3D as the recommended toolkits. Because Bamboo is capable of loading the JVM as a module, user interfaces can be developed using Java AWT. Figure 9-1 shows how Bamboo, ACE, and the various other software toolkits fit together.

Low-level networking support in Bamboo—including support for IPv4 and IPv6—are provided by the ACE toolkit, including abstractions for unicast, multicast, and broadcast. ACE has an elegant abstraction for Internet addresses, sockets, streams, and datagrams.

Bamboo's goals are ambitious. The Bamboo network software architecture is built around the following three design assumptions.

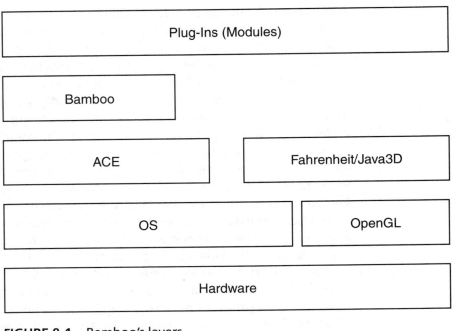

FIGURE 9-1   Bamboo's layers

1. Eventually, there will exist a persistent virtual environment shared simultaneously by billions of participants.

2. There can never be a global reboot.

3. All modifications must happen on the fly.

Figure 9-2 shows the Bamboo architecture for this grand NSA dream. This vision requires an expandable and extensible toolkit. Expandability comes from Bamboo's ability to load modules at runtime and from Bamboo's ability to implement dynamic application layer network protocols. These dynamic protocols have been prototyped [Watsen/Zyda98b].

Scalable worlds require support for an almost infinitely capable area of interest management. The area of interest management component is already running [Abrams+98]. In addition, to implement highly scalable worlds, support for a persistent universe is necessary, along with the capability to suspend and resume state. An architecture for

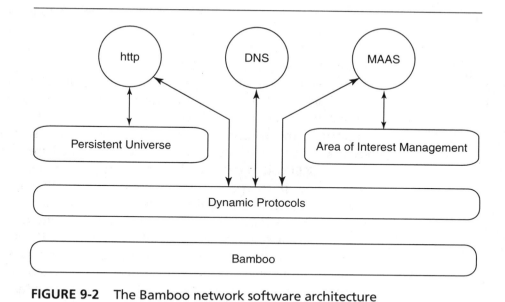

FIGURE 9-2   The Bamboo network software architecture

persistence has been developed, and synthesis is ongoing for these components of Bamboo. The Bamboo Web site [Bamboo] has information on the status of these efforts.

High Level Architecture

The Department of Defense, through the Defense Modeling and Simulation Office (DMSO), has been pursuing its own architecture for virtual environment interoperability. The High Level Architecture (HLA) effort [DMSO, Dahmann+99] aims to facilitate the interoperability and composability of the broadest range of component-based simulations. The HLA did not originate as an open standard, but it is now being recognized and adopted by both the Object Management Group (OMG) and IEEE.[2] It is particularly important because it represents the migra-

---

[2]It is interesting to note that HLA development occurred in much the same way as did the DIS standard—namely, that the initial design was produced within the DoD and then delivered to an external body (IEEE and/or OMG) for standardization. The National Research Council report discusses how this development approach can impede widespread commercial adoption of the resulting standard [NRC97].

tion path for existing DIS-based net-VEs. Indeed, further development of DIS-based simulations is scheduled to cease in 1999 as the DoD adopts the HLA, and the use of DIS-based simulations will be terminated in the year 2000.

One can think of the HLA architecture as an object-oriented net-VE design. Each simulator, known as a *federate,* is a component that represents a collection of objects, each having a set of attributes and capable of initiating and receiving events. The federate registers each of its objects with a piece of middleware called the Run-Time Infrastructure (RTI). The RTI collaborates with RTI instances on other hosts to learn about remote participants (objects) and delivers information about those participants to the local federate. The local federate, in turn, typically instantiates local objects representing those remote participants. Attribute updates and events are also exchanged through the RTI, which is responsible for handling area of interest management, time synchronization, and other low-level net-VE services on behalf of the application. The collection of federates, along with their associated RTI instances, is termed a *federation.*

Simulators in the federation send and receive state information via calls to and from the RTI. The RTI provides support for several services (Figure 9-3):

- *Federation management:* Administers the set of participating RTI instances within the federation.

- *Object management:* Registers and unregisters local participant objects within each federate; discovers remote participant objects; exchanges object state and interaction events.

- *Declaration management:* Allows each federate to designate filters on RTI notifications about the existence of particular types of remote objects, changes to particular object attributes, and particular interaction events.

- *Data distribution management:* Allows each federate to further refine RTI data distribution by providing filters scoped to particular object instances or particular regions of the simulation environment.

- *Ownership management:* Allows a particular federate to obtain and release control over the attributes of a local or remote object.

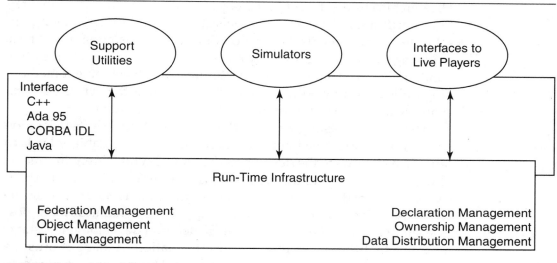

FIGURE 9-3   The HLA and the RTI

Source: From [Dahmann98]. Used with permission.

- *Time management:* Maintains a common sense of time among all federates, either based on real-time clock or based on an event-based clock.

A reference RTI implementation has been built by contractors to DMSO, although other commercial and experimental implementations exist.

The HLA architecture is defined by three sets of documents: the HLA rules, the HLA interface specification, and the object model template [Dahmann98]. The HLA rules define the relationships among federation components. The HLA interface specification defines the abstract interface exported by a conformant RTI implementation and conformant federates. This specification defines language bindings for C++, Java, and Ada. The object model template defines the set of participant object types within the federation, along with their attributes, attribute types, value encodings, and so forth.

The first step for a set of simulators that wish to interoperate via an RTI is to establish a federation [Steinman/Yu98]. The full development of the federation includes filling in all the details with respect to the

HLA architecture—the rules, the object model template, and the interface specification. Development tools are provided for completing this set of federation details. Federation development is not a trivial task, requiring the designer to specify all aspects of the net-VE. On the other hand, unlike most simulation architectures, this development methodology allows the net-VE designer to customize the set of data exchanges to meet the goals of the net-VE system execution.

The most interesting aspect of the HLA architecture is its federation concept of composable interacting simulators. Composability leads to reuse, which leads to the development of novel synthetic environments of previously unthought purpose. This goal, reusability of its expensively developed simulations, is important to the DoD. However, the HLA does not go all the way toward supporting dynamically composable simulations and universal reuse. Federation development is static, meaning that the object model and information exchanges must be completed before the simulation run begins. At runtime, federates may enter and leave the simulation at will, but only as long as they conform to the predefined object model being used by that simulation. Thus, reuse is limited to HLA systems associated with compatible object models. An HLA system, once specified, cannot support the runtime introduction of arbitrary federates and, therefore, cannot fully exploit dynamic composability.

DMSO established an architecture management group (AMG) for the development of HLA [DMSO]. This AMG has representatives from all of the major simulation programs within the DoD. The nonprofit Object Management Group (OMG) has adopted HLA as the "Facility for Distributed Simulation Systems 1.0" [OMG]. As of May 1999, the IEEE standard for HLA is under ballot as specifications P1516, P1516.1, and P1516.2. These standardization activities may further the widespread adoption of the HLA and the development of RTI software.

The HLA architecture and base RTI have been utilized to some effect [DMSO]. RTI implementations have been provided for most platforms, including Sun Solaris, SGI IRIX, Windows NT, Linux, and Java. However, the HLA faces the following two barriers to widespread adoption [Liles+98].

1. The model represents a rigid model for simulation development. It remains to be seen whether this model can be applied outside the

military domain and also whether HLA's military stigma can be shed, resulting in adoption by commercial net-VE designers (something that the DIS protocol mostly failed to achieve). Several recent commercial demonstrations indicate that the HLA model has some promise [Dahmann99].

2. Only a limited number of RTI implementations exist today. For HLA to be successful, RTI implementations supporting a broad range of simulation types need to emerge. Today, given the limited number of stable RTI implementations available, a designer may have to wait several months for a compatible RTI to become available after an operating system upgrade.

Certainly the area of RTI availability will be helped by HLA standardization.

Java-Based Toolkits

Toolkits supporting net-VE development in Java provide cross-platform delivery capabilities and also seek to maximize the ease-of-use of application development [Singhal/Nguyen98a]. Java-based toolkits allow the net-VE developer to easily integrate the net-VE application software with other standard Java services such as audio and video, transactions, and Web access [Java]. To increase composability, Java includes a component model, JavaBeans, which allows an application to receive and instantiate modules from third-party developers.

The Java Shared Data Toolkit

The Java Shared Data Toolkit (JSDT), developed and sold by Sun's JavaSoft division, provides a framework for building collaborative Java applications [JSDT]. The toolkit enables applications to allocate shared byte arrays whose contents are automatically kept synchronized with versions at other hosts in the environment. These arrays can therefore be treated as a distributed shared memory upon which each of the net-VE subsystems (see Chapter 6) can be built. The toolkit also provides tokens for synchronizating data update and provides a channel abstraction for sending and receiving shared events. Using this toolkit, one could envisage implementing a complete HLA RTI.

The IBM Shared Data Objects Toolkit

The IBM Shared Data Objects (SDO) toolkit is freely available from their AlphaWorks Web site [SDO]. Its goals are very similar in spirit to JSDT, but it provides higher-level abstractions that better enable its use for building net-VEs. A shared `session` is partitioned into multiple `places`, which may be thought of as rooms or sharing contexts. Each room may contain a collection of data objects and channels. A user, upon entering the session, may enter multiple places simultaneously. Within each place, the user may learn about the available data objects and channels, subscribe to notifications about new and deleted objects and channels, subscribe to updates of an object's state, and subscribe to events delivered by a channel.

Unlike JSDT, the SDO toolkit provides a type-safe abstraction for shared data, supporting hash tables, vectors, integers, floats, and so forth. It also provides a flexible message addressing system built around the notion of a `group` object. A group may map to a single recipient (an individual group), all recipients (the broadcast group), a designated list of recipients (a private group), or a subscribable list of recipients (a public group). The SDO model is flexible enough to support a fairly rich set of interaction paradigms, although this flexibility also limits its scalability to a few dozen participants.

Toolkits Being Developed Everywhere . . .

There are lots of toolkits under development for net-VEs, and here we can cover only some of the larger efforts and briefly state their importance. There are certainly other toolkits that we do not mention here. In a print medium, it is impossible to be current on such efforts.

The MASSIVE-2 effort continues the work of the MASSIVE-1 project [Benford/Greenhalgh97, Greenhalgh96a, Greenhalgh96b, MASSIVE-2]. MASSIVE-2 seems to be in the middle of a name change to the CRG Virtual Environment (CVE). MASSIVE-2 is a net-VE system architecture that includes

- Networking based on IP multicasting
- An extended area of interest paradigm based on third-party objects, regions, and abstractions
- Support for 3D graphics

- Real-time packet audio and text
- An extensible object-oriented API [MASSIVE-2]

The German National Research Center for Information Technology (GMD) has begun development of its own toolkit, Avocado, for networked virtual environments [Avocado]. The focus of Avocado is on networking graphics by replicating a shared scene graph among the participants in the net-VE. Sharing the scene graph is becoming a more common architecture for networking virtual environments, primarily because it is easily achievable with simple socket reads/writes. Avocado extends this by providing a "group communication system" that provides state consistency and state updates to late-arriving players in the virtual environment. Avocado is built around SGI Performer, and hence is not portable.

The Swedish Institute for Computer Science's DIVE toolkit is always under revision [Carlsson/Hagsand93a, Carlsson/Hagsand93b, Hagsand96, DIVE]. DIVE's main focus is on virtual environments as a communications medium.

The Spline system has been spun off from MERL as a commercial entity, Horizon Systems Laboratories (HSL) [Spline, Horizon]. Spline has an extremely interesting area of interest management architecture and defined the Interactive Sharing Transport Protocol (ISTP). Unfortunately, the commercialization of the toolkit has taken it from public view and, therefore, almost certainly limits its widespread adoption. Nevertheless, if HSL is successful in commercializing the toolkit, it will be of great value because of its excellent net-VE enablement capabilities.

VR Juggler is another interesting toolkit that has some networking capabilities [VRJuggler]. Unfortunately, VR Juggler papers and documents are not yet available and may become less so, since a commercialization effort appears to be underway.

TOWARD A BETTER INTERNET

The Internet was not originally architected to deal with the needs of high-bandwidth, low-latency, many-participant net-VE systems. For instance, support for multicasting was only introduced to the Internet in recent years, and even in 1999, it has not yet been fully adopted. This and other limitations to the deployed Internet will continue to be of great concern to the net-VE developers of today and tomorrow. One of the major impediments to net-VEs today is the lack of widespread support for multicasting in the currently deployed routers. As we have seen in this text, comprehensive solutions to area of interest management require that multicasting be a fundamental component of the Internet. While multicasting is not available everywhere today, experimentation with it is widespread, enabled by the MBone, which uses workstation-routers to "tunnel" multicast packets through UDP/IP packets for transmission between islands of multicasting support. All router manufacturers are now producing routers with native multicast support, and as older ones are replaced, multicasting will come to be the norm. The Internet-2 effort has multicasting in all its routers, reminding us how nice it is to throw away the prototype and then build it correctly the second time [Internet-2].

The Internet-2 effort is also working on another area necessary for networked virtual environments, that of supporting quality of service (QoS). The notion behind quality of service is that the net-VE application developer would like to be able to select the type of service to receive from the network: best efforts (like today's Internet) or various gradations of premium service (say, by specifying the absolute bandwidth required). Members of the net-VE community are working with members of the Internet-2 community to guarantee that this happens [ANS].

Multicast support at the personal computer and workstation is another unsolved problem requiring that another generation of network cards be developed and all the old ones discarded. For a small number of multicast groups, most current network cards work well. When the number of subscribed multicast groups becomes larger than a handful, most network cards today go into promiscuous mode, meaning they pass all multicast packets to the operating system for processing in software, even if no local application has subscribed to the multicast group destination of the packet. This defeats much of the reason for using multicasting and must be improved as we grow Internet-2.

Unfortunately, one of the biggest problems with today's Internet has received relatively little attention: latency. In fact, end-to-end Internet latency is getting steadily worse as network pipes become more congested. In addition, client-side latency is also deteriorating as manufacturers of client-side modems and network cards concentrate their attention on achieving higher bandwidth levels and throughput rates. We can expect an increasing number of net-VE users to be using PCs connected to the Internet by telephone lines (in the short-term) and cable modems (in the medium-term). These transmission media already have poor latency characteristics, and slow client-side hardware only exacerbates matters [Cheshire96].

RESEARCH FRONTIERS

The net-VE research community is expanding as more people recognize the value of net-VE systems for training and education, entertainment, and scientific and business collaboration. This section highlights a few of the significant themes behind the current work.

Scalability continues to be a primary area of exploration, as we learn how to build our software to accommodate large numbers of players and provide them with a compelling 3D interactive experience. We have some understanding of how to build net-VEs for small numbers of players, say, under 1,000. Many people say that 1,000 players in a net-VE are sufficient, that we will never need more, and that we will most likely need fewer.

We need more than 1,000 players when we want to build virtual environments that are stadium-sized, to enable a large crowd of spectators to watch an event. We need more than 1,000 players when we want to construct accurate battle simulations, simulations on the size of Operation Desert Storm (300,000 participants). We need more than 1,000 players if we are going to examine complex worlds, worlds built to simulate entire cityscapes. This justifies continued work in scalability. However, scalability solutions may be highly application domain dependent, and what works for one scenario may not work for the next application. The challenge, therefore, is to generalize these techniques and simplify the decisions that a net-VE designer must make when embarking on a new system.

Greater net-VE realism is also an area of continued work. Higher quality graphical representations are always desired. The challenge lies in properly allocating available polygon counts, using a combination of level-of-detail modeling and information filtering. Future net-VE systems need to model and share dynamic terrain, weather, fog, smoke, and sound. They need to do real-time collision detection and provide physical modeling to ensure accurate collision resolution. In addition, they need to support live audio and video.

We ended chapter 6 by discussing the lack of clean solutions for *graceful degradability*. Graceful degradability was first described in the 1995 National Research Council report on virtual reality [NRC95, p. 61]:

> There is a major need for systems that ensure that high-priority processes . . . [to] receive service at short, regular intervals and to provide time-critical computing and rendering with negotiated graceful degradation algorithms that meet frame rate and lag-time guarantees—this is a new computing paradigm.

Graceful degradation means that we have a solution to the multiple threads problem discussed in Chapter 6, implying that we know how to make our threads use just the right number of computing cycles and no more. For small systems with low complexity, we can build adequate virtual environments. However, as the net-VE complexity increases, the performance usually falls rapidly because the threads do not share the CPU resources effectively. In chapter 6, we talked about improving the system performance by utilizing multiple threads, but we have no good solution today for coordinating those threads to maintain interactivity and frame rate as the system increases in complexity and size.

Composability is the holy grail of today's net-VE community. Composability means that we have the ability to dynamically import models and behaviors, developed in one virtual environment, into another virtual environment. Architecting for composability is difficult. Imagine a net-VE participant bringing a new, previously unseen object into the environment and being able to see, hear, and interact with it instantly and meaningfully. Further, imagine being able to take that object with you as you leave the environment, save it on your local disk, then carry it with you into a new net-VE.

Therefore, composability also requires that each user be associated with persistent information including a 3D graphical model, behaviors, actions, possessions, capabilities, preferences, and so on. A soldier can enter a battle, depart, and return without losing either the context or his or her state information. In entertainment-based systems, users need the flexibility to select and customize their graphical representation within a *registration room* [Singhal/Nguyen98b].

As a user becomes capable of entering multiple net-VE systems provided by third-party developers, security also becomes a concern. Users will demand protection of personal information that they bring with them and distribute within a net-VE. One might even envisage trusted organizations evolving to maintain this net-VE state on behalf of the user. Security needs increase as net-VE systems support more realistic day-to-day social interactions such as shopping. There has been much interest in creating virtual storefronts or malls (composed of many independently developed stores) allowing users to browse, visualize products, and make purchases.

We can achieve parts of this composability vision today, but we do not yet have a full solution. A full solution to composability would allow

- The massively parallel implementation of comprehensive worlds, worlds we have not yet seen.
- These different worlds to be seamlessly interconnected into a single Internet-wide environment, with *portals* allowing users to seamlessly travel between those worlds.

We can imagine the entire world participating in this development, something like the participation we now see with the World Wide Web.

PAST, PRESENT, AND FUTURE

We are barely on the beginning edge of what we will experience over the next 100 years in networked virtual environments; we are not even anywhere close to what is described in classic science fiction tomes on virtual reality [Gibson84, Stephenson93, Williams98]. As of 1999, we are doing research, building prototypes, and throwing away prototypes. We sometimes field part of what we have done. Sometimes we run out of funds or have to wait for the next generation of graphics and networking hardware or the next millennium's haptic devices. We hope that this book has started someone, somewhere, toward building those networked virtual environments of which we can now only dream.

REFERENCES

[Abrams+98] Abrams, H., K. Watsen, and M. Zyda. Three tiered interest management for large-scale virtual environments. In *Proceedings of VRST '98*. Taipei, Taiwan, November 1998.

[ANS] Advanced Network and Services Tele-Immersion Project Web site: *http://www.advanced.org/teleimmersion.html*

[Avocado98] Avocado Web site: *http://viswiz.gmd.de/~hase/Avocado.html*

[Bamboo] Bamboo Web site: *http://www.npsnet.nps.navy.mil/Bamboo*

[Benford/Greenhalgh97] Benford, S., and C. Greenhalgh. Introducing third party objects into the spatial model of interaction. (Available at *ftp://turing. cs.nott.ac.uk/pub/papers/CRG97-model2.ps.gz*)

[Carlsson/Hagsand93a] Carlsson, C., and O. Hagsand. DIVE—A multi-user virtual reality system. In *Proceedings of the 1993 IEEE Virtual Reality Annual International Symposium*, 394–400. Seattle, September 1993.

[Carlsson/Hagsand93b] Carlsson, C., and O. Hagsand. DIVE—A platform for multi-user virtual environments. *Computers & Graphics* 17(6):663–669, 1993.

[Cheshire96] Cheshire, S. It's the latency, stupid. May 1996. (Available from *http://rescomp.stanford.edu/~cheshire/rants/Latency.html*)

[Dahmann98] Dahmann, J. High level architecture. I/ITSEC Tutorial, November 30, 1998. (Available at *http://www.dmso.mil/dmso/docslib/briefs/IITSEC/ 20itsec/jdiitsec.ppt*)

[Dahmann99] Dahmann, J. Personal communication, March 26, 1999.

[Dahmann+99] Dahmann, J., R. Weatherly, and F. Kuhl. *Creating Computer Simulation Systems: An Introduction to the High Level Architecture*. Upper Saddle River, NJ: Prentice-Hall, 1999.

[DIVE] The DIVE virtual environment Web site: *http://www.sics.se/dive/dive. html*

[DMSO] The Defense Modeling and Simulation Office High Level Architecture Web site: *http://hla.dmso.mil/*

[Gibson84] Gibson, W. *Neuromancer*. New York: Ace Books, 1984.

[Greenhalgh96a] Greenhalgh, C. Dynamic, embodied multicast groups in MASSIVE-2. Technical Report NOTTCS-TR-96-8, Department of Computer Science, University of Nottingham, UK. (Available from *ftp://turing.cs. nott.ac.uk/pub/papers/NOTTCS-TR-96-8.ps.gz*)

[Greenhalgh96b] Greenhalgh, C. Spatial scope and multicast in large virtual environments. Technical Report NOTTCS-TR-96-7, Department of Computer Science, University of Nottingham, UK. (Available from *ftp://turing.cs. nott.ac.uk/pub/papers/NOTTCS-TR-96-7.ps.gz*)

[Hagsand96] Hagsand, O. Interactive multiuser VEs in the DIVE system. *IEEE Multimedia Magazine* 3(1):30–39, 1996.

[Horizon] Horizon Systems Laboratory Web site: *http://www.meitca.com/HSL/*

[Internet-2] Internet-2 Web site: *http://www.internet2.edu/*

[Java] Java Development Kit (JDK) Web site: *http://www.javasoft.com*

[JSDT] Java Shared Data Toolkit (JSDT) Web site: *http://www.javasoft.com/ products/java-media/jsdt/*

[Liles+98] Liles, S., K. Watsen, and M. Zyda. Dynamic discovery of simulation entities using bamboo and HLA. In *Proceedings of the 1998 Fall Simulation Interoperability Workshop*. Orlando, September 1998.

[MASSIVE-2] The MASSIVE-2 Web site: *http://www.crg.cs.nott.ac.uk/research/ systems/MASSIVE-2/*

[NRC95] National Research Council. *Virtual Reality: Scientific and Technological Challenges*. Washington, DC: National Academy of Sciences Press, 1995.

[NRC97] National Research Council. *Modeling and Simulation: Linking Entertainment & Defense*. Washington, DC: National Academy Press, September 1997.

[OMG] Object Management Group Web site: *http://www.omg.org/*

[Schmidt93] Schmidt, D. The ADAPTIVE communication environment: object-oriented network programming components for developing client/ server applications. *11th and 12th Sun Users Group*, 1993. (Available at *http://www.cs.wustl.edu/~schmidt/SUG-94.ps.gz*)

[SDO] IBM Shared Data Objects Web site on AlphaWorks: *http://www. alphaworks.ibm.com/formula/sdo*

[Singhal/Nguyen98a] Singhal, S. K., and B. Q. Nguyen. The Java factor. *Communications of the ACM* 41(6):34–37, June 1998.

[Singhal/Nguyen98b] Singhal, S. K., and B. Q. Nguyen. Registration rooms, lobbies, and portals: Interconnecting large-scale networked virtual environments and collaborations. In *Proceedings of the 1998 Virtual Reality Annual International Symposium* (VRAIS'98), 213. IEEE Computer Society, Atlanta, GA, March 1998.

[Spline] The MERL Spline Web site: *http://www.merl.com/projects/spline/index. html*

[Steinman/Yu98] Steinman, J., and L. Yu. Adapting your simulation for HLA. *Simulation, the Journal of the Society for Computer Simulation International* 71(6), December 1998.

[Stephenson93] N. Stephenson. *Snow Crash*. New York: Bantam Spectra, 1993.

[VRJuggler] The VR Juggler Web site: *http://www.icemt.iastate.edu/research/ stools/vrjuggler/index.html*

[Watsen/Zyda98a] Watsen, K., and M. Zyda. Bamboo—A portable system for dynamically extensible, networked, real-time, virtual environments. In *Proceedings of the 1998 Virtual Reality Annual International Symposium* (VRAIS '98), 252–259. IEEE, Atlanta, GA, March 1998.

[Watsen/Zyda98b] Watsen, K., and M. Zyda. Bamboo—Supporting dynamic protocols for virtual environments. In *Proceedings of the IMAGE 98 Conference*, KA-1-9. Scottsdale, AZ, August 1998.

[Williams98] Williams, T. *Otherland: City of Golden Shadow*. New York: Daw Books, 1998.

Appendix

Network Communication in C, C++, and Java

This appendix provides code samples for how to access TCP/IP, UDP/IP, IP Broadcasting, and IP multicasting from C, C++, and Java. The code samples should be enough to get started, but more detailed tutorials are widely available. For more details on network programming, see [Comer/Stevens96a] and [Stevens98] for C and C++[1] and [Coutois98] and [JDK] for Java.

USING TCP/IP FROM C AND C++

The first step in using TCP/IP is to obtain a socket. The socket() function is used to obtain a socket that uses IP protocol and provides the

---

[1]Unfortunately, C and C++ network programs are not universally portable across different operating systems. The code samples shown in this chapter should run on most BSD-style systems with little or no modification. The networking code will require modification to run on Windows platforms, however; more details on Windows networking can be found in [Quinn/Shute95] and [Comer/Stevens96b].

TCP byte stream semantics, as shown in Listing A-1. A client can now open a connection to a server who is waiting for inbound connections. To do this, it must allocate a sockaddr_in (Internet socket address) structure that describes the destination host address and port. Listing A-2 continues the example to connect to a server at host address 10.25.43.9 and port 13214.

The connect() function call does several different things. First, it picks a free local port and binds that port to the client's socket. The client usually does not care which port number is assigned because other applications do not connect to it. Second, the function attempts to contact the server at the specified address and port. If the connection is accepted, it initializes the connection so that the application can send and receive data over the socket.

LISTING A-1   Creating a socket for network communication

```
#include <stdio.h>
#include <sys/types.h>
#include <sys/socket.h>
#include <netinet/in.h>
/* ... */
int sock;
   /* Allocate a socket
    *    PF_INET:  Use the Internet family of Protocols
    *    SOCK_STREAM:  Provide reliable byte-stream semantics
    *    0:  Use the default protocol (TCP)  */
sock = socket(PF_INET, SOCK_STREAM, 0);
if (sock == -1) {
     /* Error */
   perror("socket");
   return;
}
```

LISTING A-2   Opening a connection to a remote server

```
struct sockaddr_in serverAddr;    /* The address and port of the server */
bzero((char *)&serverAddr, sizeof(serverAddr));
serverAddr.sin_family      = PF_INET;        /* Use Internet addresses */
serverAddr.sin_addr.s_addr = inet_addr("10.25.43.9");
   /* The inet_addr() function converts an IP address string into a four-byte
      integer with one byte for each of the address values */
   /* htons() converts a 16-bit short integer into the network byte order so
      that other hosts can interpret the integer even if they internally store
      integers using a different byte order */
serverAddr.sin_port        = htons(13214);
   /* Connect to the remote host */
if (connect(sock, (struct sockaddr *)&serverAddr, sizeof(serverAddr)) == -1) {
```

```
    /* Error */
    perror("connect");
    return;
}
```

For a client to connect to a server, the server application must first have initialized a socket for accepting connections at a particular port. It first allocates a socket by calling the socket() call as above. It next binds that socket to a well-known port, as shown in Listing A-3. This code looks quite similar to the connect() call performed by the client. The bind() call may fail if another local TCP/IP application has already bound to that port. Now that the socket is bound to a port, the application is ready to start receiving connections. It calls the listen() function to tell the operating system how many inbound client connections it can queue (the so-called listen backlog).

The server finally calls the accept() function to wait for a client to connect, as shown in Listing A-4. The server actually has two sockets open at once. The acceptSock variable points to the well-known port where new client connections arrive. The sock variable references a connection to a particular client (identified by the clientAddr structure which the accept() call filled in). The server code in Listing A-4 can only process one client connection at a time because after receiving an inbound connection, it handles all requests from that connection before returning to accept() the next connection. Next, we will discuss how to support multiple concurrent connections.

LISTING A-3   Binding a server socket to a well-known port for inbound client connections

```
struct sockaddr_in serverAddr;    /* The address and port of the server */
bzero((char *)&serverAddr, sizeof(serverAddr));
serverAddr.sin_family       = PF_INET;       /* Use Internet addresses */
    /* INADDR_ANY says that the operating system may choose to which local IP
       address to attach the application.  For most machines, which only have
       one address, this simply chooses that address.  The htonl() function
       converts a four-byte integer into the network byte order so that
       other hosts can interpret the integer even if they internally store
       integers using a different byte order */
serverAddr.sin_addr.s_addr  = htonl(INADDR_ANY);
    /* See above for an explanation of htons() */
serverAddr.sin_port         = htons(13214);
    /* Bind the socket to the well-known port */
if (bind(sock, (struct sockaddr *)&serverAddr, sizeof(serverAddr)) == -1) {
```

```
        /* Error */
    perror("bind");
    return;
}
```

LISTING A-4   Accepting an inbound connection from clients

```
int acceptSock = sock;
struct sockaddr_in clientAddr;
listen(acceptSock, 4);
while ((sock = accept(acceptSock, (struct sockaddr)&clientAddr, sizeof(clientAddr)))
!= -1) {
    /* sock represents a connection to a client, clientAddr is the client's
       host address and port */
    /* ... Process client connection ... */
}
  /* Only break out of loop if there is an error */
perror("accept");
```

Once the connection is established, the client and server can send and receive data over their respective sockets. To send data, an endpoint places the data into a buffer and provides that buffer to the operating system for transmission, as shown in Listing A-5. There is a subtle aspect to receiving data from a TCP/IP socket. Recall that the TCP/IP protocol may split up the sent data into many small packets for transmission.

Consequently, the data provided in a write() call may not arrive at the destination host as one single block. Because TCP/IP only provides a byte stream interface, the destination host does not reconstruct the data boundaries created by the write() calls. The read() system call blocks the application and returns whenever any data is available on the socket. It is the application's responsibility to figure out whether it has received all of the expected data and, if not, to return to the read() call to retrieve more data. It is for this reason that the length of the data was included as the first byte in our write() buffer in the above example. The complementary receive code is shown in Listing A-6.

LISTING A-5   Sending data over a TCP/IP connection

```
int BUFFERLEN = 255;
char buf[BUFFERLEN];
sprintf(buf, "%chello!", (char)strlen("hello!"));
    /* Send data:  The write() call takes three parameters, namely the socket,
       a pointer to the data buffer, and the number of bytes to transmit from
       the buffer.  The function returns -1 if there is an error.  */
```

```
if (write(sock, buf, 1+buf[0]) == -1) {
    perror("write");
    return;
}
```

LISTING A-6   Receiving data over a TCP/IP connection

```
int BUFFERLEN = 255;
char buf[BUFFERLEN];
int byteCount = 0;     /* Total number of bytes read */
int n;                 /* Number of bytes read this time */
    /* The read() function takes three parameters, namely the socket, a
       pointer to a buffer into which read data should be placed, and the
       maximum number of bytes to read into the buffer.  The function blocks
       until data is available and then returns the number of bytes actually
       read into the buffer.  It returns 0 if no more data is available on the
       connection (i.e. the connection is closed) or -1 if there is an error.
    */
while (((n = read(sock, buf+byteCount, BUFFERLEN-byteCount)) > 0) {
    byteCount += n;
    if (byteCount > buf[0])
        break;
}
if (n < 0) {
    /* Error */
    perror("read");
    return;
}
if (n == 0) {
    /* Connection was closed */
    /* ... */
}
```

Finally, when either side has finished sending data, it can close the connection:

```
close(sock);
```

It is important to remember that the close() call only closes the local socket. To fully tear down a TCP/IP connection, both sides must close their respective sockets. In addition, the server should also be sure to invoke close() on the acceptSock when it is finished accepting new client connections.

MANAGING CONCURRENT CONNECTIONS IN C AND C++

TCP/IP-based servers typically must manage multiple client connections simultaneously, and they must also wait for new inbound connections. Unfortunately, the read() call blocks the calling thread until data has arrived on a particular socket, and the accept() call blocks until a new client has connected. While waiting for new connections in accept(), the server cannot do any processing on behalf of existing connections. In Listing A-4, this situation required us to ensure that we completed all processing on existing connections before returning to accept() the next connection. The server could therefore only handle one client connection at a time.

To support multiple concurrent connections, many servers simply allocate one thread or process for each active connection [Comer/ Stevens96a]. Each of those threads or processes handles all requests and responses on behalf of its assigned connection, and after the connection is closed, the thread or process terminates. An additional thread or process is assigned to block on the accept() call and wait for new inbound connections:

```
while (true)
    accept() new connection
    spawn a new thread/process to handle the new connection
end while
```

However, processes are expensive and introduce the need to manage concurrency and synchronization. Therefore, this approach is not practical in building servers that must handle many simultaneous connections.

The select() call allows a server to detect activity on multiple sockets from within a single process. The select() call takes a bit mask representing the set of socket IDs that are of interest. Those IDs may represent both connected and listening sockets.[2] The select() call blocks until data is available to be read on one or more of the connected sockets or a connection is ready to be accepted on one or more of the listening sockets. Upon return, the call notifies the application of which sockets can be manipulated without blocking.

The select() call also takes a timeout parameter that can force the call to only block for a limited amount of time, even if no socket becomes ready to manipulate. That timeout value can even be set to 0 to force select() to return immediately. This parameter value allows the application to "poll" a set of sockets for network activity without having to block the thread. This approach is critical for enabling single-threaded net-VE systems, as we saw in chapter 6.

---

[2]In fact, the set of sockets may also include bound UDP, broadcast, or multicast sockets.

Listing A-7 shows an example of using `select()`. Note that `select()` actually provides many more options than are shown here; [Stevens98] provides extensive coverage of these options.

LISTING A-7   Using the `select()` function to multiplex multiple client TCP/IP connections

```c
#include <sys/select.h>
#include <sys/time.h>
    /* ... */
    /* We assume that sock is the listening socket and that clSocks is
       an array of clCount client connection sockets. */
int sock;
int clCount;
int *clSocks;
struct timeval timeout;    /* How long should select() block */
int i;                     /* Loop index */
int maxSock;               /* Maximum socket number */
int returnVal;             /* Return value from select() */
    /* Allocate a fd_set bitmask of socket IDs that we
       are interested in reading.  Also, compute the
       maximum socket number of interest. */
fd_set readSocks;
FD_ZERO(readSocks);                  /* Clear it */
FD_SET(sock, &readSocks);            /* Set the bit for sock */
maxSock = sock;
for (i=0; i<clCount; i++) {
   FD_SET(clSocks[i], &readSocks);   /* Set the bit for a client socket */
   if (clSocks[i] > maxSock)
      maxSock = clSocks[i];
}
   /* Initialize the select() timeout.  In this example, we will have
      select() return immediately (timeout of zero), but the fields can
      be set to any value.  If select() should ONLY return when a socket
      is ready to read, then NULL should be passed instead of a timeout to
      the select() call. */
timeout.tv_sec  = 0;    /* Seconds */
timeout.tv_usec = 0;    /* Microseconds */
returnVal = select(maxSock + 1,    /* Socket ID range */
                   &readSet,       /* Bitmask of sockets for reading */
                   NULL,           /* Bitmask of sockets for writing */
                   NULL,           /* Bitmask of sockets for exceptions */
                   &timeout);      /* Timeout period */
if (returnVal == -1) {
   /* Error */
   perror("select");
   return;
}
if (returnVal > 0) {
      /* A socket is ready for reading.  The returnVal variable specifies
         how many sockets are ready.  The readSet variable has been
```

```
        updated to reflect which sockets are ready. */
    if (FD_ISSET(sock, &readSet)) {
        /* Accept a new client connection from sock, add it to the clSocks
           array, and increment clCount */
        /* ... */
        returnVal-;
    }
        /* Now check for data along one of the connected clients */
    for (i=0; i<clCount && returnVal > 0; i++) {
        if (FD_ISSET(clSock[i], &readSet)) {
            /* Read and process data from clSock[i].  If the client has
               disconnected (e.g. read() returns zero), then remove
               the client socket from clSocks. */
            /* ... */
            returnVal-;
        }
    }
}
else {
    /* select() returns zero if the timeout occurred.
}
```

USING TCP/IP FROM JAVA

Writing networking code in Java is considerably easier than doing it in C, primarily because many of the common operations are combined by the Java Development Kit into a few high-level primitives [JDK]. On a client, the Socket class provides an anchor to a TCP/IP connection. By instantiating a Socket object, the application directly obtains a connection to the specified server, so there is no need to call a connect() function as in C.

The Socket class provides several constructors, but two are most commonly used. One constructor takes a host name and port, and the other takes an IP address and port, as shown in Listings A-8a and A-8b. Note that in the latter example, the InetAddress.getByName() method could also be invoked using the host's true name, netVE.nowhere.com, instead of using the IP address.

LISTING A-8A   Opening a TCP/IP connection in Java using a host name

```
import java.net.Socket;
import java.io.IOException;
import java.io.DataInputStream;
```

```
import java.io.DataOutputStream;
/* ... */
Socket sock;
try {
    sock = new Socket("netVE.nowhere.com", 13214);
}
catch(IOException ioe) {
    System.out.println("Error opening socket:  " + ioe.getMessage());
    return;
}
```

LISTING A-8B   Opening a TCP/IP connection in Java using an IP address

```
import java.net.Socket;
import java.io.IOException;
import java.io.DataInputStream;
import java.io.DataOutputStream;
/* ... */
Socket sock;
try {
    InetAddress addr = InetAddress.getByName("10.25.43.9");
    sock = new Socket(addr, 13214);
}
catch(IOException ioe) {
    System.out.println("Error opening socket:  " + ioe.getMessage());
    return;
}
```

The server application needs to instantiate a ServerSocket object. This object represents a socket that is ready to accept inbound client connections, so creating the object replaces the C calls to socket(), bind(), and listen(). A ServerSocket can be constructed in three ways: (1) providing just a local port number; (2) providing a local port number and a listen backlog; and (3) providing a local port number, listen backlog, and local IP address. Indeed, in most cases, applications just need to specify the local port, as shown in Listing A-9. The Server-Socket constructor may fail if another local TCP/IP application has already bound to that port.

The server is now ready to accept and process inbound client connections, as shown in Listing A-10. This code is similar in structure to the C code version. The accept() call on ServerSocket blocks until a client connection arrives. It returns a Socket representing a connection to the particular client. The only big difference here is that in Java, the Socket encapsulates the host address and port of the client. The server can obtain this information by calling methods on the Socket, as shown in Listing A-11.

LISTING A-9   Opening a TCP/IP socket to listen for inbound client connections

```java
import java.net.ServerSocket;
import java.net.Socket;
import java.io.IOException;
import java.io.DataInputStream;
import java.io.DataOutputStream;
/* ... */
ServerSocket acceptSock;
try {
   acceptSock = new ServerSocket(13214);
}
catch(IOException ioe) {
   System.out.println("Error opening server socket:  " + ioe.getMessage());
   return;
}
```

LISTING A-10   Accepting inbound client connections at a TCP/IP server in Java

```java
Socket sock;        // The client socket
while(true) {
   try {
      sock = acceptSock.accept();
   }
   catch(IOException ioe) {
      System.out.println("accept error:  " + ioe.getMessage());
      break;   // Exit while loop
   }
      /* sock represents a connection to a client */
      /* ... Process client connection ... */
}
   // Only break out of while loop if there was an error
```

LISTING A-11   Obtaining information about the connected client

```java
InetAddress clientAddr = sock.getInetAddress();
   /* From InetAddress, call getHostName() to get the host name or
      getAddress() to get the IP address */
int clientPort = sock.getPort();
```

Using their connected sockets, the client and server can exchange data by reading and writing to input and output streams in much the same way that they write to files. Listing A-12 includes a simple example of writing some data. The DataOutputStream provides methods for writing integers, long integers, strings (Universal Text Format, or UTF), floats, and many other types. The good news is that reading from a Socket is just as simple, as shown in Listing A-13.

LISTING A-12   Sending data to a Java socket

```
try{
   DataOutputStream oStream = new DataOutputStream(sock.getOutputStream());
   oStream.writeUTF("Hello!");
   oStream.writeInt(3);
}
catch(IOException ioe) {
   System.out.println("Write error:  " + ioe.getMessage());
}
```

LISTING A-13   Receiving data from a Java socket

```
try{
   DataInputStream iStream = new DataInputStream(sock.getInputStream());
   String helloString = iStream.readUTF();
   int three = iStream.readInt();
}
catch(IOException ioe) {
   System.out.println("Read error:  " + ioe.getMessage());
}
```

Finally, when either side has finished sending data, it can close the connection:

```
try{
   sock.close();
}
catch(IOException ioe) {
   System.out.println("Close error:  " + ioe.getMessage());
}
```

Again, close() needs to be called on both sides of the connection, and the server should also be sure to close() the ServerSocket when it no longer wishes to accept client connections.

MANAGING CONCURRENT CONNECTIONS IN JAVA

Java provides no equivalent to the select() call which enables C/C++-based servers to manage multiple client connections from a single thread or process. Java servers therefore typically allocate a separate thread for each client plus an additional thread for the listening socket. Listing A-14 provides an example of this processing.

LISTING A-14   Using multiple threads to manage concurrent connections in Java

```java
import java.net.ServerSocket;
import java.net.Socket;
import java.io.IOException;
import java.io.DataInputStream;
import java.io.DataOutputStream;

public class TheServer {

    /* This inner class implements the processing for each
       client connection.  An instance is created for each
       connection received. */
    static class ConnectionProcessorThread implements Runnable {
        private Socket clientConnection;

        /* This constructor stores the client connection socket
           for later use */
        public ConnectionProcessorThread(Socket connection) {
            ClientConnection = connection;
        }

        /* The run() method is called to execute the thread.  When this
           function completes, the thread terminates. */
        public void run() {
            /* Do processing on client connection */
        }
    }

    public static void main(String[] args) {
        ServerSocket acceptSock;
        try {
            acceptSock = new ServerSocket(13214);
        }
        catch(IOException ioe) {
            System.out.println("Error opening server socket:  " +
                                ioe.getMessage());
            return;
        }
        Socket sock;        // The client socket
        while(true) {
            try {
                sock = acceptSock.accept();
                /* sock represents a connection to a client */
```

```
            /* Allocate a new thread that will run an instance
               of the ProcessThread class.  Initialize the
               ProcessThread class with the connected socket. */
          Thread t = new Thread(new ProcessThread(sock));
            /* Run the thread in the background */
          t.start();
        }
      catch(IOException ioe) {
         System.out.println("accept error:  " + ioe.getMessage());
         break;   // Exit while loop
      }
   }
  }
}
```

USING UDP/IP FROM C AND C++

As with TCP/IP, the first step in using UDP/IP is to obtain a socket. A UDP socket is obtained using the `socket()` function, except with the `SOCK_DGRAM` parameter to indicate UDP datagram semantics, as shown in Listing A-15. With this socket, the host can now start sending data to any destination. Note that there is no need to call `connect()` because UDP/IP is connectionless.[3] The local port number is chosen randomly by the operating system when data is first sent along the socket. However, in most net-VE applications that use UDP/IP, it is desirable to bind the UDP socket to a well-known local port, just like a TCP/IP server, by calling the `bind()` function, as shown in Listing A-16. The `bind()` call may fail if another local UDP/IP application has already bound to that port. It is important to note that TCP/IP and UDP/IP port numbers are independent of each other, meaning that a TCP/IP application and a UDP/IP application may simultaneously use the same port numbers on the same host.

---

[3]It is actually possible to call `connect()` on a UDP socket, specifying a particular remote IP address and port. This call does not actually establish any sort of connection, however. It simply guarantees that the socket can only communicate with the specified remote endpoint. Once `connect()` is called, communication on the socket can occur using the `read()` and `write()` calls used by TCP/IP applications. Of course, it makes no sense to `accept()` on a UDP socket because `connect()` does not actually establish a network connection.

LISTING A-15   Opening a socket for UDP/IP communications

```
#include <stdio.h>
#include <sys/types.h>
#include <sys/socket.h>
#include <netinet/in.h>
/* ... */
int sock;
    /* Allocate a socket
     *    PF_INET:  Use the Internet family of Protocols
     *    SOCK_DGRAM:  Provide best-efforts packet semantics
     *    0:  Use the default protocol (UDP)  */
sock = socket(PF_INET, SOCK_DGRAM, 0);
if (sock == -1) {
    /* Error */
    perror("socket");
    return;
}
```

LISTING A-16   Binding a UDP/IP socket to a port for sending and receiving
                    datagrams

```
struct sockaddr_in localAddr;    /* The address/port of the local endpoint */
bzero((char *)&localAddr, sizeof(localAddr));
localAddr.sin_family      = PF_INET;          /* Use Internet addresses */
localAddr.sin_addr.s_addr = htonl(INADDR_ANY); /* Use any local IP address */
localAddr.sin_port        = htons(13214);  /* Port that others can send to */
    /* Bind the socket to the well-known port */
if (bind(sock, (struct sockaddr *)&localAddr, sizeof(localAddr)) == -1) {
    /* Error */
    perror("bind");
    return;
}
```

To send data using UDP/IP, applications place data into a buffer and provide that buffer to the sendto() function, as shown in Listing A-17. When invoking this function, the application also provides a sockaddr structure describing who (which host IP address and UDP port) should receive the packet. The fourth parameter (0 in Listing A-17) specifies a set of special-delivery flags, a discussion of which is beyond the scope of this book. Note that because UDP data is sent in packets (as long as the data is within a maximum size range), the transmitted buffer does not need explicitly to include the packet length, because datagram delivery semantics guarantee that the entire buffer will be received as a single unit.

LISTING A-17   Sending a UDP/IP datagram

```
int BUFFERLEN = 255;
char buf[BUFFERLEN];
struct sockaddr_in destAddr;    /* The address/port of the remote endpoint */
sprintf(buf, "hello!");         /* Prepare data for transmission */
bzero((char *)&destAddr, sizeof(destAddr));
destAddr.sin_family        = PF_INET;        /* Use Internet addresses */
destAddr.sin_addr.s_addr   = inet_addr("10.25.43.9");
destAddr.sin_port          = htons(13214);
  /* Send data to the specified destination */
if (sendto(sock, buf, strlen(buf), 0,
           (struct sockaddr *)&destAddr, sizeof(destAddr)) != strlen(buf)) {
    /* Error */
  perror("sendto");
  return;
}
```

Receiving UDP data involves a call to the recvfrom() function, as shown in Listing A-18. This function takes a buffer for holding the received data and it fills a provided sockaddr structure with information about who (which host IP address and UDP port) transmitted the data.

LISTING A-18   Receiving a UDP/IP datagram

```
int BUFFERLEN = 255;
char buf[BUFFERLEN];
struct sockaddr_in srcAddr;    /* The address/port of the remote endpoint */
bzero((char *)&destAddr, sizeof(srcAddr));
  /* Receive data sent to the UDP port */
if (recvfrom(sock, buf, sizeof(buf), 0,
           (struct sockaddr *)&srcAddr, sizeof(srcAddr)) == -1) {
    /* Error */
  perror("recvfrom");
  return;
}
  /* Sender's address stored in srcAddr structure */
```

Finally, when either side has finished sending and receiving UDP data, it can close its socket:

```
close(sock);
```

Of course, because there is no connection, closing a socket simply cleans up local system resources. It is important to remember that the close() call only closes the local socket. Unlike with TCP, other hosts will never find out that an endpoint has closed its UDP socket, except that they will no longer see any data from that host or port.[4] The applications must have agreed to stop communicating, or they must have some other way of determining that a peer has departed.

USING UDP/IP FROM JAVA

As with TCP/IP, writing UDP/IP-based applications in Java is considerably easier than doing it in C. The DatagramSocket class provides an anchor for sending and receiving UDP/IP data.

The DatagramSocket class provides three constructors. The default constructor creates a socket bound to an arbitrary local port. Alternatively, the application can specify a local port number, or it can specify both a local IP address and port number for binding. Listing A-19 illustrates the creation of a DatagramSocket.

LISTING A-19   Preparing a DatagramSocket in Java

```
import java.net.DatagramSocket;
import java.io.IOException;
import java.io.ByteArrayInputStream;
import java.io.ByteArrayOutputStream;
import java.io.DataInputStream;
import java.io.DataOutputStream;
/* ... */
DatagramSocket sock;
try {
    // Omit the constructor argument to bind to an arbitrary local port
    sock = new DatagramSocket(13214);  // Bind to local UDP port 13214
}
catch(IOException ioe) {
    System.out.println("Error creating socket:  " + ioe.getMessage());
    return;
}
```

Using a DatagramSocket, applications can send and receive DatagramPacket objects. A DatagramPacket encapsulates all information about a UDP packet, including its data and its destination. The applica-

---

[4]However, there is nothing preventing a new application from coming along, grabbing that port, and using it. With TCP/IP, this was not a problem because the new application first had to establish a new connection and could not simply send data on an existing connection. With UDP, because connections do not actually exist, such masquerading is possible, and robust applications need to guard against it.

tion writes the data into a byte array buffer and allocates the Datagram-Packet with this buffer and the destination IP address and port, as shown in Listing A-20. To receive data, the application allocates a byte array for receiving the data and allocates a DatagramPacket. When the DatagramPacket has been received, it contains the IP address and port of the sending application, as shown in Listing A-21.

LISTING A-20   Sending data through a DatagramSocket

```
try{
    InetAddress destAddr = InetAddress.getByName("10.25.43.9");
    int destPort = 13214;
    ByteArrayOutputStream boStream = new ByteArrayOutputStream();
    DataOutputStream oStream = new DataOutputStream(boStream);
    oStream.writeUTF("Hello!");
    oStream.writeInt(3);
    byte[] dataBytes = boStream.getByteArray();
    DatagramPacket pack =
        new DatagramPacket(dataBytes, dataBytes.length, destAddr, destPort)
    sock.send(pack);
}
catch(IOException ioe) {
    System.out.println("Send error:   " + ioe.getMessage());
}
```

LISTING A-21   Receiving data from a DatagramSocket

```
try{
    byte[] dataBytes = new byte[255];
    DatagramPacket pack = new DatagramPacket(dataBytes, dataBytes.length);
    sock.receive(pack);
        // Sender information available in pack.getAddress() and pack.getPort()
    ByteArrayInputStream biStream = new ByteArrayOutputStream();
    DataInputStream iStream = new DataInputStream(biStream);
    String helloString = iStream.readUTF();
    int three = iStream.readInt();
}
catch(IOException ioe) {
    System.out.println("Receive error:   " + ioe.getMessage());
}
```

Finally, when an application is finished with its DatagramSocket, it closes it to relinquish the port.

```
try{
    sock.close();
}
```

```
catch(IOException ioe) {
    System.out.println("Close error:  " + ioe.getMessage());
}
```

Again, `close()` needs to be called on both applications, and an application receives no indication that a remote application has closed its UDP socket.

BROADCASTING FROM C AND C++

Broadcasting from C is identical to unicasting UDP/IP datagrams, with two exceptions. First, the destination address must be set to the appropriate pseudo-IP address for the broadcast:

```
destAddr.sin_addr.s_addr  = inet_addr("255.255.255.255");
```

Second, before data is broadcast using the UDP socket, the application must first register its interest in broadcasting on that socket by calling the `setsockopt()` function:

```
int one = 1;
setsockopt(sock, SOL_SOCKET, SO_BROADCAST, &one, sizeof(one);
```

Once set, the `SO_BROADCAST` option remains in force until it is changed. The actual `sendto()` call is identical to the unicast case.

Broadcast packets are delivered on any UDP socket that is waiting for packets on the corresponding port. Note that a single UDP socket may therefore receive both broadcast and unicast packets, and there is no way for the application to determine whether a particular received packet was broadcast or unicast.

BROADCASTING FROM JAVA

The only difference between unicast and broadcast Java code is in the destination IP address. To broadcast data, the application must initialize the `DatagramPacket` with the appropriate pseudo-IP address.

```
InetAddress destAddr = InetAddress.getByName("10.25.43.9");
```

The actual `send()` call is identical to the unicast case.

Broadcast packets are delivered on a `DatagramSocket` that is receiving packets on the corresponding port. As with C, a `DatagramSocket` socket may receive both broadcast and unicast packets, and there is no way for the application to determine whether a specific received packet was broadcast or unicast.

MULTICASTING FROM C AND C++

Sending multicast data from C is almost identical to sending unicast UDP data. The data should be sent to a multicast IP address.

```
destAddr.sin_addr.s_addr  = inet_addr("245.8.2.58");
```

The SO_BROADCAST socket option does not need to be set using the setsockopt() function. However, the TTL value can be specified by invoking setsockopt() on the UDP socket before calling sendto():

```
unsigned char ttl = 31;
setsockopt(sock, IPPROTO_IP, IP_MULTICAST_TTL, &ttl, sizeof(ttl);
```

Once set, the TTL remains in force until it is changed. The actual sendto() call is identical to the unicast and broadcast cases.

To receive multicast data, the application needs to subscribe the socket to one (or more) multicast addresses. The subscription is registered by calling setsockopt() with the IP_ADD_MEMBERSHIP option:

```
struct ip_mreq joinAddr;
    /* Specify which multicast address to join */
joinAddr.imr_multiaddr = inet_addr("245.8.2.58");
    /* Specify which local IP address will actually
       do the multicast join */
joinAddr.imr_interface = INADDR_ANY;
setsockopt(sock, IPPROTO_IP, IP_ADD_MEMBERSHIP,
           &joinAddr, sizeof(joinAddr);
```

Multiple subscriptions may be registered on a single socket by calling setsockopt() multiple times. However, most multicast implementations limit each socket to a maximum of 20 subscriptions. If more than 20 subscriptions are needed, the application can create and bind() multiple sockets to the same UDP port. To do this, the application must first override the operating system's security checking that would otherwise prevent multiple sockets from binding to the same port simultaneously:

```
int one = 1;
setsockopt(sock, SOL_SOCKET, SO_REUSEADDR, &one, sizeof(one));
```

It is generally a good idea to make this call before binding any multicast socket, even if fewer than 20 group subscriptions are required. This call allows other applications on the local machine to use the same port for receiving their multicast data whether on the same or different multicast group addresses.

To cancel a multicast subscription, the application makes a corresponding setsockopt() call with the IP_DROP_MEMBERSHIP parameter:

```
struct ip_mreq joinAddr;
   /* Specify which multicast address to drop */
joinAddr.imr_multiaddr = inet_addr("245.8.2.58");
   /* Specify which local IP address will actually
      do the multicast drop */
joinAddr.imr_interface = INADDR_ANY;
setsockopt(sock, IPPROTO_IP, IP_DROP_MEMBERSHIP,
           &joinAddr, sizeof(joinAddr);
```

When a socket is closed, all of its open subscriptions are automatically dropped.

MULTICASTING FROM JAVA

To use multicast from Java, the application uses a MulticastSocket, which is a subclass of DatagramSocket. The MulticastSocket is constructed in the same way as a DatagramSocket, specifying either no parameters (for a system-selected local port) or with a single integer argument (to bind to a specific port). The send() and receive() methods are available as shown previously for sending unicast and broadcast DatagramPacket objects.

To send to a multicast group, the application simply specifies a multicast address as the destination of the DatagramPacket:

```
InetAddress destAddr = InetAddress.getByName("245.8.2.58");
```

It can send the data using the regular sendto() method. The application specifies the TTL by calling the setTTL() method on MulticastSocket. Once set, the TTL remains in force until changed by another call to setTTL().

```
sock.setTTL((byte)31);
```

Alternatively, the TTL of a MulticastSocket may be overridden by specifying a TTL parameter to the sendto() method:

```
sock.sendto(pack, (byte)12);
```

This packet would be transmitted with a TTL of 12, while packets sent using the regular sendto() method will have the socket's default TTL of 31.

An application joins and leaves multicast groups by calling the joinGroup() and leaveGroup() methods on the MulticastSocket. These calls take an InetAddress representing the multicast address:

```
sock.joinGroup(InetAddress.getByName("245.8.2.58"));
  // ...
sock.leaveGroup(InetAddress.getByName("245.8.2.58"));
```

At the time of this writing (early 1999), the Java classes do not provide a way to overcome the 20 subscription limitation imposed by many multicast implementations.

REFERENCES

[Comer/Stevens96a] Comer, D. E., and D. L. Stevens. *Internetworking with TCP/IP, vol. 3: Client-Server Programming and Applications.* Upper Saddle River, NJ: Prentice Hall, 1996.

[Comer/Stevens96b] Comer, D. E., and D. L. Stevens. *Internetworking with TCP/IP, vol. 3: Client-Server Programming and Applications for the Windows Socket.* Upper Saddle River, NJ: Prentice Hall, 1996.

[Coutois97] Coutois, T. *Java Networking and Communications.* Upper Saddle River, NJ: Prentice Hall, 1997.

[JDK] Java Development Kit documentation Web site at JavaSoft, Inc.: *http://www.javasoft.com*

[Quinn/Shute95] Quinn, B., and D. Shute. *Windows Sockets Network Programming.* Reading, MA: Addison-Wesley, 1995.

[Stevens98] Stevens, W. R. *Unix Network Programming, vol. 1: Networking APIs: Sockets and XTI*, 2nd ed. Upper Saddle River, NJ: Prentice Hall, 1998.

INDEX

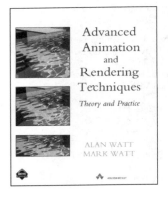

Advanced Animation and Rendering Techniques

Theory and Practice

By Alan Watt and Mark Watt

Dealing with state-of-the-art techniques in rendering and animation, this book provides a unique synthesis of advanced techniques not previously available in one coherent source. It offers a balance between theoretical concepts and implementation detail that will be invaluable to professional programmers and students alike.

0-201-54412-1 • 472 pages • ©1992 • Hardcover

Mobility

Processes, Computers, and Agents

Edited by Dejan Milojicic, Frederick Douglis, and Richard Wheeler

This book brings together in one single resource leading edge research and practice in three areas of mobility: process migration, mobile computing, and mobile agents. Presented chronologically, the chapters in this book—each written by a leading expert in that particular area—track the development of critical technologies that have influenced mobility. Introductions by the editors and original afterwords by many of the authors provide information on implementation and practical application, technological context, and updates on the most recent advances.

0-201-37928-7 • 704 pages • ©1999 • Paperback

Software for Use

A Practical Guide to the Models and Methods of Usage-Centered Design

By Larry L. Constantine and Lucy A.D. Lockwood

In this book, two well-known authors present the models and methods of a revolutionary approach to software that will help programmers deliver more *usable* software. Much more than just another set of rules for good user-interface design, the book guides readers through a systematic software development process—*usage-centered design*, which weaves together two major threads in software development methods: use cases (also used with UML) and essential modeling. With numerous examples and case studies of both conventional and specialized software applications, the authors illustrate what has been shown to work in practice and what has proved to be of the greatest practical value.

0-201-92478-1 • 608 pages • ©1999 • Hardcover

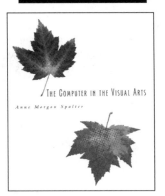

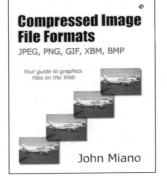

Compressed Image File Formats

JPEG, PNG, GIF, XBM, BMP

By John Miano

This comprehensive reference on the major graphics file formats and the compression technologies they employ is an indispensable resource for graphics programmers, especially those developing graphical applications for the Web. It examines the most common graphics file formats in detail and demonstrates how to encode and decode image files for each. If you want to learn how to read and write graphics file formats for the Web, there is no better reference than this book.

0-201-60443-4 • 320 pages • ©1999 • Paperback with CD-ROM

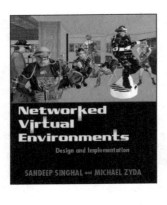

Networked Virtual Environments

Design and Implementation

By Sandeep Singhal and Michael Zyda

Networked virtual environments (Net-VEs) offer a three-dimensional, virtual "space" in which users around the world can interact in real time. Net-VE applications have already been adopted by the military and aerospace and entertainment industries. They are also used to enhance engineering design, scientific research, and electronic commerce. Written by two of the field's leaders, this book provides a comprehensive examination of Net-VEs, explains the underlying technologies, and furnishes a roadmap for designing and building interactive 3D virtual environments.

0-201-32557-8 • 352 pages • ©1999 • Hardcover

The Computer Image

By Alan Watt and Fabio Policarpo

The three main fields of computer imagery—computer graphics, image processing, and computer vision—are merging in many applications. Computer vision techniques are used in computer graphics to collect and model complex scenes; computer graphics techniques are used to constrain the recognition of 3D objects by computers; image processing techniques are routinely used by graphic designers to manipulate photographs. This book is the first to bring all three areas together in a coherent overview.

0-201-42298-0 • 752 pages • ©1998 • Hardcover with CD-ROM

Digital Illusion
Entertaining the Future with High Technology
By Clark Dodsworth, Jr., Contributing Editor

This book is the first to detail the design and implementation of computer-based entertainment. In it Clark Dodsworth has pulled together key players in the field to share their keen insights and invaluable experiences. First, the contributors describe recent developments in graphics, simulation, and animation that have led to advances in interactive entertainment. The book then describes, with examples, the infrastructure required to develop the new technologies of illusion, and it also explores some of the practical issues involved in designing virtual environments. In addition, the history and economics of the field are examined, with a critical eye to future developments.

0-201-84780-9 • 576 pages • ©1998 • Paperback

Virtual Reality Systems

By John Vince

Virtual Reality Systems is an accessible introduction to the underlying technologies used to create today's virtual environments: real-time computer graphics, color displays, and simulation software. It provides balanced coverage of both hardware and software issues and provides optional explanations of the underlying mathematical algorithms and techniques.

0-201-87687-6 • 384 pages • ©1995 • Hardcover

Multimedia Systems

By John F. Koegel Buford

This carefully edited book provides a technical introduction to key issues in multimedia, including detailed discussion of new technologies, principles, current research, and future directions. It furnishes a unified treatment of recent developments in the field, bringing together, in one volume, multimedia elements common to a range of computing areas such as operating systems, database management systems, network communications, and user-interface technology.

0-201-53258-1 • 464 pages • ©1994 • Hardcover

Addison-Wesley Computer and Engineering Publishing Group

How to Interact with Us

1. Visit our Web site

http://www.awl.com/cseng

When you think you've read enough, there's always more content for you at Addison-Wesley's web site. Our web site contains a directory of complete product information including:

- Chapters
- Exclusive author interviews
- Links to authors' pages
- Tables of contents
- Source code

You can also discover what tradeshows and conferences Addison-Wesley will be attending, read what others are saying about our titles, and find out where and when you can meet our authors and have them sign your book.

2. Subscribe to Our Email Mailing Lists

Subscribe to our electronic mailing lists and be the first to know when new books are publishing. Here's how it works: Sign up for our electronic mailing at **http://www.awl.com/cseng/mailinglists.html**. Just select the subject areas that interest you and you will receive notification via email when we publish a book in that area.

3. Contact Us via Email

cepubprof@awl.com
Ask general questions about our books.
Sign up for our electronic mailing lists.
Submit corrections for our web site.

bexpress@awl.com
Request an Addison-Wesley catalog.
Get answers to questions regarding your order or our products.

innovations@awl.com
Request a current Innovations Newsletter.

webmaster@awl.com
Send comments about our web site.

cepubeditors@awl.com
Submit a book proposal.
Send errata for an Addison-Wesley book.

cepubpublicity@awl.com
Request a review copy for a member of the media interested in reviewing new Addison-Wesley titles.

We encourage you to patronize the many fine retailers who stock Addison-Wesley titles. Visit our online directory to find stores near you or visit our online store: **http://store.awl.com/** or call **800-824-7799**.

Addison Wesley Longman
Computer and Engineering Publishing Group
One Jacob Way, Reading, Massachusetts 01867 USA
TEL 781-944-3700 • FAX 781-942-3076